Frontiers of Caribbean Literature in English

Frontiers of Caribbean Literature in English

Edited by
Frank Birbalsingh

St. Martin's Press
New York

In memory of
E. S. Birbalsingh (1901–1984)

FRONTIERS OF CARIBBEAN LITERATURE IN ENGLISH
Copyright © 1996 by Frank Birbalsingh

St. Martin's Press, Scholarly and Reference Division,
175 Fifth Avenue, New York, N.Y. 10010

First published in the United States of America 1996

Printed in Hong Kong

ISBN 0–312–12637–9 (cloth)
ISBN 0–312–12638–7 (paper)

Library of Congress Cataloging-in-Publication Data
Frontiers of Caribbean literature in English / edited by Frank
Birbalsingh.
p.   cm.
Includes bibliographical references and index.
ISBN 0–312–12637–9 (cloth). — ISBN 0–312–12638–7 (paper)
1. Caribbean literature (English)—History and criticism—Theory,
etc.   2. Caribbean Area—Intellectual life—20th century.
3. Authors, Caribbean—20th century—Interviews.   I. Birbalsingh.
Frank.
PR9205.F76   1996
810.9′9729—dc20   95–19517
                                                            CIP

First edition 1996

Contents

Contents

Acknowledgements

Chapter 2 previously appeared in *The Journal of Commonwealth Literature*, XXIII, i, 1988, 182–8.

Chapter 5 previously appeared in *Kyk-Over-Al*, no. 37, 66–75.

Chapter 6 previously appeared in F. M. Birbalsingh, *Passion and Exile* (Hansib, London, 1988), pp. 147–61.

Chapter 14, Part (1) previously appeared in *Caribbean Quarterly*, XXXVII, iv, December, 1991, 40–6.

Thanks are extended to the editors and publishers of all these titles for permission to reprint.

Introduction

In a lecture given at York University in Toronto, in 1986, George Lamming addressed an audience consisting mainly of immigrants from the Caribbean. When he described his audience as an external frontier of the Caribbean, Lamming appeared to reverse a traditional world-view in which European rulers regarded their colonial possessions as outposts on the periphery of their world – the white, rich, politically and technologically powerful metropolis of Europe and North America. According to the traditional view, ex-colonial outposts such as those in the Caribbean still survive and function, from day to day, largely because of their dependent links on former imperial centres such as London, Paris and New York.

In reversing this global structure of white centres surrounded mainly by non-white colonial outposts, Lamming was claiming that London, Paris, New York and Toronto had, in a certain sense, now themselves become outposts on the frontier of other cultures, one of which had its centre in the Caribbean. Although this new centre/outpost relationship was not colonial, it had its origin in the preceding Eurocentric, colonial structure in which large groups of non-white, colonial subjects had settled as immigrants in western European centres. Needless to say, this was not an anticipated consequence of empire; but it happened as an inevitable result of colonial subjects gravitating to imperial centres to study, visit or carry out assignments as government servants. Also, by the middle of the twentieth century, when empires began to crumble, relationships had already been fostered which made it easier for non-white immigrant communities to take shape, not only in imperial capitals, but in associated centres of affluence such as Toronto, Montreal and other Canadian cities.

In the specific instance of former British Caribbean colonies with which this book is concerned, a combination of mismanagement by post-Independence governments, British connivance with an emerging *Pax Americana* during the 1960s and 1970s, and an American foreign policy hostile to popular political expression in the region generated continuing emigration from the Caribbean. The immigrant communities evolving out of this Caribbean exodus would today number about two million people in London, Toronto and New York alone. Many emigrants left immediately after the Second World War to settle in Britain; others came in the 1970s and 1980s, mainly to Canada and the US; and both groups produced children who today remain British, Canadian or American citizens, while regarding the Caribbean, if not as their cultural and spiritual centre, at least as their place of origin.

The oldest and largest Caribbean immigrant community is in London where people from the British Caribbean flocked, especially in the 1950s because there were no immigration laws restricting their entry. When such a law was passed in 1962, in addition to stopping the flow of Caribbean immigrants into Britain, it had the effect of channelling the flow elsewhere, principally to Canada and the US. Caribbean emigration to Canada therefore follows a pattern that is the reverse of the pattern in Britain, for while it became harder for Caribbean emigrants to enter Britain in the 1960s, the Canadian Immigration Act of 1967 made it easier for them to enter Canada after the late 1960s. There is no doubt that the prime motive for Caribbean emigration has always been economic – the search for education, higher skills, employment, better opportunities and a better standard of living. After Independence in the 1960s, however, social, political and ethnic tensions joined with economic motives to spur Caribbean emigration to even higher levels than before. Hence large-scale Caribbean emigration to Canada and the US in the 1970s and 1980s.

The problems which Caribbean immigrants encountered abroad are different from those which they faced in their homeland. At home they faced poverty, exploitation, and social and political insecurity, while abroad they encountered racial discrimination, second-class citizenship and alienation. Such were the dissatisfactions abroad that, after a few years, some immigrants returned home, and others re-migrated, for instance, from Britain to North America. But, in the main, Caribbean immigrants have remained where they first landed. One reason encouraging them to remain was the reality of their children growing up outside the Caribbean, without first-hand knowledge of their parents' homeland. This reality has created an additional problem in so far as the children of immigrants have grown up with different cultural priorities and expectations from those of their parents.

The writing that has come out of the immigrant communities or external frontiers of the Caribbean is the subject of this book. The volume opens with Lamming's lecture 'Concepts of the Caribbean' which provides a historical background to emigration, and defines the term 'external frontier', after which, with the exception only of Derek Walcott's brief contribution, *Frontiers* is made up entirely of interviews with English-speaking Caribbean writers, most of whom continue to live abroad, although they may have left their homeland, in some cases, as long as half a century ago. Each interview is preceded by a brief commentary on the career of the writer, providing basic facts about his/her biography and publishing history.

What is today known as West Indian or Caribbean literature in

English[1] has come in four stages, the first of which lasted virtually throughout the first half of the twentieth century; the second from 1950 to 1965; the third from 1965 to 1980; and the fourth from 1980 to the present. These stages are approximate, each overlapping with the next, so that there is no sharp division between them: authors from the second stage, for instance, are today still active alongside those of the third and fourth stages. But the four stages offer a classification that may help to clarify the growth of Caribbean literature in English. The pre-1950 writers are generally colonial in outlook, although there are exceptions, notably C. L. R. James,[2] while the 1950–65 writers probe and question this outlook. Writers after 1965 (the third stage) espouse post-Independence interests, while writers after 1980 (the fourth stage) are concerned either with the fate of immigrants living on an external frontier, or with the fate of the others like them.

The first major figure in anglophone Caribbean literature is H. G. Delisser (1878–1944) who began writing around the time of the First World War. He was joined by fellow Jamaicans – W. Adolphe Roberts (1886–1962) and Claude McKay (1889–1948). In Trinidad, C. L. R. James (1901–89) and Alfred Mendes appeared in the 1930s, and were followed by Ralph De Boissière. Eric Walrond (1898–1967) of Guyana produced a volume of stories, *Tropic Death* (1926); but in 1927, he emigrated to New York where he was associated with members of the Harlem Renaissance.[3] Besides these prose writers, there were numerous poets, for example, Tom Redcam (1870–1933), Frank Collymore (1893–1980), Una Marson (1905–65), and Eric Roach (1915–74), all of whom contributed to the first stage of a recognizable literature by indigenous, English-speaking Caribbean writers.

Already though, even in the first stage, there are examples of emigration: apart from Walrond, there is the more notable case of Claude McKay, who left Jamaica for the US in 1912, and went on to a distinguished career, producing poetry and fiction as well as works of non-fiction. Like Walrond, McKay was associated with the Harlem Renaissance, and his writing provides the first substantial example of literature on an external frontier of the Caribbean: it is not only varied and interesting in itself, but could serve as a model for West Indian immigrants who settled in New York after McKay, notably Paule Marshall, whose parents came from Barbados, and Rosa Guy[4] (Trinidad). If before 1950, two writers – Walrond and McKay – had already appeared on the North American frontier, only one materialized on the English frontier – C. L. R. James, who became known chiefly through his historical and political writings. Thus, in the first stage of its development, Caribbean writing in English could be seen to emanate chiefly from within the Caribbean itself, and despite notable exceptions, to embody a colonial outlook that largely reflected the dominant Eurocentric values of the time.

Soon after the Second World War, although many writers still remained in the Caribbean, for example Victor Reid (Jamaica), Derek Walcott (St Lucia), and Michael Anthony (Trinidad), several emigrated to England, where they proved to be innovative and influential – Samuel Selvon, George Lamming, Edgar Mittelholzer,[5] V. S. Naipaul,[6] Jan Carew, Wilson Harris[7] and many others. In 1955 Austin Clarke (Barbados) went to Canada, where he remains the dominant black writer on that particular frontier of the Caribbean. If the pre-1950 writers tended to illustrate specific features of colonial society mainly as a reflection of reality, the post-1950 writers probed these features in a more inquiring manner that drew attention to challenging issues of personal and national identity, and their implications of political nationalism and freedom from colonial rule. To some extent the writing of these second-stage authors helped to generate the movement toward Independence in the 1960s, but it is also true that social and political forces that precipitated Independence also helped to generate inspiration for writing during this period.

The flexibility of divisions between the four literary stages discussed here cannot be emphasized enough; for there is nothing uniform or formulaic about the development of Caribbean literature. The career of Earl Lovelace, for example, belongs in the third stage, but it straddles pre-Independence issues of the 1950s, as well as post-Independence issues beyond the mid-1960s. Like the second-stage writers, Lovelace looks inquiringly at colonial oppression and fragmentation in his early work, but by and large, his novels deal with post-Independence strategies of regeneration and reintegration (the third stage). Many of Lovelace's contemporaries within the Caribbean, for example Lorna Goodison and Erna Brodber,[8] and some who emigrated after the mid-1960s – for example, Jamaica Kincaid, Dionne Brand, Cyril Dabydeen, David Dabydeen, Neil Bissoondath and Fred d'Aguiar – also straddle the post-Independence fence. Like Lovelace, these writers question colonial fragmentation and suggest processes of reconstruction and recovery; but those among this third-stage group who emigrated at a younger age – David Dabydeen, Fred d'Aguiar, Jamaica Kincaid and Neil Bissoondath – either deal more exclusively with post-Independence issues of reconstruction and post-colonial recovery, or concentrate on general themes of exile and loss as they emanate out of the lives of immigrants on their particular frontiers of the Caribbean (the fourth stage).

Since the fourth stage of writing is more exclusively concerned with the diasporan experience on external frontiers of the Caribbean, this experience may come from within the circle of Caribbean immigrants themselves, or from the (white) host community among whom the immigrants have settled. To some extent this is reflected in the work of Jamaica Kincaid and David Dabydeen, but Caryl Phillips is the best example of this type of writer in *Frontiers*. Phillips was taken in infancy to Britain where he grew up and attended school and university. His novels and plays render issues and views seen from the point of view of West Indian immigrants – the black British – as well as from the point of view of white insiders – the native Britons. But Phillips's forte is the sense of alienation, exile and victimisation affecting non-white people living in a diaspora, on external frontiers of their cultural centre.

For the greater part of this century then, from Claude McKay to Caryl Phillips, it is evident that English-speaking Caribbean writers have flourished on one frontier or another. The tradition established by McKay includes writing both about his memories of the Caribbean, and about his day-to-day life as a black person in America. This is the pattern followed by many of his successors. One exception is Caryl Phillips who, as a fourth-stage writer, had no memories of the Caribbean to invoke, and chose his early subjects from the experience of West Indian immigrants among whom he grew up in England. He introduced a Caribbean setting in his novel *A State of Independence*[9] only after he had himself visited the Caribbean. In subsequent works, Phillips considers the fate not only of West Indian exiles living on external frontiers of the Caribbean, but of other exiles – Blacks and Whites – who share a legacy of oppression and displacement. Caribbean frontier or diasporan literature reflects a broad pattern of Caribbean subjects – usually memories – yielding to typical immigrant experiences of discrimination and alienation, and later taking on more abstract themes of victimization or oppression, as experienced by anyone who may share the Caribbean prototype of displacement from the Old World, exile to the New World, and a second exile to frontiers further afield. As quintessential aspects of Caribbean experience, displacement and exile reappear constantly during the interviews in *Frontiers*.

At least from the time of Ovid, the Latin poet, artists have endured exile, either willingly, or because it was forced upon them. Ovid was banished by the emperor Augustus and, despite numerous pleas for his freedom, remained in exile until his death. Since he wrote lyric poems of great depth and poignancy while in exile, it is tempting to believe that Ovid's exile had a positive influence on the quality of his writings; but it may just as well have had a negative influence, or no influence at all. Nor do examples of exiled artists since Ovid prove conclusively that exile has any effect on art.

In the first half of the twentieth century, two major figures in English literature – James Joyce and T. S. Eliot – lived in exile during most of their writing career. Also, the upheaval of the two World Wars temporarily or permanently displaced many European artists, for example, Vladimir Nabokov, Thomas Mann, Bertholt Brecht, Jerzy Koszinski and Ruth Prawer Jhabvala. Even if exile cannot be shown to have influenced the achievements of these writers, their work reflects the pattern observed in Caribbean

frontier literature of dealing both with specific concerns about their homeland or country of settlement, and later with more abstract themes of
international or philosophical significance. Before Eliot and Joyce, this
pattern is evident in the work of other exiles like Joseph Conrad or Katherine
Mansfield, although it is true that Conrad tended to deal with abstract issues
of morality anyway. But Katherine Mansfield, who left her homeland, New
Zealand, to live in England and Europe, first wrote stories about New
Zealand, then established her main reputation through fiction often set in
public places such as hotels or railway waiting rooms, and dealing with
general psychological or philosophical issues. Henry James is an even
better example of a novelist who, like many Caribbean writers, was born in
a colonial milieu, and later thrived in exile. Although his native United
States was, in political or national terms, already one hundred years old
when James left it to live in Europe, it was a colonial society in cultural
terms, dependent on Britain for cultural models and artistic standards.
James himself, in his biography of Hawthorne, identifies what he calls
'items of high civilization' which did not exist in the United States in the
nineteenth century, and made it difficult for a major writer to survive there.

Almost one hundred years later, Naipaul made similar remarks about
the Caribbean. Whether James and Naipaul were justified or not, their
feelings about the perceived colonial inadequacy of their native cultures
encouraged them to cherish exile, and devote their major creative energies
to writing on an external frontier of their native cultures. Mistakenly or not,
what James perceived in the 1870s, and Naipaul in the 1970s, was that their
cultures of origin were not mature enough, and in Naipaul's case, neither
large nor rich enough to support their imagination. The disconcerting, not
to say demeaning nature of this perception inevitably contributed to
conflict between James and his more patriotic contemporaries such as
William Dean Howells, while it has similarly conspired to make Naipaul
persona non grata in the Caribbean.

In James's *oeuvre* the early novels deal largely with American social
manners and characters, the middle novels with Euro-American relationships involving Americans living in Europe, and the late ones with symbolic meanings that only partially involve Americans. This pattern
generally matches the course of Naipaul's fiction, which begins with vigorous, earthy, and aromatic evocations of Trinidad society, and moves via
Africa and other places, to *The Enigma of Arrival*,[10] which celebrates the
English countryside in an expertly tailored style that contrasts sharply with
the ironic evocativeness of his earlier writing. It is significant that other
Caribbean writers who live on external frontiers do not show Naipaul's
versatility either in subject or treatment. This may be one reason why,
although he is not interviewed in *Frontiers*, Naipaul's name is brought up
frequently, not always admiringly.

It is through his non-fiction rather than fiction that Naipaul is usually accused of offending Caribbean and third-world people. *The Middle Passage*,[11] which describes Naipaul's travels in the Caribbean, is a notorious work in this respect. But today, after we have observed the destructive impact on Caribbean society of leaders such as Forbes Burnham[12] (1923–85) and Eric Williams[13] (1911–82), it is conceivable that Naipaul's criticism of Caribbean people for destructive, 'picaroon' behaviour for example, may no longer be regarded as harsh. Burnham's party ruled Guyana continuously since 1964, flouting electoral or democratic procedures, and reducing Guyana to the status of the poorest country in the western hemisphere. Yet Burnham and his party were re-elected five times! And there was never any widespread movement aimed at removing Burnham's government, as there was in 1962–64 to remove the government of Dr Cheddi Jagan.[14] Eric Williams also ruled Trinidad and Tobago continuously for a similar length of time, with similar results.

If Naipaul's criticisms are too harsh or cruel, one must also recognize that they are not unique. Other Caribbean writers have expressed similar views, and in this volume, Lamming's hypothetical portrait of a Caribbean politician in 'Concepts of the Caribbean' exhibits some of the 'picaroon' characteristics of unscrupulous and unprincipled self-interest that Naipaul has identified. Salkey's comments in the final section of his interview, and Lorna Goodison's lament over Jamaican cultural deficiencies illustrate much the same thing. Jamaica Kincaid's *A Small Place* also levels charges against Antigua that are not dissimilar to those levelled by Naipaul against Trinidad and the Caribbean. Yet none of these writers has incurred the wrath heaped on Naipaul.

Perhaps the angry response to Naipaul may be due to the rather strident tone of *The Middle Passage* which tends to report alleged Caribbean inadequacies with a prophetic sort of zeal rather than with regret or sadness. Another factor may be that *The Middle Passage* appeared at a time when independence was in the air, and self-criticism, however accurate – more so if it was accurate – went against the grain. More importantly, in a society historically sensitized to feudalistic notions of race, colour and class, one cannot overlook the fact of Naipaul being Indian as a possible factor in the response to his writing.

By the 1950s there were many brown and not a few black West Indians, from the upper middle class, who held views that were critical of West Indians and were therefore regarded as pro-imperialist. These were generally well-to-do, educated or professional people, some of whom may have been trained in Britain, where their anglophile views either originated or gained strength. Sneeringly called 'Afro-Saxons', such people were accounted as self-hating, eccentric, irrelevant, anachronistic, though not dangerous except to themselves. But Naipaul did not fit into this harmless if irritating or self-destructive mould. This is partly because he belonged to a Caribbean social sub-group – Indians – who formed less than 20 per cent of the English-speaking Caribbean population and who were consequently marginalized in social and political terms. But Indians did not uniformly make up 20 per cent of the population in each English-speaking territory. In Jamaica, for instance, they were about 2 per cent, whereas in Guyana and Trinidad they were 51 and 40 per cent respectively. Yet Indians were marginalized no matter what percentage of the population they represented in a particular Caribbean territory.

Even if the minuscule proportion of Indians outside Guyana and Trinidad offered a mathematical justification for their marginalization in places such as Jamaica and Barbados, there are historical reasons why this marginalization persisted in territories where Indians were either a clear majority or close to it (Guyana and Trinidad). Firstly, Indians did not arrive in the region until 1838, later by a few years than smaller indentured groups such as the Portuguese, and much later than the overwhelming majority of Caribbean people, those descended from African slaves who had provided labour in European-owned Caribbean plantations for three centuries before. Secondly, by coming as indentured labourers to replace the freed Africans on the sugar plantations, Indians automatically assumed a position at the bottom of the social ladder. For these reasons, Indians were underdogs in the ensuing competition to acquire basic skills such as mastery of the English language, western education and Creole social manners. Their consequent marginalization is well-documented in fiction by Indo-Caribbean writers like the Naipaul brothers, Selvon, Ismith Khan or Lauchmonen, and in novels by Creole writers such as H. G. Delisser – *The Cup and The Lip*;[15] and Edgar Mittelholzer – *Corentyne Thunder*.[16]

By 1962, when *The Middle Passage* first appeared, it is true that Indians were being rapidly creolized. But they still retained distinct aspects of marginalization as Lamming hints in 'Concepts of the Caribbean'. Imagine the reaction if an Indo-Trinidadian not only came out with a book like *The Middle Passage,* but himself achieved the status of an international literary celebrity which ensured that his books would be more widely read than those of any other Caribbean author. Naipaul was perceived as rubbing salt into the wounded pride of a people who had suffered all too grievously from three centuries of slavery. Were it not for obvious differences between the composition and structure of British society and those of the West Indies, the reaction of the British social establishment to the writing of D. H. Lawrence might well be compared with West Indian reaction to Naipaul. Lawrence's criticism of upper-class emotional impotence and philosophical decadence in his novels, should not have come from a miner's son. Even as liberal a member of the British establishment as Bertrand Russell tended to dismiss Lawrence merely as someone who only spoke about 'Blood! Blood!' all the time. It is unlikely that Russell's reaction would have been just mildly dismissive, if he came from a social group that was smarting from the effects of three centuries of humiliation, oppression and enslavement.

Of the twelve writers who are interviewed in *Frontiers*, seven have been based in England at one time or another – Andrew Salkey, Samuel Selvon, Jan Carew, George Lamming, Roy A. K. Heath, David Dabydeen and Caryl Phillips – while Austin Clarke, Cyril Dabydeen and Dionne Brand live in Canada, Jamaica Kincaid in the US, and Lorna Goodison in Jamaica. These twelve writers come from diverse backgrounds, and do not represent frontier experience in any uniform sense. The inclusion of Lorna Goodison in *Frontiers* should illustrate any links or contrasts between Caribbean frontier writing and literature currently being produced in the Caribbean.

Lamming's interview provides insights into intimate cultural links that have always existed between Africa and the Caribbean. The second author represented in *Frontiers*, Derek Walcott, is not interviewed: his chapter consists of a reading of the poem 'The Sea is History' which Walcott gave to students at York University; the chapter also contains Walcott's introductory remarks and answers to questions that followed the reading. As someone whose writing career has lasted longer than that of most West Indian writers, Walcott's views on the definition of history and drama are of particular interest. Walcott has always taken a catholic view of the mixed nature of Caribbean culture without assigning more significance to one element or group than another.

Andrew Salkey has written fiction, poetry, children's fiction, travel writing, and criticism besides producing numerous anthologies and journalistic pieces. He has also served as friend, confidant, adviser, correspondent and informal agent to many writers. Salkey had the confidence of the fifties writers in London – Naipaul, Lamming, Mittelholzer, Mais, Carew, Hearne and Harris – and his work as an interviewer and journalist brought him into close contact with such leaders as Dr Eric Williams, Forbes Burnham, and Dr Cheddi Jagan. Salkey uses the phrase 'bright as blisters' to describe the achievement of some of the best writers (V. S. Naipaul, Derek Walcott, and Jamaica Kincaid); but he adds disquieting remarks about the prospects for many other West Indian writers.

Along with Samuel Selvon, Jan Carew is probably the most gifted storyteller among Caribbean writers. Carew has strong political instincts. Like Lamming and Salkey, his books appeared regularly up to the late 1960s. Then, if Salkey is to be believed, Carew and his second-stage contemporaries discovered that their manuscripts were no longer acceptable to metropolitan publishers. This resulted in a decline in the production of literature on external Caribbean frontiers in the late 1970s and 1980s.

During this time, Carew has continued to lecture widely, and in recent years, has turned his attention to history rather than fiction. 'The Wild Coast', the title of Carew's second novel, is the original name of Guyana, and, as such, it expresses the author's commitment to Caribbean art and culture which derives from his intense Guyanese patriotism.

Salkey's claim is that so long as Carew and his contemporaries supplied fresh memories of the colonial or pre-Independence Caribbean, they were considered marketable; but when their memories became overshadowed by Independence and its consequences, their market value dropped. At the same time, these writers had to compete with indigenous writers in the frontiers on which they lived, that is to say, with (white) English, Canadians and Americans or with younger Caribbean writers such as the children of fellow Caribbean immigrants whose accounts of growing up on external frontiers were more authentic and acceptable.

Selvon's record of publication seems to bear out Salkey's claim. His rate of publication dropped off markedly after the 1950s. Selvon's writing has always appealed through its use of Caribbean linguistic structures and devices to score comic points related to particular characters, or particular features of race, colour or class discrimination. For this reason, Selvon's subjects have remained thoroughly Caribbean, whether he is writing about the Caribbean itself, or about immigrants on a frontier. Through their language Selvon's books have contributed greatly to the development of a West Indian national consciousness. It is unfortunate that his description of this consciousness as 'open' should be contradicted by a sharp polarization of attitudes in many Caribbean societies since Independence, and in Guyana by racial riots and killing.

Roy Heath migrated to England in 1950, like Lamming and others; but whereas Lamming and company began publishing more or less immediately after they reached England, Heath's first novel did not appear until nearly twenty-five years after his arrival in England. While by chronology, Heath belongs with his second-stage contemporaries, his publishing history places him among younger post-Independence writers. In his interview, Heath seems to regard his long residence on the English frontier as a kind of penance for the publication facilities which he enjoys in England and which he would miss in Guyana. His novels deal mainly with his memories of Guyana, and remain in the second stage of Caribbean writing in English. In what he regards as a realistic appraisal of the predicament facing the Caribbean, Heath believes that third-world societies will continue to be at the mercy, if not of colonizing powers, as in the past, of 'people with the money'.

Living on the Canadian frontier, Austin Clarke began his career by transforming memories of his homeland into fiction. Then followed novels and stories reflecting the conditions of Caribbean immigrants who live in

Toronto victimized by race and colour prejudice and by police brutality. In his interview, Clarke probes into the nature of Caribbean experience in Canada seeking out, in a tone that is both chastened and militant, better prospects for the future.

Clarke's colleague Cyril Dabydeen did not emigrate to Canada from Guyana until 1970. Dabydeen is greatly concerned about mixing memories of his homeland with his experiences in Canada. He considers it a central feature of his creative process to juggle his memories of Guyana, or 'there' as he calls it, with reactions to his present circumstances 'here' in Canada. It is partly because of this juggling that Caribbean aspects of his language are adapted to become more accessible to a Canadian audience. This matter of audience is discussed in almost every interview, suggesting its critical importance to writers who live in exile.

Dionne Brand is the final Canadian representative in *Frontiers*. She came to Canada (from Trinidad) in the same year as Dabydeen, and is more unambiguous than him in approaching her audience. She freely uses Creole or Caribbean forms of speech and expression, despite any difficulties that they may pose to a non-Caribbean audience. This difference of approach to language illustrates an important issue of writing on external frontiers of the Caribbean. Should such writing be directed at the author's frontier audience or at his/her home audience in the Caribbean? There are also the implications of acceptance for publication in Britain, Canada or the United States. Along with her insights into this issue, Dionne Brand reflects on her self-declared Marxism, lesbianism and feminism. The title of her collection of poems *No Language is Neutral* illustrates her belief in the power of ideology to influence language and shape the world.

Kincaid's writing is deeply psychological, which may account for its literary success. Her first book *At the Bottom of the River* (1983), is a collection of stories which utilizes memories of her homeland (Antigua); but *Lucy* (1990) includes American characters in an American setting. Although in chronological terms, Kincaid belongs with the third-stage writers, she is sharply critical of post-Independence Antigua as well as America, suggesting a point of view too broad to be easily classified. Lorna Goodison's passionate commitment to Jamaica highlights attitudes of detachment or alienation which may enter the work of her colleagues in exile. Not that Goodison herself shuns international subjects; for she writes with equal passion about racial injustice in South Africa; but her reference to specific Jamaican subjects, especially women of the poorest class, carries a unique sense of contemporary authenticity. Yet her inspiration is more spiritual or mystical rather than social or political: hence her yearning for 'heartease', a kind of mystical nirvana. Goodison's charge of inauthenticity against Roger Mais's language recalls Kincaid's comments on Lamming's patriarchal language in *In the Castle of My Skin*.

Unlike his cousin Cyril, David Dabydeen went from Guyana to England where he attended school and university and became a university lecturer. He has published scholarly works as well as three collections of poetry, *Slave Song* (1984), *Coolie Odyssey* (1988) and *Turner* (1994). Dabydeen's memories of post-Independence Guyana are vividly recorded in *The Intended* (1990), a novel that portrays rural Guyanese life chiefly among Indians or 'coolies'. David Dabydeen and Caryl Phillips are the two youngest writers interviewed in *Frontiers*. They come a full generation behind Lamming or Carew. Although Dabydeen grew up in the same rural part of Guyana as Carew, his childhood is separated from Carew's by forty years, and his report on racial riots and the evacuation of ethnic groups to safe areas, is a world away from Carew's rather idyllic version of a Guyanese countryside, in which he and Martin Carter[17] read poetry by moonlight, and discussed philosophy in the open air.

Dabydeen's *The Intended* and Phillips's most recent novels do not employ conventional techniques such as a third-person omniscient narrator, or a linear sequence of events based on chronology. In his interview, Phillips praises the technical innovations of Latin American writers for reflecting the social and cultural diversity of Latin America and the Caribbean more accurately than conventional techniques used by English-speaking Caribbean writers. Innovative techniques not only mirror Caribbean diversity: they place the region within a realistic, historical framework of colonial fragmentation in the process of evolving into the complex society of today.

Phillips's novels, plays and non-fiction reflect a highly promising talent. Somewhat like Kincaid, he can look at the Caribbean subjectively as well as objectively. The result is writing that provides uniquely balanced and perceptive insight into the condition of black people in the modern world. This condition is so deep-seated that, as Phillips suggests, it has direct links with Shakespeare's study of Othello nearly four hundred years ago. Phillips's promise is further illustrated by his evident growth during the five-year period separating his two interviews in *Frontiers*. A comparison of the two interviews will show some widening of the range of his ideas and a deepening of insight. Since the second interview starts off, in publishing chronology, from the point where the first ends, they should be read as parts of one whole.

As a literary form, the interview is essentially an oral version of literary biography. The interview unites biography, criticism and literary history, attempting to show how these genres are interrelated, and how their interrelationship might illuminate the creative process of the writers and the quality of their work. Since a good inverview can capture some of the spontaneity, directness and naturalness of the human exchange between writer and interviewer, there is a fine line between being spontaneous enough, yet not so spontaneous as to report mere gossip or irrelevance. Insofar as it can convey a subjective, personal sense of the writer's creative process, the interview is more effective than the critical essay.

While the best critical essays may stimulate more objective or intellectual excitement, it is unlikely that a critical essay can reproduce the combative vigour of some of the more personal comments and reactions expressed in these interviews. Similarly, an essay could not capture exactly the raw sense of violation in Jamaica Kincaid's reaction to V. S. Naipaul's description of a black man in *The Middle Passage*. Kincaid's reaction, in her own words, properly belongs to the realm of autobiography; but when combined in her interview with her criticism (and the interviewer's) of her own work, and the work of other writers, the result is a fuller commentary with human interest not normally available in a critical essay.

Like a critical essay, an interview cannot include every detail about a writer or his/her work. One has to select biographical facts as well as texts. One also has to take account of the writer's preferences. In *Frontiers*, for example, Roy Heath did not wish to comment either on his work, or on writing by other Caribbean authors. In Salkey's case, with three dozen works of poetry, fiction, essays, children's stories and travel-writing to draw on, his interview ran the risk of being either a mere bibliography, or so selective as to be pointless: in the end, it focused on him as a resource of literary history. Consequently, the method in *Frontiers* might appear too impressionistic, or anecdotal, and run the risk of presenting an incomplete view of each writer. But these interviews do not attempt to give a complete view of each writer: through the selective process of combining biography, criticism and literary history, they attempt to give an impression of the development of writing on external frontiers of the English-speaking Caribbean.

The interviews are arranged in a rough chronology that begins with the second-stage writers who emigrated to England in the 1950s, and ends with those in the third and fourth stages, who emigrated to England, Canada or the US after Independence. The interviews were recorded in three separate periods: in 1985/87 – Selvon, Lamming, Carew, and Phillips (l); 1990 – Roy Heath and David Dabydeen; 1991 – Salkey, Clarke, Cyril Dabydeen, Dionne Brand, Jamaica Kincaid, Lorna Goodison, and Phillips (2). Lamming's lecture 'Concepts of the Caribbean' was given in 1986, while Derek Walcott's reading of 'The Sea is History' occurred in 1989. The interviews with Carew, Selvon, Lamming and Phillips (l) were previously published.

I am grateful to Pat Cates and the staff of Academic and Technical Support Group (Arts) at York University for transcribing the interviews. Thanks also to Majorie Davis of the University of Warwick for transcribing two interviews. For editorial assistance I am grateful to Yvonne Vera,

Robin Potter and Venka Purushothaman. Thanks also to Jan Pearson for typing the final manuscript, and to the Dean of Arts, York University, for providing me with two research grants. My most grateful thanks, however, must go to the writers themselves, to whom I am deeply indebted for their infinite kindness and generosity.

Notes

1 *Frontiers* considers Caribbean literature in English by those who were born or raised in the Caribbean. Such writing began appearing before 1900, but did not attain a solidly distinctive quality until the early 1900s. Of course, there was a long tradition of writing about the Caribbean by visitors and travellers going as far back as the sixteenth century to figures like Sir Walter Raleigh. It is ironic that by the last decade of the twentieth century, Caribbean literature has come full circle to include writers like Caryl Phillips, who can now be regarded as a traveller or visitor to the Caribbean, although he is of Caribbean origin.

2 For James, see Chapter 2, note 15.

3 The 'Harlem Renaisance' is the name used to describe a goup of black American poets, essayists and novelists who emerged in New York shortly after the First World War. The work of these writers represented a 'rebirth' of black American writing. Some of the best-known names were James Wheldon Johnson, Countee Cullen and Langston Hughes.

4 Paule Marshall's Barbadian parents settled in New York during the First World War. She was born in 1929 and grew up in Brooklyn. *Brown Girl, Brownstones* (1959), her first novel, gives a dramatic portrait of Blacks in New York during the Depression. Paule Marshall has produced other works of fiction, including *The Chosen Place, The Timeless People* (1969) and *Praisesong for the Widow* (1983).

   Rosa Guy was born in Trinidad, but grew up in Harlem, New York. She was actively involved in the struggle of American Blacks for freedom, especially during the Depression. Rosa Guy has written several novels that dramatize black American experience in New York, for example, *A Bird at My Window* (1966) and *A Measure of Time* (1983).

5 For Mittelholzer, see Chapter 4, note 1.

6 V. S. Naipaul was born in Trinidad in 1932. He attended Queen's Royal College where he won a scholarship to Oxford University. He has lived in England since the 1950s, and has established an international reputation as a novelist, travel writer and author. Naipaul's first two novels were *The Mystic Masseur* (1957) and *The Suffrage of Elvira* (1958). He has written eighteen other volumes of fiction as well as non-fiction. Naipaul has won numerous awards for his writing. He has also been knighted. Many writers in *Frontiers* express opinions on Naipaul's writing, notably Jamaica Kincaid in Chapter 11.

7 Wilson Harris was born in Guyana in 1921. He attended Queen's College, and later worked as a land surveyor in the Guyanese hinterland which provides the setting for many of his novels. In 1959 he settled in England. Since his first novel, *Palace of the Peacock* (Faber and Faber, London, 1960), Harris has produced about twenty other works of fiction and non-fiction. His writing is regarded as rich, multi-layered and profound, though not easily accessible.

8 For Erna Brodber, see Chapter 2, note 10.

9 Caryl Phillips, *A State of Independence* (Faber and Faber, London, 1986).

10 V. S. Naipaul, *The Enigma of Arrival* (Viking Penguin, London, 1987).

11 V. S. Naipaul, *The Middle Passage* (André Deutsch, London, 1962).

12 For Burnham, see Chapter 1, note 13.
13 For Eric Williams, see Chapter 2, note 22.
14 For Dr Jagan, see Chapter 1, note 14.
15 H. G. DeLisser, *The Cup and the Lip* (Ernest Benn, London, 1956).
16 Edgar Mittelholzer, *Corentyne Thunder* (Secker & Warburg, London, 1944).
17 For Martin Carter, see Chapter 5, note 12.

George Lamming:
Concepts of the Caribbean

George Lamming was born in Barbados in 1927. He attended Combermere School, and in 1946 moved to Trinidad to teach. In 1950, he emigrated to England. His first novel, In the Castle of My Skin, *was published in 1953, and was followed in quick succession by three other novels and a travel book,* The Pleasures of Exile *(1960). More than a decade passed before two more novels appeared. Soon afterwards, Lamming returned to Barbados where he still lives, although he spends extensive periods lecturing or serving as writer-in-residence at various colleges and universities abroad. Lamming's first novel is now regarded as a West Indian classic, and his later novels probe West Indian political issues with perhaps greater perception than any other body of fiction. His novels, essays and lectures give Lamming a reputation as one of the most reliable commentators on West Indian subjects. Lamming has travelled widely, and won many awards, including an honorary doctorate from the University of the West Indies. (Lamming's lecture 'Concepts of the Caribbean' which follows, and his interview in Chapter 2 were recorded in Toronto on 12 November 1985.)*

A concept of people or place does not arrive out of the blue. How you come to think of where you are, and of your relation to where you are, is dependent on the character and nature of the power of where you are. You yourself do not decide who you are and what your relationship should be to where you are: a certain prevailing power does that. Therefore, if you are trying to think of concepts of the Caribbean, these concepts will undergo change, and will be offered differently according to either the centres of power that are shaping them, or the centres of resistance that are re-shaping them. So if you read history innocently, and hear about a sailor called Columbus whom you receive as hero and discoverer of worlds, your reading is a concept that has been shaped by some other authority.

A curious thing about the West Indies is that we started mis-named, and much later, we decided it was too late to change it. The tremendous movement of Columbus, who found himself mistakenly in a part of the world which he didn't know, was seen from a Europe that was making discoveries, and was therefore assessed positively and heroically: Columbus's movement could not conceivably have been seen in quite the same way by the people he encountered.

Before Columbus arrived in the Caribbean at the end of the fifteenth century, there was a very viable culture and civilization in these islands. There was an aboriginal population made up of people such as the Arawaks and Caribs who were moving from the mainland of South America or through the islands from Trinidad up to Cuba. Within a matter of twenty-five or thirty years of Columbus's arrival, this aboriginal population was almost totally destroyed. In other words, what we know about the modern Caribbean is that it is an area of the world that began with an almost unprecedented act of genocide. So when you look at history, its movement, and the concepts with which you define historical events, you realise that your perception depends on the defining centre of power or the re-defining centre of resistance.

The early European arrivals may look very heroic for what they did. The Europeans were remarkable men, and their achievement in navigation is not to be devalued or undermined. Yet the history of their arrival has been reconstructed in very strange ways, such that there is no greater collection of lies than what has been written about it. Columbus's journal speaks about meeting a Caribbean aboriginal on arrival and conversing with him. Yet, as far as I know, Columbus spoke not a word of any aboriginal Caribbean language, and the aboriginal spoke neither Italian nor Spanish; it is peculiar that they could understand each other: what Columbus really did was to create what he ordered, because he represented power.

For a hundred years after Columbus, every European power, some great, some small, moved into the region. There was no area of the New World over which European nations, in their discovering and thrusting out, did not engage in battle with each other to claim ownership of some part of the region. The concept of discovery – a false concept, in a sense – because there already were people living there – now shifts to the Caribbean where, for a long time, we have lived in what one can call the imperial frontier. In other words, these territories did not exist in themselves for themselves. They were conquered, settled, and maintained on behalf of those who owned them. There were early experiments in little peasant holdings with white people living in the islands. Then, this monster, sugar – this thing associated with sweetness – comes in and dominates the labour of the masses. Sugar has no respect for colour. When sugar, as a crop, was experimented with, it was found that it would require a large labour force, and in Barbados, St Kitts, Antigua and other places, small white land holders were driven off, some to settle in the southern United States. Sugar means land. So the concept of the imperial frontier had to shift to coincide with what we have since come to know as plantation society.

The movement of the people was absolutely necessary in order to justify the existence and expansion of the area as a plantation society. An extraordinary experiment took place from the end of the fifteenth century through to the nineteenth with the movement, first of Europe, then Africa, and Asia, into the Caribbean. Peculiar meetings took place, and various kinds of associations were formed amongst these cultures,[1] all meeting more or less under the same zonal authority, that is, according to who was in charge in a specific area; and by the end of the seventeenth century and the first two decades of the eighteenth, sugar had the kind of value that oil has acquired in our own time. At one stage the Dutch tried to exchange New York for Barbados, and the British refused. What De Gaulle rudely called a speck of dust (a West Indian island) had value in those days.[2]

As a result of struggles within plantation society, centres of resistance developed to the original concepts that were imposed. One such centre of resistance was to the idea of the Caribbean as an imperial frontier. This idea was powerfully held by both the British and the French, though less so by the Spanish who did not appear too interested in settling in the Caribbean. Francis Drake,[3] for example, a man whom we would today call a thug and vagabond, was greatly interested in Panama as the imperial frontier from which he could deal with the movement of Spanish gold. In resistance to such imperial ideas the concept grew that the Caribbean was a landscape re-made by the labour force of all those who had been brought into it from one place or another. Therefore, when we speak of the Caribbean, we are looking at a common historical experience that remains true for all parts of the region, whether they are French, English, or Spanish-speaking. In other words, the most authentic meaning of the word 'Caribbean' is the organiza-tion of labour within the region by people particularly from Asia and Africa, and the responses of their labour to imperial rule, including the way in which they organized successful rebellions against this rule.

Although people in the various territories had no direct experience of each other, a common kind of preoccupation comes out in the literature of all Caribbean territories, whether French, Spanish or English-speaking. The experience, in terms of organization, is one of plantation slavery, with its tremendous base of African labour, and the experience of indentured labour after emancipation. Into Guyana and Trinidad, Asia came, in different circumstances, but for purposes that were substantially the same. Whatever may be identified as cultural differences, including religion, between what you may call Indians and Africans in the Caribbean, their one common experience is the culture of labour. Both groups of people came into the society to perform precisely the same function, and for a long time had precisely the same relation to the domestic centre of power whatever the territory they were in.

When we hear of divisions between these people in a particular territory, we must consider the extent to which race may not have been a political device used to reinforce division; because what they have in common, as an historical experience, is the common culture of labour, precisely the same kind of labour relation to the land. This is one of the things I want to emphasize. Let us not be distracted by this notion – a powerful legacy – that we are dealing with something called the French-speaking Caribbean or the English-speaking Caribbean. What we are dealing with is the particular manifestation of people with a common historical experience. Caribbean history and sociology have suffered because they have been constrained by the notion that the English-speaking Caribbean scholar is one who is concerned with the English-speaking Caribbean, and sometimes one who does not even deal with the English-speaking Caribbean, but with some very specific territory like Jamaica or Barbados.

I emphasize this because I have a vision of the Caribbean which is shared by many people, and because we are talking about a reality that is still to be discovered. There are various reasons why we have not been able to discover that reality. One has to do with the early political fragmentation of our people. It is only very recently that we can make moves from territory A to territory B. It is not so long ago that if you were telephoning from Barbados to Martinique, the call had to go through London and Paris, although Barbados is just across from Martinique. This is one of the technical manifestations of the political fragmentation that we have suffered in the Caribbean. But fragmentation is opposed both by our common historical experience, and by a centre of resistance that has been planted and is expanding. In a way, there are elements within the university structures of all the territories which have been agents of this expansion, creating and fertilizing this concept of the Caribbean as one zone of historical experience, with very fundamental cultural linkages which are still to be identified and explored.

Resistance to this concept sometimes comes from certain powerful elements that dominate the social formation of the region within each territory. Everyone must be born somewhere, and although there are some strange people who may have forgotten where that is, everyone is subject to and dependent on influences from their place of birth. Things planted in your head by those influences sometimes remain there permanently. This is the basic definition of culture – 'cultivation' – that which is planted and tended and grows. I have a functioning relationship with labour movements in the region for the simple reason that I believe that labour is the basis of culture.[4]

The earliest meaning in the English language of the word 'culture' is the tending of plants and the raising of animals. (It is only later that it shifted from the physical and material world to be used also as a metaphor for the cultivation of the mind.) In other words, if you are interested in the culture of a society, in whatever period of time, one of the first things that you must look for is the means by which the people feed themselves. This is very obvious, because if there is no food, you cannot come to the university to read; you cannot do anything; you may fast for a while, but you will not survive for long. So, in a way, 'culture' has never lost its original meaning: the means whereby men and women feed themselves. The history of cultural development must be very closely related to the history of labour and to changes in the forms of labour in a society.

It is not an emphasis that is often made by historians and sociologists, but it is an example of how they can, within certain areas of what is called scholarship, distract us from some of the fundamental realities of human experience. Just think of the history you read, how heavy it is in what is called constitutional or military affairs, or matters which have to do with the decision-makers in that society! But the history of labour, as told by the forces of labour, is not very prominent in official texts of history. I do not know whether literary scholars make the connection, but one of the functions of the novel in the Caribbean is to serve as a form of social history. The novelist thus becomes one of the more serious social historians by bringing to attention the interior lives of men and women who were never thought to be sufficiently important for their thoughts and feelings to be registered. (If you are poor and black, the notion that you are a subject of study only makes sense to the police.)

I have been trying to share with workers how I see the formation, or rather deformation of the governing élite in most of Caribbean social life. The governing élite is fairly new, and extremely nervous; and because it is new, it is also very dependent and vulnerable. I wish to give what you might call the etiology of one member of this élite, a minister, perhaps of finance or agriculture.[5] It is the portrait of a man who is called 'Honourable Member', and whom many of you may have some reason to admire. He was born some forty-odd years ago in an urban village with a local primary school. Later, he attended two secondary schools, before going on a government scholarship to a university abroad. He qualified as a lawyer, and had a passing interest in the study of economics, but was persuaded by his godfather, a senior public figure, to return home where his chances of a political career looked promising. He had moderate success at the bar before he successfully contested an election. Today, he has served as a minister of the Government, and has represented his country in various international negotiations.

This minister owns four houses and a chicken farm. There is also rumour of substantial investments in an auxiliary transport service locally known as the Mini Bus. He has shares in various tourist resorts. His known assets are estimated to be in the region and figure of not under two-and-three-quarter million dollars. He occupies a large five-bedroom house in the rural suburbs, with an ample view of six parishes and an horizon of sky that disappears in the deep blue water around. His tastes have been influenced by foreign travel. The furniture in the house is modern Scandinavian, and there is a conspicuous assortment of Moroccan rugs, exquisitely patterned in crimson and gold. These were acquired after a brief romance in southern Spain. The walls on all sides are disfigured by juvenile souvenirs of illuminated nights in New York, eating out along the bay in San Francisco, racially mixed couples who play around the kidney-shaped swimming pool. There are no books anywhere.

The family has two cars, one Italian and the other Japanese. Our minister's cultural preference is magazine reading and film. He is careful in his choice of clothes. Abroad he was known to wear pink carnations in his buttonhole, but probably dropped this style of decoration since flowers on a man provokes serious questions in the Caribbean. He lunches frequently in restaurants on the south coast, dines twice weekly on the West coast. Much of his eating has to do with political and technological business. He has two children, a girl who went to St Hugh's high school from a junior school called St Gabriel's, and a son who had problems at home and was placed in a minor public school in the south of England. Neither child has seen the inside of a government, local, or elementary school, and neither has any recollection of ever travelling by bus or other forms of public transport.

I refrain from offering physical descriptions, since our minister is of the type who bitterly resents any reference to the skin. It is sufficient to add that his wife is a lady distinguished by her hair. They have both retained travel documents which allow them indefinite residence elsewhere. Many of his contemporaries have had similarly privileged schooling, and have been less enterprising; but they have all made notable contributions in education and at the upper levels of the civil service. Some have been chairs of corporations, senior functionaries in the development of various kinds of banking systems. A few are in general medical practice. None of his acquaintances have gone into business. Let us identify him as the 'Honourable Member', a man who sees his achievements as the basis of an expanding personal prosperity in the years ahead. To understand the true history of this man, in relation to his public duties, we cannot concentrate on the period of those forty years of which you have heard, nor can we view him exclusively in the context of his personal life, without any reference to his social formation. Such a limited perception can only lead to fruitless and self-defeating conclusions.

It is more helpful, instead, to examine the process of evolution which produced the success that he, and a whole class of men like himself, now embrace as the most desirable reward of their efforts – social power and material wealth. His great-grandfather was born in the parish of St George in 1876, the year of the Confederation riots.[6] He was put out to labour as an estate hand at the age of nine. Twelve years later, an ox-cart crippled him for life. Despite the fact that he already had a son of four, it would have been useless in those days to argue a case for compensation. He lingered until the age of 40, elaborating on the theories he had heard in his childhood about the great insurrection that engaged a turbulent class of workers against elements of the dominant class of that day.

It was a time when plantation families fled their homes to seek refuge on ships at anchor. In his parish alone, St George, assorted labourers had stolen or captured over 14 acres of produce. Their adversaries, even in 1877, said it was the work of communist agitators. That charge, as you will see, has been the official explanation of any disruptive social action for more than a century. It is amazing that, to this day, people can still success-fully make the danger of communism their main appeal in what are thought to be free and fair elections; for example, as Edward Seaga did in Jamaica.[7] The 'Honourable Member' would be in this category. His grandfather, who was born in 1894, continued to pass on his father's recollection of the Confederation riots. He could never, for example, understand why Gover-nor Hennessey should have chosen the outrageous proposal that the mental asylum in the parish of Barbados should be open to lunatics from other islands.[8]

His grandfather had distinguished himself as a cooper. He made and repaired every kind of wooden cask and tub you could imagine, and through his skills, made himself and the artisan class he represented, indispensable to the technical functioning of the plantation. This artisan class of coopers, carpenters, and masons were stubborn men who had cultivated an immense pride in the excellent quality of the things that they made; they had a simple, genuine dignity. The 'Honourable Member' would hardly remember him; but it was this grandfather who preached the necessity of education. He perceived the school as the only possible means of rescuing his offspring from the humiliation his ancestors had endured. The book, the lesson and the pen were taken seriously. That is why his son, the 'Honourable Mem-ber's' father, born in 1940, was destined to be an elementary school master. The elementary school became their chapel, Queens Royal College and Jamaica College their cathedral, and the English University the kingdom of heaven.[9]

Our 'Honourable Member' and his class – bright, ambitious and often patriotic men – assumed their challenging tasks without any historical or social experience of the ownership and control of the means of wealth and production in their own country. They are just functionaries who take care of other people's business. It makes for a certain frigidity at the heart of all their protestations about unfair terms of trade, when a subtle or not-so-subtle bullying by capitalist powers makes them shape a foreign policy that may not be in the interest of their people.

It is therefore important for working-class people, in this situation, to recognize what is the main bastion in the people's national defence. It is neither the army, police, nor any other arm of the state power, but those whose productive labour is the foundation of the country's survival, who constitute the major factor that will determine objective needs, and how these should relate to a genuine social climate. There is little or nothing functionaries or mercenaries can do before members of a united working class who know, with absolute clarity, what they have to do. If we were to follow the lifestyle of the 'Honourable Member' – the style that now threatens to be dominant for all people – we would stumble into a way of living in which we would consume what we do not produce, and produce what we scarcely consume.

I must now ask questions about the extraordinary interest which certain countries take in forms of democracy. I often wonder why capitalist imperialism should be so concerned about the electoral democracy that their vassals practice. How is it that these alien spirits, who have always been indifferent to the hunger of our children, should suddenly be so eager to rescue us from a lack of democracy? Is it not that they understand very well the arena of politics in which the 'Honourable Member' and his class organize their parades, and that they find in the national cock-fight we call elections the easiest and safest entry into our domestic affairs? I put it simply as a speculation and no more: the imperialist salesmen of electoral democracy recognize that the contending political parties, in their fierce pursuit of office, create an effective division within the ranks of working people, and make the power of labour that much easier to control. The fundamental basis of sovereignty should therefore be the workers' control of their place of work, where every choice of programme and personnel, from management to the floor, remains decisively within their hands. That would be an authentic arena for elections.

I do not want to discuss religion in terms of the vulnerability of a new governing élite that has never had any historical experience with being a ruling class. Religion, at a certain level, is custodian of the society, and it calls for serious reflection. We must not only contend with democracy, but also with a very serious challenge that comes from the evangelical movement. The most sinister vandals who have worked across the Caribbean are agents of this movement, and they have nothing whatsoever to do with religion, Christianity or Jesus. They are politically motivated, and I am convinced – when the work of identification is done – politically handled. It is a very serious matter. An amazing amount of radio-time, from one end of the Caribbean to the other, is taken up by these 'religious' broadcasts. There are some territories – for example, Dominica – where an entire station is devoted to such broadcasts 24 hours each day. Foreign evangelists recognize that there is a deep and genuine religious sensibility in that region.

This is one of the mistakes that people of the left have often made. You have to speak very carefully about God when dealing politically with 90 per cent of the people of the Caribbean. Your own views and your own position can put you in jeopardy if you try to equate that sensibility with something superficial or backward. Quite often there is a political intelligentsia that has not really worked out the language of communication to be adopted when dealing with that sensibility. But having spotted it, these politically motivated evangelical movements, have found that it is not a very difficult soil to exploit and abuse in the name of Jesus.[10]

At one time, the Caribbean may have been seen as an imperial frontier, but there is a vision now emerging in which we can speak of the region as a wider concept. It does not exist exclusively within the sea and at the shores that we geographically call the Caribbean. There is a Caribbean world that exists, in a very decisive kind of way, in many metropolitan centres, whether in North America or in Europe. There is a Caribbean in Amsterdam, Paris, London, and Birmingham; in New York and in other parts of North America. These centres comprise what I call the external frontier, and this frontier, particularly the visionary progressive elements within it, has a very decisive role to play in the future cultural and political development of the Caribbean. What that role will be might yet have to be worked out. But wherever you are, outside of the Caribbean, it should give you not only comfort, but a sense of cultural obligation, to feel that you are an important part of the Caribbean as external frontier.

Lamming answers questions from the audience

Q: You mentioned that after the Emancipation of African slaves, indentured labourers were brought over from India. Why did they bring this labour? Why didn't they just hire the blacks who were freed?

A: That is a very important question in Caribbean history. In a way, it would have been much cheaper to deal with the labour that was there, because there was no shortage of it. But since the labour was free, it was more difficult to deal with because it would not any longer work on the terms of the plantation. The very expensive exercise in indentured labour served to pay for control of the local African labour. Unfortunately, the agony of indentured labour has not been dealt with sufficiently. Some think it is only black people who have suffered in the Caribbean. In his last book, *The History of the Guyanese Working People*,[11] Rodney tries to draw our attention to the extraordinary struggle and pain of the Indian people, during that period of indenture. They arrived literally chained or locked into plantations; they could not move, and therefore they were used. It was a very expensive way of doing things, and its only justification was that it was the means by which plantation owners could control the force of labour which existed in that situation. It produced very serious tensions in the society.

Q: Are you saying then, that if indentured labour had not been brought over, that because the blacks were free, the price of labour – the wage rates – might have risen to a level that could have caused a crisis?

A: It might have become more expensive. The plantations would not have had the power to control labour as it did with the presence of the indentured labourers, because you could not predict when the blacks would work or when they would not. They had already started to withhold and regulate their labour. The survival of what remained of the plantation system depended, to a large extent, on regular and consistent labour at specific times. Sugar cane has to be cut when it is ready, and taken to the factory in time. Economically, in terms of saving money, I do not think indenture saved money. What was saved was the ability to control the Africans. This was psychologically very important – the actual social control of the African labour force. Regarding the Jamaican situation – within the period between 1838 to 1865 there was the remarkable development of ex-slaves buying land on the hillsides, and building their own schools. Jamaica, in a sense, was set for extending that kind of peasant smallholding society. But since you could not expand the wealth of blacks without also extending and increasing their political control, these smallholding extensions had to be contained or curtailed. If blacks acquired property, and thereby the right to vote – for that was the criterion on which voting privileges were based at that time – it meant that blacks would eventually achieve political control of the society. lacks formed an overwhelming majority of the population and to expand the experiment of peasant smallholdings was tantamount to accepting eventual political control by blacks.

Q: Experience in Africa was that Asians were given better jobs than the Africans. Although you say Asians and Africans shared the common experience of labour in the Caribbean, was the Asian not more favoured?

A: There are considerable differences in the development of these two sets of people – Africans and East Indians. If I look at the two areas with which I have had some acquaintance – Trinidad and Barbados, I would say that there appears to be, as people move off from the land, a preference for the African-descended person, as far as the controlling system was concerned. For example, up to forty years ago, it was a very rare thing, in Trinidad, to see a civil servant, not to speak of a senior civil servant, who was Indian. It was a very rare thing to find any senior officer in the police force who was Indian. In terms of some of the schools that I have mentioned here, up to the forties, there would not have been any substantial presence of Indian children in the privileged government secondary schools and colleges. That would have been the difference. So that although later, both in Trinidad and Guyana, there would develop a small – I don't think that it is as big as people make out – Indian, entrepreneurial class in both countries, in my view, today, the overwhelming majority of Indo-Guyanese and Indo-Trinidadians remain largely a working class. Indians have done more or less what the Africans have done. The old African grandfather who had a piece of land, invested heavily in education. Similarly, Indo-Guyanese now invest in products of education. But the situation is such that you have two major groups of people, with equal claim to the landscape, engaged in a very serious rivalry for political rights. That is where there is tension.

Q: If the difference between the Africans and Asians is not cultural, and since you have said there is no difference in their performance of labour, why does the rivalry persist?

A: There are differences in the sense that both people came with cultural legacies. One difference too is that the Indian came later, and therefore the Indian element makes the Indo-Guyanese and Indo-Trinidadian feel closer to each other than they might to other Guyanese and Trinidadians. They entered the society in the third or fourth decade of the nineteenth century, and continued to come in until about 1917. Their situation is well depicted in Selvon's novel *A Brighter Sun*, and in V. S. Naipaul's novel, *A House for Mr Biswas.*[12] Later generations are faced with the battle of identifying where they stand in relation to that process of creolizing through contact with their Afro-Caribbean environment. What I meant by a common culture of labour is that the overwhelming majority of Indo-Guyanese, for example, have the same relation to the agents who are controlling their society as the majority of blacks. In both Guyana and Trinidad, Indian labour is about the lowest-paid, because they are still there as labourers. When you say Indians are making this and that, what you are doing is selecting or identifying a small element within the group. It is like hearing that a man called Lamming had a million dollars, and then coming to me to say I was fooling you all the time. That has led to much tension.

In Guyana, race was used as a means of social control since the colonial period. If the newly-freed African labour was going to sabotage anything, they could not do it because of this new force. So that kind of challenge could be set up between them, and it continued to be used long afterwards. I am convinced that the long survival of Mr Burnham as Prime Minister and President of Guyana depended on the manipulation of race as a device.[13] Other people argue the other way around. But what Burnham succeeded in doing, very cleverly and carefully, is getting elements, particularly among the black plutocrats, to believe that he was the only person who could rescue them from Indians taking over. That was very carefully plotted, and that is how he used the device. When a device has been used for so long, by the way, it is very difficult for anybody in the situation to be wholly free from its influence. I do not myself share the view, but I know it is seriously argued by adversaries of Dr Cheddi Jagan,[14] that he was not himself exempt from manipulating race as a device for election purposes and for control of the total Indian constituency. When a particular method pervades a society for so long it doesn't matter how pure you are, it will be very difficult for you to be exempt from its influence.

In 1953 the People's Progressive Party, under the joint leadership of Burnham and Jagan, played a decisive role in Caribbean history, in terms of the politics of race.[15] They won an election and came to power, and this was so potentially dangerous to the colonial authorities that they were not allowed to stay in power. Within about three-and-half months, the constitution was suspended and most of the leaders jailed. The only member of the leadership who was not jailed was Burnham. What was the meaning of that exemption in 1953, and was it a factor in 1965 or 1966 when Burnham did become leader of the government?

Q: What are the prospects for Caribbean unity?

A: I consider the forging of regional contacts between each territory to be a very urgent task. I do not believe in what people call a national identity. No individual can realize this national identity creatively unless it takes place in a liberated Caribbean region.

Notes

1   For more than three centuries, Europeans in the Caribbean brought slaves from Africa to work on their plantations. Sexual liaisons between white masters and female slaves produced, in time, a mixed-blood population who occupied an intermediate position in the feudalistic social hierarchy of the plantation system. When slavery was abolished in the nineteenth century, labourers were brought from India to work on plantations vacated by the freed slaves. Lamming refers here to the multi-ethnic complexity, and social and cultural diversity that developed out of centuries of social mixing and cultural association between different ethnic groups in the Caribbean.

2   European nations engaged in fierce rivalry over their West Indian possessions. Territories were conquered in battle, or exchanged in treaties after the end of a war. Because of this, some territories changed ownership many times. Interest in the West Indian colonies was mainly economic.

3   Sir Francis Drake (1540–96) played a prominent role in the defeat of the Spanish Armada, and frequently attacked Spanish possessions in the Caribbean. Lamming refers to Drake's attack on Spanish ships *en route* to Spain, carrying gold and other valuables from Spain's colonies in South America.

4   In the 1970s Lamming had a close association with the Barbados Workers Union, and used to organize programmes for their Labour College.

5   The minister described is imaginary, a composite of traits most Caribbean people will recognize in individual politicians they have known. Lamming's portrait may be compared with Naipaul's description of the 'picaroon' in *The Middle Passage* (p. 79).

6   These identifiably Barbadian details suggest that Lamming's imaginary minister has

grown up in Barbados. For Confederation riots involving governor John Pope Hennessey, see note 8 below.

7 In 1980 Edward Seaga, leader of the Jamaica Labour Party (JLP) won elections against the ruling People's National Party led by Michael Manley. Seaga espoused free enterprise, anti-communism, and generally pro-Western policies that sharply contrasted with the previous Manley government's socialist policies, and its links with communist Cuba. Seaga's policies found favour with the Reagan administration in the US, and Seaga was one of the Caribbean leaders who supported the American invasion of Grenada, mounted in 1983 against the 'communist' government of the New Jewel Movement that had been led by Maurice Bishop.

8 John Pope Hennessey was appointed Governor of Barbados in 1875, when he tried to implement a proposal to form a Federation of the Windward Islands, including Barbados. The Federation was opposed by both whites and blacks in Barbados, who registered their opposition to the establishment of a mental hospital in Barbados to serve the Windward Islands as a whole. Riots ensued, and Governor Hennessey was transferred to Hong Kong in 1876.

9 Most British Caribbean colonies had one government Secondary School for boys, and one for girls, which were accessible mainly to children of the social élite (white and Coloured), whose families could afford to pay. Poorer children could enter only if they won scholarships. Trinidad had Queens Royal College; Jamaica, Jamaica College; Barbados, Harrison College; and Guyana, Queens College. These schools were staffed mainly by expatriate teachers with university degrees and a few local people who were university graduates.

10 The Christian evangelical sects to which Lamming refers are mainly American in origin. Suspicion of political involvement has been attached to these sects for a long time, for example, in Guyana, during the 1960s, when some sects were believed to harbour agents of the United States Central Intelligence Agency, intent on suppressing the threat of Marxism or Communism in Guyana. It is certainly plausible that these sects could serve the political interest of United States foreign policy which, at least until recently, had a paranoiac fear of popular, Marxist or Communist movements in Latin America and the Caribbean. See Index for Austin Clarke's reference to Evangelical sects.

11 Walter Rodney, *The History of the Guyanese Working People, 1881–1905* (Johns Hopkins University Press, Baltimore and London, 1981).

12 Samuel Selvon, *A Brighter Sun* (Allan Wingate, London, 1952). V. S. Naipaul, *A House for Mr Biswas* (André Deutsch, London, 1961).

13 Linden Forbes Sampson Burnham (1923–85) became Prime Minister of British Guiana in 1964. The country achieved Independence from Britain in 1966, and its name was later changed to Guyana. As head of government, Burnham changed his title to President, and the country became a republic within the British Commonwealth. Burnham remained as head of government and leader of the ruling party, the People's National Congress (PNC) until his death. The PNC is supported mainly by Afro-Guyanese. See note 15 below.

14 Dr Cheddi Jagan was born on a sugar plantation in Guyana in 1922. He trained as a dentist in the USA and returned to Guyana where he founded the People's Progressive Party (PPP) in 1950. The PPP, with Dr Jagan as leader, won elections in 1953; but the government was dissolved by the Governor after only 133 days. Dr Jagan and his party won elections again in 1957, and yet again in 1961. After 1964, Dr Jagan was leader of the opposition until he became President in 1992.

15 The electoral victory of the PPP was significant partly because the elections were based on a constitution that permitted universal adult suffrage for the first time in Guyana's history, and partly because the PPP presented a united front that included members from all sections of Guyanese society. It was after the government was dissolved, and the

constitution suspended, that fighting within the PPP caused the party to break in two. Burnham then took a wing of the PPP that followed him to form the PNC. Thus, with an Indo-Guyanese as leader of the PPP, and an Afro-Guyanese as leader of the PNC, the electorate became racially polarized, and Jagan was seen to represent Indians, while Burnham was identified with the interests of the Afro-Guyanese. See Chapter 7, note 38.

CHAPTER 2 | George Lamming: Africa and the Caribbean

Q: In the 1950s we had many colonial hang-ups, and Africa was a place about which all West Indians, including those of African descent, were very mixed up.[1] Since then we've had many commentators, in particular Edward Brathwaite,[2] the historian and poet, who have greatly illuminated the African past of the Caribbean. How has the subject of Africa in Caribbean consciousness affected Caribbean literature?

A: I think one must always look at these influences as evolving forces. I would say that that [African] influence has deepened a little more in Caribbean consciousness, not for literary reasons, but because there has been a greater awareness of Africa at the political level. Up to about when *The Pleasures of Exile*[3] was written, I would guess that no African leader had ever visited a Caribbean territory, or vice-versa. In the twenty years or so since then, masses of people in Jamaica, Barbados, and Trinidad have seen Nyerere, Machel, and Kaunda; and Zambia knows Manley.[4] So, in a sense, there has been something more concrete than the previous romanticism. Masses of Caribbean people have actually seen and heard these African leaders. Then, getting nearer to questions of creative expression, I would say that we have also seen during that period (about 1960 to 1980) African writers who have visited the Caribbean. This is very important, because it used to be very much a one-way traffic, of the Caribbean man or woman going to Africa. We've had Ngugi[5] who has been to Grenada and Barbados in recent times. There has also been a Nigerian, Omotoso,[6] who has spent a rather long time in Barbados and in Jamaica, and I think in Trinidad as well. He was working on developments in popular theatre in the region. Then there was Abiola Irele, a Nigerian academic whose major work was on Césaire and the French-speaking Caribbean.[7] I would say that there is a sense in which there has been a concretization of the Afro-Caribbean connection, and that, of course, will expand. It won't contract. From here on, it is likely to get wider and wider.

In terms of creative expression, I would say that the most powerful influence on Caribbean literature by way of linkage between concepts of Africa and the Caribbean, has been through the rapid development of the Rastafarian movement. The Rastafarian movement[8] is a most extraordinary and powerful phenomenon which was founded in Jamaica in 1930; from the 1950s when it was still an almost exclusively Jamaican phenomenon, it has now become a regional, cultural force. Now, there isn't a Caribbean territory where it does not exist, and where it has not had a strong influence. It has had its influence on Walcott in *O Babylon*.[9] There is also a very fine novel by Erna Brodber,[10] a Jamaican; and I would think there are further influences in a variety of ways. Of course, in the music of the region, I think, by linkage, there has been that influence too. It takes the form of people still searching for this Africa and not yet being clear about it.

Q: So it's a dynamic process.

A: I would think so, yes, because it still raises the question of what is the cultural base of the society. It raises the question of what forms of collaboration are to take place.

Q: One might focus on one particular aspect of the African connection, namely the African oral tradition and what that has meant for Caribbean literature itself, for instance, in the structure of *In the Castle of My Skin*.[11] I think critics tend to talk a bit loosely about the influence of an African oral tradition on any Caribbean narrative that is not structured in a strictly chronological way. Were you aware, in a formal sense, of an African oral tradition when you were writing *In the Castle of My Skin*?

A: No, I don't think so. Remember, *In the Castle of My Skin* was written very early. I was aware of a very powerful oral tradition, in the village in Barbados, but I wouldn't think that there was any conscious linkage to Africa. I think that there is a very conscious linkage with Africa through the old people, and I would have been aware of the image of Garvey[12] which would probably have had something to do with my awareness of Africa.

When I was writing *In the Castle of My Skin*, which would be in 1951 or 1952, I had become very aware of Africa. The first time I met Africans was in London,[13] and I think there was a lot of influence there. I was a regular visitor to the West African Students' Union, where we had a lot of discussions. These discussions were largely about the common predicament of colonial peoples and the kinds of struggles, cultural and otherwise, that had to be endured. I suppose it would make sense to draw on – I don't know if you will call them African – influences, but I was not conscious of them. Still there is a lot of such influence. This is one of the things that Brathwaite has been trying to identify – and later Maureen Warner Lewis[14] – that there is indeed a lot of African behaviour in Caribbean society, of which the people practising that behaviour are not themselves aware.

Q: While we are on the subject of attitudes toward Africa, you speak with great admiration of C. L. R. James,[15] as we all do. He is our first great intellectual; there is no question about that. Recently, in the *Third World Book Review*, when an interviewer asked him about the African past and Caribbean culture, James said:

I do not know what are the African roots of the language and culture of Caribbean intellectuals. I am not aware of the African roots of my use of the language and culture. I pay a lot of respect to Africa. I have been there many times. I have spoken to many Africans. I have read their literature. But we of the Caribbean have not got an African past. We are black in the skin, but the African civilisation is not ours. The basis of our civilisation in the Caribbean is an adaptation of Western civilisation.[16]

It seems an astonishing statement for the author of *Black Jacobins*.[17] Do you know about that aspect of James's thinking? It is not an unknown opinion in the West Indies, even now in the 1980s when there are still people who try to reject the African past, despite all the analyses and the illumination that we have had about the historical African reality.

A: There is a lot of complexity in James's situation. There was another occasion, much earlier, when he was describing what we would call his intellectual physiognomy, that is, how his mind worked. It is true that James came out of a region whose literary classes would have been shaped by a Victorian ethos of the gentleman as scholar. This was then radicalized by the politics of skin, which was unavoidable if you lived in Trinidad in the 1920s and the 1930s. What he is saying is that there were seminal, critical ideas within that European tradition that enabled him to understand what he understands about Africa and its relation to the world, and that those ideas were his guide. He did not find those ideas in Africa; he found them in that particular social mould in which he grew up.

Q: But those ideas would have projected a misguided view of Africa as being a dark place of non-achievement.

A: I don't think he believed that. I don't know him on that.

Q: He has never said that, and I am not saying that. But I am pointing out the danger of that kind of educational process, which could have influenced a black Caribbean intellectual in that way, at that time.

A: James also was going to be a pioneer among non-Africans. He was going to be a pioneer figure in arguing the case about the African capacity for ruling his world. It is that idea too which influences the organization of *Black Jacobins*. James finds a way in which he equates the struggle in Haiti with events which have been taking place in Africa with the Kikuyus, who have been fighting against British colonial rule since the 1920s. I don't think he has any doubt about that. I think he explained that it was much later that he got to reading about and trying to understand the content of African civilizations before their contact with Europe. That was not on the agenda when he was growing up.

Q: On a more personal level, I followed your career from *In the Castle of My Skin* (1953) to *A Season of Adventure* (1960), and observed the steady growth of an important Caribbean writer. Then I noticed a gap between *A Season of Adventure* and *Water with Berries* (1971).[18] Could you tell me a little about what happened in that period? Were you engaged in journalism or travel and, if so, why not fiction?

A: I think people are inclined to see a career in terms of publishing events, but the fact that there is a gap in publication does not mean that work is not going on: it might take time. There is an interval, and I might have to speculate about that myself, because I am not at all sure that I have the answer to your question.

I do remember that, from the 1960s onward, my career was involved in a lot of travel, the kind of travel that was greatly involved in the Caribbean. I was going to and fro and getting involved in what I call extra-curricular activity. For example, I think it was in 1965 or so that I spent a year for the New World group as the guest editor of the two issues about Barbados and Guyana Independence. To the best of my recollection I had also started, probably before '65, to write *Natives of My Person*.[19] It had a long gestation and long organization period. That probably took longer than any other book. I remember that sections of it were written when I was Writer-in-Residence at the Mona Campus (Jamaica) of the University of the West Indies, in 1967. So there is a long period during which *Natives* was being worked on.

Q: This long gestation period might be related to what was said about Africa before. Is it possible that the genesis of this novel is a matter of your wrestling with the African past, and ordering it in your own imagination? A later critic did say that in *Natives of My Person* you are studying the etiology of the causes that hinder present-day Caribbean social development. The causes or things that hinder such development are surely to be found in the historical relationship of the Caribbean to Africa – slavery, and so on.

A: I think there are different approaches in looking at my published work. My work has a very strong thematic base. There is a sense in which, from *In the Castle of My Skin* to *Natives of My Person*, you can read my work really as one book. If you see *In the Castle of My Skin* as the re-creation of a colonial childhood and adolescence, it applies not only to Barbados, but really to the whole region. Already that book has a regional character. At the end of it, the boy leaves for Trinidad, and then the next book picks up on the stage of movement in our history which is the migration to England. Those long speculations and so on between the men on the deck in *Natives of My Person* are really an extension of the long speculations of the boys on the beach in *In the Castle of My Skin*. The groupings are almost similar – this talking about a world which exists only as an idea in your head and you can see the men on the deck as the extensions of the boys on the beach, that movement out, people searching and feeling. That was Stage Two.

Then we get the first explicit political novel, *Of Age and Innocence*,[20] which looks at the kinds of struggle that would be taking place in what were the last stages of the colonial experience. It is about people getting ready to rule, and the problems that are going to come up. The terrain that is really at influence there is Guyana, with that close relation between the African and the Indian leader and the arguments that go on around that. There is also a whole sub-plot of the secret society in which the Indian boy, the African boy, the Chinese boy are in fact living out the future that the adult world is talking about.

Then *A Season of Adventure*[21] brings us to the predicament of these peoples after the fall of colonial rule, namely, that independence is going to collapse because it has no base. I say all this to suggest that the span of the novels, from the re-creation of the colonial childhood to the fall of the first Independence government, encompasses a whole era of experience. Being a thematic writer, the question was what was the next stage in that cyle, and the next stage – it came up logically when I look back on it – was to find a metaphor that rounded the whole thing off, a sense in which, in one way, *Natives of My Person* might have opened that cycle, although I would not have had the intellectual experience or the skills to organize that kind of book at the time I was writing *In the Castle of My Skin*. So the end is the beginning in that sense, and *Natives of My Person* is not about the six-teenth–seventeenth-century age of reconnaissance: it is a critical explora-tion of what was happening in the twentieth century post-Independence period. You could interpret the commandant in *Natives* as a composite figure of the Caribbean boss leader. The commandant could be a composite of Williams,[22] Burnham,[23] Manley,[24] that figure who came up and was chosen, but once in the seat of authority, ruled in that kind of way. The democratic process never got internalized in Caribbean society. Structures that might be called democratic were established, but they were never fully accepted as workable for normal, day-to-day living.

Notes

1   Up to the 1950s there were very few exchanges between Britain's colonies in Africa and those in the West Indies. The first African country to gain Independence was Ghana in 1957. That promoted freer exchange.

2   Edward Brathwaite was born in Barbados in 1930. He read history at Cambridge Univer-sity and lived in Ghana for eight years. His trilogy, *The Arrivants*, published in the late 1960s, provides a comprehensive treatment of the relationship between Africa and blacks living in the Caribbean and the Americas. Cf. Chapter 4, note 40.

3   George Lamming, *The Pleasures of Exile* (Michael Joseph, London, 1960).

4   Julius Nyerere was President of Tanzania; Samora Machel was President of Mozambique till his mysterious death in an air crash in the early 1980s; Kenneth Kaunda was born in

1924 and was president of Zambia until 1991. Michael Manley, son of Norman Manley, was Prime Minister of Jamaica from 1972 to 1980. He then became leader of the opposition. Manley was re-elected Prime Minister in 1989 and resigned because of ill-health in 1992. Cf. Chapter 1, note 7.

5　Ngugi wa Thiong'o, the Kenyan novelist, wrote a critical work, *Homecoming and Other Essays* (Heinemann, London, 1972), based on his experience in the Caribbean.

6　Kole Omotoso is a Nigerian scholar, novelist and author whose *The Theatrical into Theatre* (New Beacon Books, London, 1982) is a full-length study of drama in the English-speaking Caribbean.

7　Professor Abiola Irele was teaching at the University of Ibadan, Nigeria at the time. He now teaches in the US.

8　Rastafarianism is a fundamentalist religious philosophy linked to social protest. It has its roots in Jamaica in the 1930s, but did not become popular until the 1960s and 1970s. The name 'Rastafarian' signifies one who believes that the former Ethiopian Emperor Haile Selassie or 'Ras Tafari' is Christ reincarnated. Rastafarian beliefs are based on the biblical account of King Nebuchadnezzar who ruled the kingdom of Babylon, and sacred Jerusalem. Rastafarians regard themselves as living in captivity, in Babylon – present-day Jamaica.

9　Derek Walcott's play *O Babylon* portrays members of the Rastafarian community in Jamaica. The play was written in 1975, revised in 1976, and published by Farrar, Straus and Giroux in New York, in 1978, in the volume *Joker of Seville and O Babylon*.

10　Erna Brodber is the author of two novels, *Jane and Louisa Will Soon Come Home* (New Beacon Books, London, 1980) and *Myal* (New Beacon Books, London, 1988).

11　George Lamming, *In the Castle of My Skin* (Michael Joseph, London, 1953).

12　Marcus Garvey (1887–1940) was born in Jamaica. He established the Universal Negro Improvement Association in Jamaica in 1917. In 1916 he moved to the US where his black self-help movement became widely known through his many speeches, editorials, essays, manifestos, and petitions.

13　London in the 1950s was an international centre especially for Commonwealth students, writers and scholars. There, as a West Indian, Lamming would have had his first opportunity of meeting Africans or Asians – fellow Commonwealth citizens.

14　Maureen Warner Lewis teaches at the University of the West Indies in Mona, Jamaica. Some of her critical writings explore Afro-Caribbean connections, especially in the field of linguistics. See her *Guinea's Other Sons* (1990).

15　Cyril Lionel Robert James (1901–89) is the most distinguished man of letters ever to emerge from the English-speaking Caribbean. James was born in Trinidad and educated at Queens Royal College. His formidable scholarship and prolific writing on history, politics, culture, literary criticism, fiction and sport are, astonishingly, the product of his own self-education. James's novel *Minty Alley* (New Beacon Books, London) was published as early as 1936, but his reputation is based more on his historical and political writings. *The Black Jacobins*, a history of the successful San Domingo revolution by black slaves, appeared in 1938, and is regarded as a classic of historical writing. James emigrated to England in 1932. He spent 1938–53 in the US. In 1958 he went to Trinidad and played an active role in the struggle for Independence, but in 1962 he returned to England where his final years were spent.

16　Angus Calder, 'An Audience with C. L. R. James', *Third World Book Review*, I, ii. 1984, p. 6.

17　C. L. R. James, *The Black Jacobins: Toussaint L'Ouverture and the San Domingo Revolution* (New York: Dial, 1938; New York: Vintage Books, 1963).

18　Between 1953 and 1960, Lamming produced four novels. It was another eleven years (1971) before his fifth novel appeared, *Water With Berries* (Longman, London).

19 George Lamming, *Natives of My Person* (Longman, London, 1972).
20 George Lamming, *Of Age and Innocence* (Michael Joseph, London, 1958).
21 George Lamming, *Season of Adventure* (Michael Joseph, London, 1960).
22 Dr Eric Williams (1911–82) was Prime Minister of Trinidad and Tobago from 1956 to
    1982. Williams was born in Trinidad and attended Oxford University in England where he
    read history. He wrote several historical works, the most famous of which, *Capitalism and
    Slavery* (1964), argues that there were economic rather than humanitarian motives for the
    abolition of slavery.
23 See Chapter 1, note 13.
24 See note 4 above.

CHAPTER 3

Derek Walcott: The sea is history[1]

Derek Walcott was born in St Lucia in 1930. He studied at the University College of the West Indies in Jamaica, and settled in Trinidad where he worked for the local newspaper the Trinidad Guardian. *In 1959 he founded the Trinidad Theatre Workshop and remained its director until 1977. His plays were produced at the Workshop and in other parts of the Caribbean, as well as abroad. Walcott's earliest poems appeared in the West Indies during the 1940s and 1950s. His first major collection of poems to be published in Britain was* In a Green Night *(1962). Since then Walcott has produced several other collections of poems and plays which have increased his reputation as one of the finest of contemporary poets and a leading dramatist. Certainly he is the major figure among anglophone Caribbean poets, his only serious rival being Edward Kamau Brathwaite. Walcott also writes perceptive reviews and literary essays. It is interesting that Walcott achieved international eminence as an author before he left the West Indies to live in the US in the 1980s. He was awarded the Nobel prize for literature in 1992. (His reading was recorded at York University in Toronto on 18 January 1989.)*

The word called 'history' is the question. I'm talking neither about the idea of revisionist history, from the reverse view of the victim now becoming articulate, nor about the idea of history from the view of the ex or current master, or ex or current slave. I'm talking about the idea of history becoming a deity, a force, as much as science has become a deity. History obviously has to do with the idea of time, and the idea of time varies. People who have confidence to dominate the idea of time, or nations who have ideas of dominating the future, or of hallowing the past, do it under the name of this alleged force called history.

There's no history in art, for example. The criticism of art is historical, but art itself does not contain history. I am not talking about ruins. There are too many people who are horrified at the idea of what would turn out to be the bad taste of the Greeks, because our concept of Grecian sculpture is a bleached-out Elgin marbles[2] frieze in which everything is dripping with weather, and some eyes are missing, and an arm is gone. That is a ruin sanctified by time; and the people who behold ruins sanctify them through the eyes of history. But that statue or frieze, if it were seen in its own time, would horrify the elegant taste of people who now cherish it.

You wouldn't want to believe that Greek statues were painted in the way that Catholic icons are painted, or that they had eyes and simulations of lips, and flesh colour, or bright clothes. But Greek statues were not Victorian: they were Asian objects, painted brightly, simulations, in proportion, of actual human figures. In other words, if we looked at Greek sculpture now, we would judge it to be bad art. Our hallowing of what is archaic is a process of the presumption of dominating time through memory; and I think it affects everything. It affects concepts of art. It certainly affects concepts of people seeming to be unable to produce art in the way that people who make art think it should look. For countries that are generally described as emerging, or third world, that is an affliction that is very hard to get rid of.

The Greek actress Irene Papas[3] said that in her opinion the closest thing to a Greek play was the musical *Hair*:[4] it had all the noise, vitality, choreography and the unity of a production like *Hair*. Our image of Greek theatre is of bleached-out, stately, dusty, real, moving statues, and we prefer to preserve it; but as long as aesthetics are tainted by this temporality of an idea of art and time, then ordinary things like concepts of progress and development, and what is a greater achievement, by comparison, become minimal to the idea of aesthetics being affected by time. Unless some approach, not necessarily disrespect, but some deflection of the way of looking at time happens in people, then all they can do is yearn to imitate, change, or radically alter, which is just as bad as imitation in a sense.

I've often asked myself if I say this because I'm embarrassed about the past. If you look at the past of the Caribbean, there's much to be ashamed of, because every racial group in the Caribbean has come from a situation of degradation. Most of the white people in the Caribbean, for instance, are descendants of convicts. Then there were slaves, indentured servants and so on. But this is temporal, just a few centuries. Unless the artist can work his way through this, then he's going to be under the same burden of science, politics and the state.

There is a quotation from Joyce's *Ulysses*: 'History is the nightmare from which I'm trying to awake' (Knopf and Random House, New York, 1961, p. 34) and I don't think he simply means the peculiar, special, provincial history of Ireland: he is talking about time: the consequential idea of time. For the artist to deliver himself from the bondage of time, which is called 'history' is the only way he himself can burst through. And the bondage of time involves language. It involves the idea of language being the tool that dominates the colonial. The Irish situation is exactly what I'm talking about, in which it is not simply a matter of losing your language. In the idea of language is included the idea of time. If you think of the development of literature in epochs, or treat literature as if it were a science, then every epoch should lead to a literary discovery, and the discovery of penicillin would become like the appearance of Dante. Literature would develop progressively in the same way that the history of science does. But this is not true. We have never had another Dante. So how can you judge the idea of literature in the temporal sense? The idea of art has no tense apart from the present. Dante, for a poet, *is*. That is related to the same idea that God *is*. God doesn't have a past or future tense. And art does not have a past or future tense.

The poem I shall read gives a compressed, though not chronologically accurate, portrait of Caribbean history and how it progresses. When somebody asks you where is your history or where is your culture, or what have you done, the question comes from a presumption of people who believe that history represents achievement: it can therefore be chronicled successively by epochs as a record of achievement. That's a Faustian idea that leads to Nazi Germany, or to empires. Empires claim time. Hitler and Napoleon claim time. These people have a destiny. They feel that they are produced by history, and therefore can dominate it. History is only an aspect of the kind of territory, one of the territories that they dominate. So if someone asks me, as a Caribbean person: 'Where is your history?' I would say: 'It is out there, in that cloud, that sky, the water moving.' And, if the questioner says: 'There's nothing there,' I would say: 'Well, that's what I think history is. There's nothing there.' The sea is history.[5]

It's one thing to have said what I said; it's another thing to admit and show what I've tried to do in this poem ['The Sea is History']. It's not only an idealized, romantic, or bitter view of history, because towards the end what is abused and what is excoriated is the decay, and the fact that the people who now run the Caribbean are acting on the same view of history: they are re-enacting this linear idea of possession, of rule, of using the same methods to govern as their predecessors did. In other words, the most imitative aspect of the slave is when he rules and imitates the conduct of the master. That's the worst aspect of colonialism. And it is not only confined to the Caribbean: it's in the history of the Western hemisphere. It's there in the history of the American Indian; in the history of the Mexican. It's in Nicaragua. If it were possible to look at the Nicaraguan from the point of view of not having a concept of destiny, such as the American empire has, then things would be perhaps a little clearer. That does not mean that I'm idealizing a sort of pastoral, nostalgic or futuristic dream world, because the end of the poem is perhaps even more furious than the beginning.

Derek Walcott answers questions from the audience

Q: Is your voice the voice of the entire Caribbean people?

A: It's an historical question that confines itself to whether the authority of the poet's voice is part of an authority to speak for the people, and that is a political trap, a trap of ambition, and of the spirit. No, because I'm not the only writer in the Caribbean. I would imagine that fury, anger, or a sense of injustice can produce in a writer the wish to be articulate; but that is a very dangerous trap. I'm not even interested in sharing the feelings of the people, because those who have been asked to share the feelings of the people are the ones who get shot first. Joyce talked about this. What he said was not: 'I'm going to speak for my people.' He said: 'I want to be the uncreated conscience of my race.'[6] That's the crucial thing. Not to be prophetic and messianic, but to make the conscience.

I think Shelley meant the same thing when he said: 'poets are un-acknowledged legislators of the World'.[7] Again it is like a Greek statue. The idea of seeing Shelley as some ethereal fairy up in the clouds with a trumpet blowing is absurd. That is not what he's saying. Shelley was a very commit-ted, actively political person in his work. So when he talks about poets being unacknowledged legislators, he is not saying anything romantic: he is saying something radical. The trumpets do call to battle, so long as you don't think of every voice as a trumpet. It may be a flute, or something else. It's not different from what the Russian or Irish poets have suffered. They *are* the unacknowledged legislators. And Shelley is not saying that they will remain unacknowledged. But if they are acknowledged, it would not be to their glory, for then we would have in the world a sense of that acknowledgement that might deprive the poets of the need to say what they had to say.

The last thing I would want to hear myself being described as is '*vox populi*', because that's a politician's trip. If I felt at the time that I lived, that I tried to say something about the West Indian race which is not only black, but Chinese, Indian – everything – then, if I even said anything touching any of these races, I would really have been in a situation where I might have tried to make a small utterance for people who are represented by all the continents in the world. It is politically seductive to do that, and that is the danger of what is commonly called political poetry: because it immedi-ately takes on temporality. It says: 'This is necessary, it's for now: we need it now.'

Q: You talk about growing up as a child and watching life around you, and learning from it. But you also talk about creating something new. In what sense is your writing new?

A: I don't think that I was trying to find a new way to do anything, because if I was to find a new way to do something, I would be *avant garde*; but I had this generation of writers around me – Lamming, Naipaul, Brathwaite.[8] What happened was not like somebody coming into a clearing in which suddenly there was a vista. The Caribbean is a very old society, historically older than America: Barbados is older than New York.[9] But what was around us had not been written down. It's hard to believe the fear and excitement you felt if you wrote the word 'breadfruit' in 1945; because breadfruit was comic. It was not an apple that had been celebrated by Cézanne.[10] You didn't read a sonnet which said 'Shall I compare you to a breadfruit tree?' Yet, the sculpted shape of a breadfruit is extremely beautiful. The breadfruit leaf is also beautiful. But the word did not have history.

If this was a Latin culture, and I came and said the word 'potato', you'd burst out laughing, because the word has no history. If I said 'breadfruit' in 1945, the word would not have been treated with historical respect. That is why we as writers felt a tremendous excitement; because we were putting that word down, and at the back of it was this absence of any profound literary or artistic association. It was not like somebody trying to write because a missionary had told them how to make a 'w'. It was simply that these were gifted writers who had this tremendous, exhilarating, open thing ahead of them. And none of them was like the other. Because if they were all part of a political school, or even a racially united movement, West Indian literature would not be so various. The characteristic temperament of Naipaul is very different to that of Reid, or Lamming, or Hearne, or Selvon; and different in terms not of race, and not even of being from Trinidad or from Barbados. This was the real originality of these writers – that they gave a name and dignity to a thing like the breadfruit which was not even named before them. But nobody felt authoritative doing it. In that sense the thing was new.

Q: Before your plays, was there any drama in St Lucia?

A: When I was recently in St Lucia I was talking about theatre in the street. It wasn't restricted and didn't have a proscenium and so forth. It was natural. On Boxing Day, in St Lucia, there was a man who was called Flavier, or Flavier Jab; Flavier Diable; Flavier the Devil. His job in life was to play the devil on Boxing Day. He had the same function and hierarchy as Japanese Kabuki. Another man played the She Devil, and they had a troupe of imps around them. You knew that on Boxing Day Flavier was playing the devil, if you were in your house and you heard far off a lot of children chanting different chants. One of them would go: 'Woy woy mwe diab-la! Woy woy mwe diab-la!' which means, 'Look! Look! Here's the devil.' Then the devil would say: 'Voyer send de l'eau water ba give me,' and the children would repeat: 'Mwe ka bruler, I'm burning. Throw water on me, I'm burning.' This is the devil saying it. And the devil would continue: 'Voyez de l'eau ba mwe', and the children would say: 'Mwe ka bruler', and they would vary the melody until it got into a kind of counterpoint.

What is happening is that the devil is walking along, and he is surrounded by his imps and a Lucifer figure, who is his lieutenant. Then the children follow him; not only the children, but virtually a street. So he was in charge of the town. In other words, if you stayed at home and heard it, you were petrified. His costume was a combination of Santa Claus, the devil, and Greek-African. He had an exaggerated pair of comically large balls. Then he had a tail, sisal beard, and horns. He had the right to go anywhere. He would lead people. When he stopped, they would stop. He would turn. They would wait. Then he could charge them right down the block. And they'd run and he'd be chasing them. And the whole drama, the whole choreography of this man acting this role on Boxing Day was that this town belonged to him. There's no theatre in the world where that happens now: that anybody has a town to themselves and is given complete respect and has the authority to smear or chase you.

I remember we used to look through the jalousies and say 'Well, my God, Flavier is coming!' And we would see some dignified bourgeois going down the road, and he would hear this chanting, far down the street: 'Woy, woy mwe diabla!' and he would quietly turn right around and go back home, not because he was scared, but because it created that whole aura of dramatic participation. One of the most amazing performances was that at every crossroads they came to, they and the imps would put down a sisal sack, and enact the Fall of Lucifer. I think his name was Seewo, but he did the exact thing that Lucifer did, which is to challenge the authority, not of God, but of the devil. The mythology gets very mixed up. They would then enact a resurrection. Father Christmas and X and Y and all those things were concentrated in a combination of Catholic and African mythology.

There's no theatre like this: it was not spontaneous, and it was not exuberant; it was codified, rigid; and it had its own rules of conduct. The equivalent would be if a playwright had an audience which he could tell: 'Follow me around the town. Here's my play.' The only way to do this play is to completely re-enact it with the audience. Performed by itself on stage it becomes meaningless. But performed in the street, and followed by a crowd like in a golf game, that would be the theatre that I am describing.

Notes

1 This chapter consists of remarks made by Walcott before and after reading the poem 'The Sea is History', which is taken from his collection of poems: *The Star Apple Kingdom* (Farrar, Straus, Giroux, New York, 1979), pp. 25–8.

2 The Elgin Marbles are Greek sculptures brought from Athens, in 1816, by Thomas Bruce, 7th Earl of Elgin, while he was in the British diplomatic service. They are now exhibited in the British Museum in London, and have been reclaimed by the Greek government, so far without success.

3 Irene Papas is a Greek actress who has appeared in classical Greek drama in the theatre and on film.

4 *Hair* is the 'American tribal rock musical' first produced off-Broadway in the 1960s, then on Broadway by Bertrand Castelli (lyrics by Gerome Ragni and James Rado). The musical captures the radical spirit of the 1960s' cultural revolution.

5 Walcott reads his poem 'The Sea is History' at this point.
6 James Joyce, *Portrait of the Artist as a Young Man* (Penguin, 1976, London), p. 253.
7 The last line in Shelley's 'A Defence of Poetry'.
8 See Index for Lamming, Naipaul and Brathwaite.
9 Cf. Phillips's remarks on the age of the Caribbean in his interview.
10 Cézanne (1839–1906), a French Post-Impressionist painter, is regarded as one of the founders of Cubism.

CHAPTER 4 | Andrew Salkey: Bright as blisters

Although Andrew Salkey was born in Panama, his parents were Jamaican, and he grew up in Jamaica. He was born in 1928, and educated at St George's College and Munro College in Jamaica, before going to England in 1951. He studied English literature at the University of London, then followed several careers as a schoolteacher, broadcaster, interviewer and scriptwriter for the BBC (British Broadcasting Corporation). Salkey's first novel, A Quality of Violence, *appeared in 1959. He produced four more novels, several children's novels, two travel books, and four volumes of poetry, as well as nine anthologies of Caribbean literature. Salkey acknowledges producing more than 33 books, and six manuscripts that are still in preparation. In 1976, he left England to teach at Hampshire College, Amherst, Massachusetts, where he still lives. Salkey has won several honours and awards. (This interview was recorded in Amherst on 15 February 1991.)*

Q: What are your impressions of West Indian writers of your generation?
A: When I went to England in 1951 the only published West Indian writers in London, at that time, were Lucille Iremonger and Edgar Mittelholzer.[1]
Q: How did you meet Mittelholzer?
A: I met him at the BBC when I went there to see Henry Swanzy who used to produce the radio programme, *Caribbean Voices*.[2] Poems and stories would be collected from us in the Caribbean and sent to England, then read back to us in the Caribbean on *Caribbean Voices*.
Q: How did you get on with Mittelholzer?
A: I liked him enormously. He was such a professional story-teller; he knew about the shapeliness of a story, and important things about technique. He once explained plotting, and I use that definition still in my classes at Hampshire College. He said that it was a narrative matter of cause and effect: you set up a storyline, something linear, and out of it there's an occurrence of causation. It's like upright dominoes that tilt and touch, and then fall. It's a matter of one event causing another to happen, and that one, in turn, causing yet another event to happen, and so on.
Q: He remains, to this day, our most prolific fiction writer.

A: Yes, and a master of technique. A highly-polished storyteller. A spell-binder.

Q: He could control different genres of writing such as the social realism in *Corentyne Thunder* and *A Morning at the Office*, the historical fiction of the Kaywana trilogy, the ghost story in *My Bones and my Flute,* and what one of his characters in *Of Trees and the Sea*[3] calls 'poetical-comedy-fantasy'. As you say, he was a skilled and versatile technician. Yet something went wrong.

A: He didn't like himself. He was full of self-loathing. He would complain about his wrists being scrawny, his face too pinched, freckled and dark. Apparently his childhood was tormented. His father was authoritarian, prudish, and finicky about most things – his and Edgar's personal conduct, beliefs and so on. Edgar took things to extremes. He used to describe himself on the back of his books as being of Swiss-German ancestry. He thought it a terrible waste to be born in the West Indies.

Q: In *A Swarthy Boy,*[4] he mentions his father's disappointment in him as a baby, because he was born a darker colour than expected. Problems of race and colour began from way back and seemed deep-seated in him. Was he tense and serious all the time? Did he have hobbies?

A: He loved German fiction and music, especially Nietzsche and Wagner.

Q: That is seen in his writing.

A: He loved what he thought was Germanic discipline too. He would have five cigarettes in his little, silvery, old-fashioned cigarette case; always precisely five to last him for precisely a week. And when he did a day's work, he would count up the words and put the total at the bottom of the page, and close the folder and go for a brisk walk, come back, and go to bed.

Q: Jan Carew[5] tells a story about the first book Mittelholzer wrote in Guyana; he went from house to house selling it. And when you think of all those rejection slips he got in the 1930s and 1940s, along with feelings of isolation, inadequacy and insignificance in a tiny, distant colonial outpost! Yet he never gave up; he never stopped; he wrote and wrote, storing up all those rejected manuscripts, until they came out in the 1950s. The self-loathing was there, and it took him in the end, alas; but there was still the activity, the dogged effort.

A: Oh, there was a terrific drive, a special heroic impetus to fulfil himself as a writer. And he did it. He may not have fulfilled himself as a husband, father, or friend; but he did so as a writer. I was his only friend in London. He would say that often to my wife. He disliked George Lamming[6] and the others. He would turn up at my flat with a record of Wagner's opera *Parsifal* and he would say: 'Now, I know you have no such thing in your house, Andrew. Every time I come, play it for me, will you. And it's not yours; it's really mine.'

Q: Does the self-denigration emanate out of his colonial situation itself? Does it belong only in the Mittelholzer's generation of writers?

A: It was specifically Edgar's malady. His pain was uniquely his. There are several wellsprings of self-loathing, I suppose. One is nationality; then, there are class and race. His suicide pointed to the fact that he felt abjectly unclean: that is why he burnt himself alive.

Q: What about Wilson Harris?[7]

A: *Palace of the Peacock* was sent to me in manuscript. I had just done *West Indian Stories*[8] for Faber and Faber, and my friend Charles Monteith, who was John Hearne's[9] editor, sent the manuscript to me. I didn't know that they had also sent it to six other persons at All Souls College, Oxford. These were friends of Charles Monteith. They were all baffled. They thought the novel had something, but what? When I read it I was bewitched. There was not much characterization; the dialogue was awfully stilted and literary: it hadn't the suppleness and verisimilitude of spoken exchange. Why had I enjoyed it so much? Why was I transported by it? It's those questions that I answered in my report, 14 pages long, and the novel was published. I had not known Wilson at the time. When the book was published, it had the most extraordinary reviews. Before its publication, during the writing of my report, there was a challenge I had decided to face. At that time, Faber had just done William Golding's *Lord of the Flies*;[10] and I said if Faber could trust Golding's *Lord of the Flies* with all those endless subordinate clauses, they could risk publishing Wilson's novel. I let them know that they were not to expect to earn a pretty penny out of it, but they would earn kudos for publishing a man who was a very difficult but exceptional author. Then I met Wilson and fell in love with his curious mind. He started being an open but layered book to me, and I realized that I had put in my publisher's report all sorts of things that I had only suspected, but for which there was already evidence in the man's life, for instance, the land-surveying, the politics, the reading of Jaspers,[11] and the whole metaphysical side of his remarkable intelligence. I mentioned all this because there were pieces of evidence in the text that led me to coax it into a fairly well-ordered essay: it was more of an essay than a publisher's report. I knew that Wilson was his own man. Even his narrative sentence was not the usual sentence that English or West Indian novelists write. But I worried about those books of eighty to ninety pages: they were long short stories, really, maybe novellas. Then he moved to Scotland, and *Black Marsden*[12] came out of that. Without the benefit of those Guyanese trees, boulders, rivers and forest, that iconography of landscape, I wondered how he was going to draw on the cityscape in Scotland. How was he going to do that wonderful juxtaposition of shadow and substance? But he managed it, although I confess that I haven't seen his most recent books. His writing ties my expectations in knots, and goes far beyond them.

Q: Do you think his vision has grown larger, or is it more or less the same vision repeated from book to book?

A: No. I see embellishment and extension.

Q: I certainly agree about his technical contribution to the Caribbean novel in English. He employed in 1960 what Latin American writers now call 'magical realism'[13] and regard as an innovation. It is astonishing that, apparently working by himself, he was able to devise a technique in which the borders of conventional reality were broken down to reveal a more complex and mixed reality. This was wholly original, even if it sometimes resisted or defeated comprehension.

A: Yes, very true. I took a walk with Wilson in 1970, in the grounds of Government House in Guyana – Burnham's house.[14] He scuffed the ground and stirred up what looked like sea sand. He stared at it and said: 'You know, Andrew, there are places here that if you got to know them, you wouldn't be surprised at my writing. We have places so high up, Roraima,[15] for instance: there's sea sand up there, fossils of fish; because in fact it was under water at one time.' Then he talked about a boat in the top of a tree, where the water had subsided and left it, and the Amerindians swimming on dry land. It was so different from my Jamaican mind-set, which is insular, island-bound and straightforward. His mind-set reminded me of the concentric mazes of Gabriel García Márquez, Alejo Carpentier and Angel Asturias.[16] One of the things hidden from the English critic is the real origin of the Latin American storytelling mind. The origin is Moorish-Arabian. I wasn't surprised when Salman Rushdie[17] confessed that the whole impetus of his writing came out of *The Thousand and One Nights*, and *Scheherazade*. Wilson's genius for entering his own concentric mazes and taking us along with him resembles very much the energy of Latin American magical realism.[18] His variety is not so lush, exuberant, or luxuriant, but more on the stark side, compressed and metaphysically taxing. Wilson's travels in the mazes are nevertheless the very empyrean of ambiguity.

Q: What about Roger Mais?[19] Is there not a sentimental streak in his detached, middle-class sympathy for poor, downtrodden, black Jamaicans?

A: That may be there; but he always had a feeling that the poor and downtrodden needed representation. Let me give voice to that washer-woman, or woodcutter. Let me give voice to the tenement-yard person, the pregnant woman who has no husband. The diabetic who has a constant sore foot and lingers outside the Chinese shop, has dreams too. Roger's writing had a clear political emphasis.

Q: He was active with the PNP?[20]

A: Yes. Edna Manley was his personal friend, and Norman Manley[21] cherished Roger. I acted in two or three of his plays as a young man. He also wrote poetry and short stories, and was a good oil-painter. He was heavily influenced by the prose that we have all imbibed from the Bible. I've always felt that those characters of his needed him. He was going to provide for them a space in which they would be noticed. His plays were almost tracts to tell you the truth, serious political tracts, but suffering no loss of metaphorical meaning.

Q: So the fact that his inspiration was political was not necessarily negative.

A: No. Of course not.

Q: John Hearne's[22] is a peculiar achievement. Technically, he is an immensely gifted writer; but I feel he went to waste.

A: He is closely akin to Edgar Mittelholzer, and a tragic figure too.

Q: Yes, very tragic, although he is still alive. [Hearne died in 1994.]

A: John's Jamaica was plantation Jamaica. He told me himself that when he looked around in his day, he saw a British governor, the colonial secretary, and his friends who were Jamaican Whites. He wanted to remain part of that, and did it terribly well. But he also knew how to write: he was a devil at the mechanics of composition. But I knew that it would lead to enormous pain and dissatisfaction, because the Jamaica that he knew and wrote about just evaporated in front of his eyes, during the 1960s and 1970s.

Q: Did you yourself start writing in London?

A: No. I started in Jamaica, and some of my very early pieces, poems mainly, were published in *The Daily Gleaner*.[23]

Q: Is it correct to say that your reputation as a writer rests on the novels that you wrote at the beginning of your career in London?

A: I've also done a fair amount of children's writing – novels[24] published by Oxford: about ten of them; and the two travel books, one on Guyana, and one on Cuba.

Q: But if we look at those first five novels, and their preoccupation with identity, was that not very much a 1950s or pre-Independence concern? In *Escape to an Autumn Pavement*,[25] for example, Johnnie Sobert asks Fiona plaintively: 'Can't you see that I don't belong anywhere? What happened to me between African bondage and British hypocrisy?' (p. 41). Johnnie is preoccupied throughout the novel with being 'a colonial boy with only slavery behind [him]' (p. 182). Does that type of preoccupation come from an historical phase that has now gone, or do West Indians still write about such concerns?

A: I don't think people write about them now. Look at Caryl Phillips's[26] work: he's categorically turned away from our concerns of the 1950s. It's no longer the colonial lament. Even though there is a certain amount of pain at the centre of what he's describing, and in the images that he delineates, it's not the same old-fashioned pain. His characters seem to know who they are. They may still be very unsettled, still quasi-colonial beings; but they seem to have an inner strength that makes his work different from ours. Caryl Phillips, Neil Bissoondath[27] and the other eighties writers are excellent storytellers, sure of their craft and identity; it's hard to keep up with them. They've gone ahead of me.

Q: Your work dealt with the matter of self-definition, with finding out who we were as Caribbean people, who had an overlay of British culture. We were bicultural and bilingual; we could speak our own Creole, as well as the official language – standard English – and we were creatures of this dual system. Anybody writing at the time obviously dealt with that. Phillips grew up in England: he's British in a way that you and I were not; he went to British schools, then Oxford. He now has a problem recovering what we all took for granted: our speech and all the sights, sounds, and Caribbean experience that, in fact, some of us considered a disadvantage at the time.

A: That's why I consider him to be a breakaway writer who is new, and has a crisp, daring voice. I'm happy to know that he appeared in my time, and that I can enjoy his work. I don't really see anything negative in his work; there's no strain; he really operates as though he knows and feels what he writes about.

Q: Yes. You are quite right. I don't mean to suggest he is one-tracked. Despite his British upbringing, he is able to handle both British and West Indian characters or situations with equal authority, which the fifties writers did not.

A: We resisted it, to tell you the truth. The only one who never resisted it was Vidia (V. S. Naipaul): he seemed to have taken a conscious decision to turn away, substantially, from what he felt was pulling him back into a colonial nightmare.

Q: George Lamming has said that Naipaul's novels on foreign subjects, for instance, in *A Bend in the River* and *The Enigma of Arrival*[28] still project a Caribbean point of view: in other words, Naipaul still interprets life through West Indian or Caribbean eyes.

A: Vidia genuinely liked what he read at school. He fell in love with English literature. He handles its diction uniquely, with genius, in every-thing he writes. No wonder they say he's the best writer of the English language. Most of the critics in England have said that. He is a very fine stylist. His sentences hook you, because they seem to be colloquial, but are not. Vidia has a finger like the ancient mariner, and you feel that you're the only one being addressed or spoken to. It's something about the quality of his sentences: they are indeed skilfully honed, marvellously grammatical; but, at the same time, loose-limbed. They have a very supple quality, which catches so many people, and makes them feel as though he's actually talking to them. That's why he handles epigram and paradox so expertly. He really understands how the English language works in satire and irony.

Q: When I go through the English parts of *Enigma of Arrival* I see all that you say, about the beauty of the sentences, and their supple grace; but when he talks in West Indian sections, about travelling from Port of Spain to New York, for instance, or about his first experiences as an immigrant in London . . .

A: Nobody does it better. Yes. You're right. And you know what else nobody does as well as he does: he is a master of Trinidad Creole. Sam [Selvon] agrees about that, too. He once told me half-jokingly that Vidia was challenging him – he meant as a writer of Trinidad Creole.

Q: You've been productive in many genres – fiction, poetry, travel-writing, children's stories, anthologies – which do you prefer doing?

A: At first, I wrote to find out what I could write. I wanted to test myself. As a primary school lad, I would read things like Cardinal Newman's *Idea of the University*[29] and I wouldn't even understand the first sentence. I really loved reading; then I wondered if I could write something like that novel or short story I had just gobbled. I started when I was about eight years old with an imitation Bulldog Drummond[30] story set in Jamaica. But the writing that I enjoy perhaps more than any other form is poetry. I also rather fancy the idea of entertaining the child reader. There is something about telling a story for young readers that makes me feel good. I become responsible when I'm writing for them. I try not to give in to little self-pleasing things. I try to come on as a fairly honest entertainer. I dig very deep into my past history as a boy at home, into my old relationships with the boys and girls I knew at the elementary school and secondary school. I also enjoy short stories because I find that I want to experiment when I dip into that particular form. I become restless and I use my Anansi[31] a great deal. The short story is akin to the lyric poem: it's condensed, and tight, and you've got to choose characters very adroitly; you mustn't go in for gratuitous, long descriptions. I also like the travel book, especially Vidia's kind of travel book which I could never write.[32]

Q: Your *Havana Journal* and *Georgetown Journal*[33] have sections in them where you interview people and then give a diaristic commentary which I think is very good.

A: Vidia has now turned to that kind of thing with his book on the South of the United States; it is full of interviews, like his more recent book on India, *India: A Million Mutinies Now*.[34]

Q: *Georgetown Journal* and *Havana Journal* contain very good observations and vivid pen-pictures. You maintain a fine objectivity: you stand aside and listen, then report as accurately as you can.

A: I tried to do that, yes.

Q: And now that the events in the two *Journals* have long passed, your books have become valuable works of social history. There are stories about Burnham,[35] and other leaders, and accounts of various issues that have now lost their significance, but were important then: they are stored up in your *Journals*. I don't wish to belittle your fiction or children's stories, or any other part of your achievement; but I think the two *Journals* will endure.

Since you have observed the full flowering of modern Caribbean writing in English, at close quarters, from its beginning in England, in the 1950s, do you feel satisfied now, or are you worried? After all, Naipaul and Walcott are just about the best in the world at what they are doing. And there are many excellent young writers, including female writers, springing up. You must feel great satisfaction.

A: No, I'm worried. I'm very seriously worried. Publishers have turned away from us, towards Africa. It's purely commercial. The money is now in African schools and African society. Oxford and Heinemann are now picking up Nigerian writers the way that they picked up George Lamming, Samuel Selvon and me in the 1950s. Recently, we have hardly been able to get a book published. O. R. Dathorne[36] was complaining the other day. Sam Selvon has been suffering very badly, and George Lamming has had a tough time of it. So there is a terrible crisis. Don't think that I am blaming anybody like Vidia. But it's as though they found their man, their star, and they stopped looking. I know the manuscripts have been going in, because people write asking my advice about publishers to send their manuscripts to. Then they get them back. We're no longer telling stories any longer that will be a critical success, or put money in the pockets of the conglomerates. And when we come to America, we are oddities.

Q: How do you account for Jamaica Kincaid's[37] success then?

A: Jamaica Kincaid was assisted by her husband and his father who was the fiction editor of *The New Yorker*. She was a child of *The New Yorker*. She got a wonderful springboard there. Good luck to her.

Q: Let me ask you the same question about the progress of West Indian politics, as I asked about West Indian literature. We all grew up in British colonies, and saw British rule as the great obstacle to self-development; then we got rid of the obstacle, and put in rulers of our own. What have they achieved in thirty years?

A: That's when we started to grow up, when we took over the reins. I greatly admired Eric Williams[38] and one day at the BBC, he said to me in front of Ernest Eytle[39] and two English broadcasters: 'Well, you know what's wrong with you, Andrew? You're an idealist, and when you're a politician you have to deal with the reality of politics.' He knew he had failed in a certain essentially human way.

Q: If our leaders have failed, where does that leave us? Are West Indian people to remain like Sam Selvon said, long ago, 'citizens of the world', or, as Eddie Brathwaite[40] said, 'harbourless spades'?

A: That's how we are as people who are inured to a very small, trifling economy: we learn to rely on other people's economies. It's a natural thing for us to do for survival. We place our backsides in a factory in very cold Alberta, or freezing Newcastle upon Tyne, and are quite satisfied. We send our children to school and do all the right things, and one day, take a trip back home to Antigua or Jamaica; but we do not yearn and deeply pine for the place. I don't know why we're like that: it's as though the economy fashioned us rather than anything else. The economy is the Bible that fashioned us, not the folk culture. Deprivation, poverty, our continuing client-status, trying to manage: these are the defining elements in our lives.[41]

Q: That sounds bleak. It is similar to what Naipaul said in *The Middle Passage*,[42] thirty years ago. But I regard you as probably the most complete man of letters that we have produced, considering not only your fiction, poetry, anthologies, children's stories, broadcasting and so on, but also your close association with so many writers for forty years. You have said that you are worried about the present state of West Indian writing because of its neglect by publishers, but what about your own writing? Not that your career is over, by any means, but how do you think you will be remembered?

A: That's a difficult question to answer. Maybe I am not the one to answer it. But I'm a promoter, in a sense. I should like it to be known that I promoted the doers of my generation. I just love talking about them, writing letters, finding publishers. I will continue to contribute the odd book myself. But I love the idea of our literature. I can't tell you how fascinated I was that we could write books – novels, short stories, poems, plays. I have one of the most representative collections of West Indian and African books. They are in London. I am going to leave them for my wife, if I die before her, and ask her to hand them over, in time, to the University of the West Indies. I suppose that's how I would like to be remembered, as a kind of mad, letter-writing, publisher-finding, non-charging agent-hustler on behalf of my fellow writers, and many of them haven't been only West Indians. Yes, I'd be well satisfied with that sort of memorial description. Very proud, indeed, to have had a definitive something or other to do with V. S. Naipaul's first book for André Deutsch; Wilson Harris's for Faber and Faber; one of Samuel Selvon's children's books for Nelson; and others of the then London-based brood and the non-West Indian outsiders to it. Now, all this sounds so exemplarily altruistic and noble as chieftains, doesn't it? Not a bit of it! I've written and edited well over 33 books (with six manuscripts in preparation), and if just one is read or recalled, with some slight interest, I'd be quite happy, on the other side, thank you! I wouldn't mind if it were merely a single line from a poem or some incident in a short story or novel. Of course, the really important thing about our writing is that it *must* continue; our literature *must* 'keep on keeping on'. What with the jaundiced eye of the conglomerates looking askance at our manuscripts and what with the star system burning bright as blisters (*one* Naipaul, *one* Walcott, *one* Kincaid), the immediate future looks pretty overcast. Mind you, Caryl Phillips, Neil Bissoondath, and the coming nineties writers are more than capable of grasping the baton and carrying it forward, with assurance and accomplishment.

Q: You have shown extraordinary energy and dedication to our literature, and altruism to our writers. More than one of your books, I am sure, will continue to be read – certainly the two *Journals*. Your novels provide the best urban Jamaican version of our identity crisis, and your children's books supply a deeply-felt need. Do you have a final word?

A: Yes; a plea to all West Indian, Guyanese and Belizean broadcasting stations to insert in their cultural programming an hour or so, like the BBC's *Caribbean Voices*, as a source of literary encouragement – a clearing-house for the talent of beginning writers (storytellers, poets, playwrights, journalists). I ask the same of the newspapers, but the radio has a dynamic, far-reaching, aural effect on our hinterland populations, quite other than that of the published dailies, weeklies and magazines. We did begin with Henry Swanzy's *Caribbean Voices* (really, officially the BBC's), and I'd like to close on a note of caution: that is, beginning over again with home as the centre rather than London or New York or Toronto, and beginning with a complementary adjunct to our long-proven, vigorous oral tradition: radio. Let the quintessential capital for native West Indian publishing follow, as it may!

Notes

1   Lucille d'Oyen Iremonger (1920–90) was Jamaican, and the author of two novels, *Creole* (1951) and *The Cannibals* (1952), as well as several works of travel and biography. She was married to the British Member of Parliament Thomas Iremonger.

   Edgar Mittelholzer (1909–65) was born in New Amsterdam, Guyana, where he attended Berbice High School. He spent much of the Second World War in Trinidad, then in 1948 migrated to England. He is the author of 25 books, all of which are novels except for an autobiography, *A Swarthy Boy* (Putman, London, l963); and a travel book, *With a Carib Eye* (Secker and Warburg, London, 1958). Mittelholzer's novels vary from the solidly realistic *Corentyne Thunder* (Secker and Warburg, London, 1941) and *A Morning at the Office* (Hogarth Press, London, 1950) to the bizarre *Shadows More Among Them* (Lippincott, Philadelphia, 1951), the ghostly *My Bones and My Flute* (Secker and Warburg, London, 1955) and the macabre *Eltonsbrody* (Secker and Warburg, London, 1960).

2   *Caribbean Voices* was a literary radio programme which was broadcast over the BBC Overseas Service for Caribbean listeners in particular. *Caribbean Voices* was started by the British Foreign Service on 11 March 1945 and went off the air on 7 September 1958. Henry Swanzy produced and edited *Caribbean Voices*. In this capacity, he helped to launch the careers of several West Indian authors and poets, including Edgar Mittelholzer, George Lamming, Samuel Selvon, Jan Carew, V. S. Naipaul, and Derek Walcott.

3   See Note 1 for *Corentyne Thunder*, *A Morning at the Office* and *My Bones and My Flute*. The Kaywana trilogy consists of: *The Children of Kaywana* (Secker and Warburg, London, 1952), *The Harrowing of Hubertus* (Secker and Warburg, London, 1954), (later republished as *Kaywana Stock* and *Kaywana Blood* (Secker and Warburg, London, 1958).

The Kaywana trilogy constitutes Mittelholzer's major contribution to West Indian literature. Together these three novels provide a fictional reconstruction of the history of Guyana from 1616 to 1953. In addition, there is *Of Trees and Sea* (Secker and Warburg, London, 1956).

4   See Note 1 above.

5   For Jan Carew see Chapter 5. For example, cf. Carew's comments on Mittelholzer.

6   See Index for George Lamming.

7   See Index for Wilson Harris, and Introduction, note 7 for *Palace of the Peacock*.

8   Andrew Salkey (ed.), *West Indian Stories* (Faber and Faber, London, 1960).

9   Charles Monteith was a Fellow of All Souls College, Oxford University. He was senior editor, and later Chairman of Faber and Faber. He was also editor, mentor and friend of John Hearne and Wilson Harris.

    For John Hearne, see note 22 below.

10   William Golding, *Lord of the Flies* (Faber and Faber, London, 1954).

11   Karl Jaspers (1883–1969) was a German philosopher regarded as one of the formative influences on modern existentialist thought. Jaspers himself was strongly influenced by Kierkegaard and Nietzsche. It is remarkable enough that Harris should have heard of Jaspers in Guyana. To have digested Jaspers's work so that it influenced his own writing is little short of miraculous. See Index for references to Wilson Harris in Jan Carew's interview and elsewhere.

12   Wilson Harris, *Black Marsden* (Faber and Faber, London, 1973).

13   See note 16 below.

14   See Index for Burnham. Also Chapter 1, note 13.

15   Mount Roraima is one of the highest mountains in Guyana. It is 9219 ft high, and forms the highest peak in the Pakaraima range of mountains in the county of Essequibo.

16   Gabriel Garciá Márquez of Colombia won the Nobel Prize for literature in 1982. His most widely-read work is the novel *One Hundred Years of Solitude* (1967) which considers the horrors of war and evils of imperialism while, stylistically, marking a break with traditional realism. This style has been called 'magical realism', a term that is also applied to the work of other writers who eschew conventional realism.

    Alejo Carpentier (1904–80) is a Cuban writer whose love and knowledge of French and Spanish music and architecture, can be traced in his works. He lived in Paris (1929–39) and wrote surrealist short stories. His *The Kingdom of This World* (1949) is considered a historical novel or legendary chronicle, which considers the Haitian past. His work, as a whole, is noted for its 'magical realism'.

    Miguel Angel Asturias (1899–74) was the first Latin American novelist to be awarded the Nobel Prize (1967). The complexity of his work derives from an intricate use of the linguistic resources of poetry, of narrative form, and of indigenous mythical structures. Asturias pioneered 'myth creation' as a device and grasped the significance of surrealism as a perception of reality.

17   Salman Rushdie, born in India, lives in Britain; he achieved fame/infamy when his novel *The Satanic Verses* (1989) was condemned by Ayatollah Khomeini of Iran. Khomeini placed Rushdie under an Islamic sentence of death for blasphemy, and Rushdie went into hiding. Rushdie's novels such as *Midnight's Children* (1981) and *Shame* (1984) are praised for technical innovations which derive at least partly from Oriental, Arabic literature; for example, the story within a story, changing narrators, and the mixture of fantasy with fact. Rushdie's technical innovations are typical of 'magical realism'.

18   See Index for comments on Latin American literature by Carew, Heath and Phillips.

19   Roger Mais (1905–55) was a Jamaican novelist, dramatist, short-story writer and painter. He died of cancer. His novels are inspired by revulsion against social injustice and oppression, especially *The Hills Were Joyful Together* (Jonathan Cape, London, 1953)

and *Brother Man* (Jonathan Cape, London, 1954). A third novel, *Black Lightning* (Jonathan Cape, London, 1955), deals with more spiritual and symbolic issues.

20 The People's National Party (PNP) is one of the two leading political parties in Jamaica, and currently forms the island's government.

21 Norman Manley (1893–1969) was Prime Minister of Jamaica from 1955 to 1962. As founder and leader of the PNP, in the 1950s and early 1960s, Manley had to preside over Jamaica's secession from the Federation of the West Indies. Manley's wife Edna was a sculptor and an important patron of the arts in Jamaica. Norman Manley wrote an introduction to the collected edition of Mais's three novels. Cf. Chapter 2, note 4.

22 John Hearne is a Jamaican novelist and journalist. As one of the group of West Indian novelists in England in the 1950s, his first novel *Voices Under the Window* (Faber and Faber, London, 1955) underlined themes of identity and oppression in Jamaica. But Hearne's later novels moved gradually away into a more unrealistic mode of writing, until he collaborated with Morris Cargill to write three suspense or detective novels that seem to have little significance beyond entertainment.

23 *The Daily Gleaner* is Jamaica's main daily newspaper. Well-known Jamaican writers such as H. G. DeLisser and Vic Reid have worked on the paper, while others, including Andrew Salkey and Lorna Goodison, published their early works in it.

24 Some of Salkey's children's novels are *Hurricane* (Oxford University Press, London, 1964); *Earthquake* (Oxford University Press, London, 1965); *Drought* (Oxford University Press, London, 1966); and *Jonah Simpson* (Oxford University Press, London, 1969). The travel books are *Havana Journal* (Penguin, Harmondsworth, 1971); and *Georgetown Journal: A Caribbean Writer's Journey from London via Port of Spain to Georgetown, Guyana* (New Beacon, London, 1972).

25 Andrew Salkey, *Escape to an Autumn Pavement* (Hutchinson, London, 1960).

26 For Caryl Phillips, see Chapter 14 and Index.

27 Neil Bissoondath was born in Trinidad and studied at York University in Canada. He has lived in Canada since 1973. He is the nephew of V. S. Naipaul, and the author of two collections of stories, *Digging up the Mountains* (1985); *The Eve of Uncertain Tomorrows* (1990); and two novels, *A Casual Brutality* (1988) and *The Innocence of Age* (1992).

28 V. S. Naipaul, *A Bend in the River* (André Deutsch, London, 1979). For *The Enigma of Arrival*, see Introduction, note 10.

29 Cardinal John Henry Newman (1801–90) was a fellow of Oriel College, Oxford University. He was ordained priest in 1846, and appointed Rector of the New Catholic University of Dublin in 1854. In *The Idea of a University Defined* Newman argued that the duty of a university is instruction rather than research.

30 Bulldog Drummond, hero of crime stories by Cyril McNeile (1888–1937), enjoyed wide popularity up to the 1950s; they include *Bulldog Drummond* (1919), and *Bulldog Drummond Strikes Again* (1933).

31 Anansi, the spider trickster of West African origin is perhaps the most popular hero in Caribbean folklore. Anansi's ability to succeed, through trickery and ingenuity, despite human frailties and his status as an underdog, appealed to slaves who were also underdogs and who therefore relied on their wits rather than physical force to confront their white oppressor.

32 V. S. Naipaul has produced several travel books, including *An Area of Darkness* (André Deutsch, London, 1964) and *India: A Million Mutinies Now* (Heinemann, London, 1990).

33 See note 24 above.

34 See note 32.

35 See Chapter 1, note 13.

36 O. R. Dathorne is a novelist and editor who was born in Guyana. In addition to scholarly works, he has written two novels: *Dumplings in the Soup* (Cassell, London, 1963); and *The Scholar Man* (Cassell, London, 1964).

37 For Jamaica Kincaid, see Chapter 11 and Index.
38 See Chapter 2, note 22.
39 Ernest Eytle was born in Guyana and trained as a barrister. He also broadcast on the BBC. He is remembered as the author of a biography of Sir Frank Worrell: *Frank Worrell* (The Sportsmans Book Club, London, 1963).
40 Edward Brathwaite, among numerous other works, has written a trilogy, *The Arrivants*, consisting of *Rights of Passage* (Oxford University Press, London, 1967); *Masks* (Oxford University Press, London, 1968); and *Islands* (Oxford University Press, London, 1969); and a second trilogy consisting of *Mother Poem* (Oxford University Press, London, 1977); *Sun Poem* (Oxford University Press, London, 1982); and *X-Self* (Oxford University Press, Oxford, 1987). Brathwaite is also a historian, an influential literary critic, and a respected commentator on Caribbean culture and society.
41 Cf. Chapter 8, note 44.
42 See Introduction, note 11.

CHAPTER 5

Jan Carew:
The wild coast

Jan Carew was born in Guyana in 1925. He was educated locally at Berbice High School, and at universities in Europe and the US. In 1962 he briefly returned to the Caribbean before going on to Canada. He later went to the Caribbean for another, briefer stay, before finally settling in the US. In the United States, Carew was professor of African-American Studies at Northwestern University until he retired in 1987. His first novel Black Midas *(1958) was followed in quick succession by three other books, including* Moscow is not My Mecca *(1964), a work describing the author's disillusionment during a visit to Moscow. Carew's first two novels,* Black Midas *and* The Wild Coast *(1958) are set in Guyana: but his third,* The Last Barbarian *(1961) is set in New York. This indicates a movement in Carew's work away from purely Caribbean interests to general issues of racism and imperialism in an international context. Carew has written fiction, poetry, drama and history, and has won many awards. In 1975, Princeton University did him the signal honour of establishing the Jan Carew Annual Lectureship Award. (This interview was recorded in Toronto on 20 June 1987.)*

Q: Was there any literary interest on either side of your family?
A: My father was very creative. His greatest passion was to paint and draw.
Q: But you grew up with your mother?
A: Effectively yes. She was the dominant figure in the lives of my sister and myself. She saw that we were educated because my father did not really care whether we were educated or not.
Q: Berbice High School[1] is connected with Indians and the Presbyterian Church. Why did your mother not send you to Queen's College?[2]
A: I think this was very good to her. We had remarkable masters, like J. A. Rodway[3] who also taught Derek Walcott.[4] The most vivid thing I remember about Rodway was his love for art and literature. I remember him bringing to our class Renaissance paintings and giving us long talks about their meaning. He used to communicate his enthusiasm and lend us books – English poetry, Dickens – writers he liked. So it was a very literary relationship, which I would not have got at Queen's College, because it would have been more structured there. Then there was Ben Yisu Das.[5]

When he walked up and down and lectured, the whole room lit up. Whatever he was lecturing on became fantastically interesting. He taught history, and I really liked history. We did the history of the British empire for the Cambridge exams.[6] We were identifying with Drake[7] and Hawkins[8] and Frobisher[9] and so on, when Yisu Das gave us, in translation, Spanish histories of the same period to read. The heroes of English history were no different from the heroes of Spanish history. He did not say anything. He just left it like that. It stunned us. If he had preached at us, it might not have had the same effect. So that gave me a clear insight on how subjective this imperialist business was. But the school was interesting. It was a residential school. Barefoot peasant boys would come out of the Corentyne[10] to Berbice High School and be transformed. In Berbice I was exposed to the whole multi-ethnic way of Guyana: the lore of the Corentyne, which I loved, the landscapes, the people, their relationships, and their vendettas. The Corentyne was like the Wild West in those days. People would ambush you in the back alley. I used to go out sometimes with armed outriders around me. There was cursing and killing. Yet it was a beautiful period of growing up.

Q: We get some of this experience in *The Wild Coast*.[11] Did Mittelholzer also go to Berbice High School?

A: Yes, but he was expelled when he was 13 years old for kicking a white (English) master at the school. The man had made an insulting remark about the natives.

Q: A small area around New Amsterdam produced Martin Carter, E. R. Brathwaite, Edgar Mittelholzer, Wilson Harris[12] and yourself. Was it pure accident, that one town in British Guiana, in the 1930s, produced all these writers?

A: New Amsterdam used to be the old Dutch capital, and Berbice was quite different from Demerara where the English had settled mostly. There was more of a cohesive cultural matrix in New Amsterdam. Traditions were fiercely guarded, although New Amsterdam was an absolute backwater in terms of Georgetown. There were no industries to speak of. It was a joke about how people used to peek behind the curtains in New Amsterdam when they saw a stranger. But in the 1930s there was a great deal of art, painting, literature, music, poetry and reading in New Amsterdam. Mittelholzer, for example, like me, was first a painter. He came into prominence when he sent in a watercolour to a British Empire art exhibition and won a prize.

Q: His beginning as a writer has always seemed to me utterly courageous, almost incredible to have happened in Guyana at that time.

A: It bordered on madness. The whole town was against him. He wrote a variety of things. He wrote lyrics for calypsos, and because he came out of New Amsterdam, he was steeped in the folk culture. All other things came out of this. *Creole Chips*[13] was a collection of local legends and stories out of the old tradition. It was a profound ethnographic study. He went to work at one time for Davson, a commercial firm, and every morning a white company director would come in and everybody had to stand. Mittelholzer was sitting with his leg up on the desk, waiting. The man said 'Good morning', and Mittelholzer said nothing. They fired him. All of these rebellions added to his reputation. Then you heard that he was a writer. He published *Creole Chips* at his own expense, and sold it from door to door. It was the first major publication in the modern Guyanese renaissance of writing.

He wrote a lot of stories. There used to be ads in foreign magazines which said, 'Send me a short story and I will criticize it free of charge,' in order to induce you to buy something. So Edgar used to write short stories, send them to these people, and get their criticism. That spurred him on. The only critical eye he had on his work was these magazines hustling subscriptions. That went on for years – endless submissions and endless rejections. Yet undiminished optimism kept him on. He did not let it crush him; until finally *Corentyne Thunder*[14] was accepted by an English publisher in 1941.

Q: When did your own writing begin?

A: Rodway encouraged me to write essays at school. Then we moved to Georgetown where I worked in the civil service as a customs officer. I was writing for the local magazine, the *Christmas Annual*.[15] I also did a lot of drawing and painting. I really thought that painting would be my main focus, not writing.

Q: Did you know Wilson Harris or any other Guyanese writers at that time?

A: I knew Wilson very well because he was courting my sister in Georgetown. He married my sister. Wilson and I became very close – night and day, shouting, arguing, discussing, reading – Marx, Spengler, Nietzsche, anything. Of course, it was a formative period. The context in which we were arguing was completely wrong. We just did not have the education. Nonetheless, it was a very alive and exciting period. I knew Wilson when he was a surveyor, and there were other surveyors like him who had a lot to do with shaping my vision. The surveyors were an interesting breed. They had to break out of the structures of Georgetown, go into the interior, and spend long periods by themselves. So it was complete isolation without the kind of intellectual exchange that would go on in the normal course of things. Wilson lived with this for about seventeen years. It explains some of his writing in *Palace of the Peacock*.[16] That is the writing of someone accustomed to talking to himself in the Guyana bush for seventeen years! Andrew Salkey[17] was one of the key figures in getting that book out.

Andrew helped both Harris and Naipaul to get published. He wrote an analysis of *Peacock* and recommended it.

Q: I think it is rather nice that struggling West Indian novelists stuck together and helped each other in the beginning. Later, they branched out. This is natural; then rivalries and conflicts came.

A: There were always links. Sam Selvon and I were always friends. There was never any rift. Lamming, too. V. S. Naipaul and I had an extremely good friendship. We always got on well.

Q: There was no formal rift with Naipaul?

A: No, we were friends right up to the time we last met.

Q: When you left Guyana, where did you first go?

A: I went on a long leave to Trinidad and bluffed my way into getting a job in the Price Control Board which was set up during the Second World War to control profiteering and inflation. They paid me about three times what I was earning in the civil service in Guyana. Then I left for the US wholly on my own. I had saved that money, the only time in my life I saved money in that fashion. I lived in the country and I saved most of my salary and paid my own way. The family gave me some subsidies. So I left for Howard University in Washington, DC.

Q: You got entrance while you were in Trinidad?

A: Yes, I wrote and got accepted. I went to Howard around 1946, immediately after the war, when the Americans doubled up their university programmes to accommodate servicemen who had missed out. In one year you could do two years of study by going right through the year without holidays. You just had one week off. So I went on that programme, to do two years' study in one year, because I feared that my resources would not hold out.

Q: How long were you at Howard?

A: One year.

Q: So you did not get a degree?

A: No, I hated it.

Q: Why?

A: I hated the racial discrimination in Washington, the ghettoized existence of blacks and West Indians.

Q: How did you find Howard itself as a university?

A: At Howard it was all right because there were many West Indians who cut across a lot of lines which would have existed for them in the Caribbean. Then you had Afro-American friends too. The race situation bewildered me. I couldn't stand it after a while, and decided to head up north. I had heard about Case Western Reserve University in Cleveland from a classmate at Howard who was from Cleveland. It was a big white university. I took the Greyhound bus one night and headed up to Cleveland. I was at

Case Western Reserve for two years, and while there I met the son of the Czech Consul-General, who was a classmate of mine. He told me there were scholarships for third-world students at Charles University in Czechoslovakia. He got the application forms from his father. I applied and they gave me a scholarship. I did not graduate from Case Western Reserve because I got this scholarship, and I would have had to put out so much money to graduate that I was glad to get out.

Q: What studies did you do at Case Western Reserve?

A: I did pre-medicine studies.

Q: So it was all scientific work.

A: Yes, I never did anything in the arts except one course in journalism at Howard. At Case Western Reserve I took economics and geopolitics. My major was science. I was doing physics, chemistry, math, biology.

Q: Up to your early twenties, did you envision a medical career?

A: No, I did not envision a medical career. My mother sort of pushed me into it. But I resisted. I didn't want to be a doctor. At Case Western Reserve, I began to write and paint seriously. I thought then that I would take to painting. But something happened while I was studying, and I realized that I was not going to make the kind of sacrifice that would be necessary to bring painting to a point where it would completely satisfy me. I left Case Western Reserve, got the scholarship to Czechoslovakia, but first went to visit Guyana. This was in 1949. I stayed in Guyana for eight months.

Q: Your mother was still there?

A: My mother was there, and Wilson was there. Cheddi Jagan[18] had just come back from America. I heard him speaking at a street-corner one night in Georgetown. He was analyzing the role of the peasant in Guyanese life, and his relationship to the big estates; how they steal his own land and only cultivate small portions of it, how they control water and land, and penalize the independent peasant. No one had ever done that kind of analysis. It had a tremendous effect on me.

Q: Did you know of him before?

A: No. After I heard him speak, I went to his house that night and said to him, 'Look, nobody has ever talked like that before in this country. I want to join you right away, and help out in any way I can.' That was when I met Martin Carter and Sydney King.[19] We became very close. *The Political Action Bulletin* was the predecessor of *Thunder*.[20] I began to write for that paper and go to meetings at night with Cheddi. Wilson Harris was very much a part of the movement then. He was a great admirer of Cheddi, and Cheddi used to rely on him. So that was a lively time, bulging with all sorts of things. We used to read poetry to each other at night; we would write a poem and then read it to the group who would criticize it. Martin read his poems, and Wilson would read and explain his in a convoluted fashion. Wilson was a man who was never aware of his surroundings. He walked through the Guyanese jungle for 17 years without even a penknife for protection. Wilson was comparing the long savannahs to the plains where Achilles and Hector fought, and in a poem he wrote about Hector, you could actually see Hector on the long savannah. It was really incongruous. How could you bring Hector into this rain-forest bush? Tigers would be snarling at night with Wilson sitting at his campfire, arguing about Spengler.

Q: Was it not perverse, Wilson importing all this extra-cultural material – Greek and Roman myths – into the Guyanese landscape?

A: That is the thing: how Wilson made it totally believable! He made it seem a natural part of our world. After the ferment of those times, I wrote *Streets of Eternity*,[21] a book of poems. It was very important in my literary career because it was like a catalyst: it led me to prose writing.

Q: All this was in that eight-month period around 1949! It must have been very productive!

A: It was tremendously important and stimulating. Wilson and I took Martin up to Canje.[22] All day long and at night as well, we talked about books and poetry. The creative thing was really getting us. The political aspect was profoundly affecting the creative part. There was a symbiotic relationship. Then I left for Prague via Paris. It was in Paris that I began to mingle in the society of writers. There was the Brazilian painter Tiberio. I became very close friends with him. I wrote a play about him and he was a character in *The Last Barbarian*.[23] Tiberio was a close friend of Picasso. I met Picasso through him when Picasso came to open an exhibition. Subsequently, I met Picasso again in Czechoslovakia, when he came to our Writers' Class. So the Tiberio encounter was very important for me. I also heard for the first time about Jorge Amado;[24] then I later met him in Prague. I began studies in Prague, in the Faculty of Natural Science, researching into radio isotopes: it was postgraduate work. The Communists had taken over. I used to write for journals in Prague, and at one point I sang in a nightclub. Then I left Prague and went back to Paris. I began to write in Paris, and wrote my first novel, *Rivers of this Night*.[25] It was a line I took from one of Wilson's poems. Seymour[26] published a piece from that novel. That began it. I showed the manuscript to André Gide.

Q: This would be in 1950–51?

A: Yes. Gide read the manuscript and said, 'If I were you, I would not show this to anyone else.' It really was devastating. I went back and worked at it again, and showed him another manuscript. He said, 'Look, you will be a writer. Writers have to develop thick skins. This story is not bad; it has some flashes. You still have a long way to go.' I sent a lot of things to the BBC *Caribbean Voices*. Then I went to Holland and was in Amsterdam for two years. There was an artists' club there and I became an honorary member. In Holland I helped to edit a journal in a special edition of which I brought out some poems by Wilson (Harris) and Cy Grant.[27]

Q: Was all this before you went to England?

A: I went back and forth to England, but I never liked England. I was a British subject, or maybe you should say a British object. I finally realized I had to go to England to work. I went into the Olivier company as an actor. After the Olivier season, I went down to Guyana. Wilson and I went up the Potaro.[28] On that trip, the cook in our party, Herbert Stockman, would tell me stories which were seminal material for *Black Midas*.[29] Wilson put in his interpretations too. So between Stockman and Wilson, I left with a manuscript, which was going to take me five years to unravel and fictionalize. The echo of these fellows was more of an impediment than anything else. I wrote about four versions of *Black Midas*. Then there came a certain point when I began the fifth version of *Black Midas*, and from the first few sentences, I knew I had really mastered the craft of writing. I was in the middle of all sorts of things when *Black Midas* was being born. My first wife and I had broken up, and I was seeing Sylvia Wynter[30] whom I later married. About the same time I met Jimmy Burns-Singer, the Scottish poet who was also a critic writing regularly for *The Times Literary Supplement*. Jimmy said to me, 'What about this novel you are supposed to be writing? I'd like to see it.' The next day he took it to Secker and Warburg, who read it and wrote me a letter accepting the book. That moment changed my whole life. So I finished *Black Midas*, and I am always sorry I did not do the full novel, because in the manuscript it was twice as long as the book which was published. *Black Midas* was a tremendous success. Jimmy Burns-Singer reviewed it on the front page of *The Times Literary Supplement*, with a big headline. Then Kingsley Amis and John Wain went out of their way to attack me personally because Singer was saying that the finest writing in English was coming from outside England.

Q: So you were associated in the minds of those critics with V. S. Naipaul?

A: No. Naipaul was nowhere in the picture. Lamming had published his first two novels. Selvon had published several books, and Vic Reid's *The Leopard*[31] had just come out. *Black Midas* was really a kind of nexus for the West Indian novel, giving it a much broader public attention. Then *The Wild Coast* was snapped up by Secker and Warburg. I had written it before *Black Midas*.

Q: After *Black Midas* there was *The Wild Coast*, *The Last Barbarian* and *Moscow is not my Mecca*[32] about your trip to Moscow. Those books came out rather quickly, and by then you were an established writer.

A: Then there was a fallow period – I know writers always like to find excuses for fallow periods – but I really was fed up with humiliations,[33] dealing with publishers.

Q: I am fascinated by the Caribbean or Guyanese subject of *Black Midas* and *The Wild Coast*. The themes are large, but the subject matter is Guyanese or Caribbean. Then, *The Last Barbarian* seems to go outward in subject matter, taking in New York, and speaking for Black, third-world, oppressed people. There is a widening of the subject matter, coming from a colonial context to a wider international context. Now, you have become a spokesman for victimized, Black, third-world people. Is that just a natural consequence of not living in Guyana anymore? Is that why you see things from a wider context?

A: I think that is partially true, but it also has to do with personal choices. Take someone like Roy Heath. We grew up together in Agricola.[34] Roy remembers every single detail of life in Guyana, after forty-five years away from it.

Q: Why do you think it took so long to come out?

A: It hibernates. It takes a long time. You cannot get away from something you are so deeply rooted in. My own experience, my own intellectual growth is such that I am best at living in a wider world. That is good. I really like travelling.

Q: There is a lot of your own experience in *Black Midas*?

A: It is someone else's story. I was not Sharpe. *The Wild Coast* is my most autobiographical book. The boy was myself. Then in *The Last Barbarian* Don is me, but I found the character unsuccessful and unsympathetic because I hated myself so much that I could not create a wholesome image of myself in the character. I disapproved of Don as I was writing. Then *Moscow is not my Mecca* goes off into writing about someone into whom I could put some of my own experiences. Now I think this has crystallized. I can plumb that experience.

Q: You will write an autobiographical novel?

A: Yes. I am putting it in novel form. Everything I do gets to that form. That history of Grenada[35] is really a novel, taking history and its facts and putting it in that form.

Q: We are speaking of forty years of writing and thirty years of being published, from 1958 to 1986. You have seen West Indian writing emerge and become established. How do you feel about those early years when Harris and you would talk? What are your feelings about our literary history in the last thirty years?

A: I think that this is a great period in the history of Guyana. The criticism of our literature, which is fundamentally anti-colonial and aims at liberating a colonial imagination, has never caught up with that nexus or upsurge. They are putting it into contexts that are askew. Criticism has to understand the eruptive force of the anti-colonial movement. 'The anti-colonial movement' almost sounds like a cliché. This is not exactly what I mean. I mean this awakening of the human spirit, this feeling when I went with Cheddi into the countryside of Guyana, when we were setting up the Youth Movement for the PPP, and I could hear the peasants talking poetry to me, or

I could hear Martin Carter reading his poems in the car, by lamp, at night in the Canje, while the people talked back to him in poetry. All these things were phenomena. If you did not live through them, you would not know.

Q: Do you think literature gave expression to the political feelings of the period in the early fifties?

A: Yes, it has some apprehension of the power of this upsurge through Wilson Harris, and through Martin Carter. It does not matter what direction they go in now. It was the times which spewed them out. They go in all creative directions of the compass. One of the things is that, being from Guyana, we are in Latin America. The Latin American imagination[36] feeds on exile without losing its kind of creative force. But in the English-speaking Caribbean, authors do not have the same umbilical binding to roots that the Latin American authors have. Well, of course one makes that theory, then you think of Roy Heath who has been away for forty-five years and goes back with that meticulous detail into the psyche of the 1930s, in Georgetown. It is unbelievable.

Q: But I would have thought the best writing by our best writers is about their home experience. Naipaul's best book is *A House for Mr Biswas*.[37]

A: And the short stories.

Q: *Miguel Street*[38] is fantastic.

A: Because in it there is still a kind of tenderness and compassion in the middle of the satire; there is great warmth and feeling. When he wrote about B. Wordsworth for instance, he was in love with the poetic spirit of this character. I agree completely in that sense. However, what I am trying to say is that I am more rooted in Guyana after forty-five years, through certain experiences which entered my psyche and framed the language that I use and the images I carry. You cannot get away from that, no matter how many places you go to. What you must learn in this long, painful period, is how to see everything else in the world through this spectrum. Sometimes the mirror is blurred, and you can't see through it. Your early Caribbean experiences and present life are separate things: you have to struggle to bring them together.[39] It has never really been done before, and we, the third-world writers, all of us, are humanizing the process. When Ernest Hemingway[40] writes about Africa it infuriates me. He is using Africa as a kind of Hollywood, epic background, and his characters are parading against this backdrop. In a way, when Forster[41] is writing about India, India is just an exotic backdrop. India is not India. They do not know the dreams, the hopes, the deep roots of that Indian psyche, which only an Indian can know. When Mulk Raj Anand[42] writes a story, even a bad one, it is still better than anything those fellows have written. He understands the people. The West Indian experience has always been a very eclectic experience. Uprooted from the four ends of the earth and dumped there, we have not really come to terms with synthesizing all the cross-currents.

Q: When you think of all our writers, Sam Selvon is probably the one who has worked most consistently with that local experience, plumbing it all the time. Living away from that setting as you have done, as Sam has done, how can you be true to that experience? You say it is still energizing your writing. But what would a young Guyanese think of you now? I have lived outside of Guyana for almost thirty years – less than you. Yet I see a difference between myself and younger Guyanese.

A: That is true. But I think the great question is one of being true to yourself, ruthlessly assessing who you are, where you stand, what your experience has been. I realize I am alienated from those younger generations in Guyana, at certain levels. But there are still other levels. When a young Grenadian comes to me and tells me that he read my book and it moved him tremendously, that is because I am still in the same area as he is. It is not possible for anyone else to do that, to bring us back to the fold. You lose some things. I lose essences of the smell of the earth, and the dreams of the people in a very contemporary sense. What they are thinking now often baffles and surprises me. But I am coming to terms with it. There is not one of us who does not carry in his heart a desire to go back. But there are not the conditions to go back.

Notes

1 Berbice High School was established in New Amsterdam, Guyana, by the Canadian Presbyterian Mission Church during the early years of this century. The Canadian Presbyterian Mission worked mainly with Indians in Guyana, and a majority of the students in Berbice High School were Indian.

2 Queen's College was the main government secondary school for boys in Guyana. It was situated in the capital city, Georgetown. Cf. Chapter 1, note 9.

3 J. A. Rodway was from St Lucia, where he taught Derek Walcott in school.

4 For Derek Walcott, see Chapter 3 and Index.

5 Ben Yisu Das was one of the first Indian teachers at Berbice High School.

6 Up to the 1970s, secondary school students in the English-speaking Caribbean sat for examinations administered by Examination Boards in Britain. The Cambridge School Certificate Board of Examinations was one of the most popular.

7 For Drake, see Chapter 1, note 3.

8 Sir John Hawkins (1532–95) was the first English slave trader. He was regarded with hostility by the Portuguese and Spanish, and died in a raid on the Spanish West Indies.

9 Sir Martin Frobisher (1539–94) was an English navigator and explorer who made discoveries in searching for a Northwest Passage to India and China. He fought against the Armada, and was Vice-Admiral to Sir Francis Drake's expedition to the West Indies in 1585.

10 Corentyne is a rural district, in the county of Berbice, in Guyana. It forms the setting of Mittelholzer's novel *Corentyne Thunder*. See Index under Mittelholzer.

11 *The Wild Coast* (Secker and Warburg, London, 1958).

12 New Amsterdam is in the county of Berbice, in Guyana.
    For Mittelholzer, see Chapter 4, note 1.

For Harris, see Introduction, note 7.

Martin Wylde Carter was born in Guyana in 1927, and wrote, among other works, *Poems of Resistance* (Lawrence and Wishart, London, 1954); *Poems of Succession* (New Beacon Books, London, 1977); *Poems of Affinity* (Release Publishers, Georgetown (Guyana), 1980); and *Selected Poems* (Demerara Publishing, Georgetown, 1989). He has been a radical voice in anglophone Caribbean poetry, his politics having been shaped by the anti-colonial protest, in Guyana, during the 1950s, when he was jailed for a short period because of his support of the People's Progressive Party. Carter was later Minister of Information and Culture in Prime Minister Burnham's government, and represented Guyana at a Commonwealth Poetry Conference in Cardiff, Wales.

E. R. Braithwaite was born in Guyana in 1922, and was a fighter pilot with the Royal Air Force during the Second World War. After demobilization, he became a schoolteacher in London, and out of his experiences as a teacher, he wrote the bestselling book *To Sir With Love* (The Bodley Head, London, 1959), describing his experience of racial discrimination in postwar London. Since then he has held varied jobs, for example, as Head of the Guyanese Mission at the United Nations, and as Guyana's ambassador to Venezuela. He has also written several other volumes of autobiography, and one novel, *A Choice of Straws* (The Bodley Head, London, 1965).

13   *Creole Chips* (Lutheran Press, Georgetown, 1937). This book is out of print. Only a few copies still exist, for example, in the archives of the Government of Guyana.

14   See Introduction, note 16.

15   The *Christmas Annual* was a literary magazine that appeared every Christmas, and was published by the newspaper *The Daily Chronicle*. It contained stories, articles, poems, photographs, puzzles, recipes, almost everything. It was different from *Kyk-Over-Al*, which was literary and artistic; but the *Christmas Annual* reached a larger audience, for many of whom it was their only visible example of local literature or culture.

16   See Introduction, note 7.

17   For Andrew Salkey, see Chapter 4, especially note 8.

18   See Chapter 1, note 14.

19   For Martin Carter, see note 12 above.

Sydney King is an Afro-Guyanese politician who has changed parties and fought elections many times. He was a minister in the PPP government which was overthrown in 1953. He later joined the PNC briefly. He is still politically active, and has changed his name to Eusi Kwayana. His current party is the Working People's Alliance (WPA).

20   *The Political Action Bulletin* was the organ of the Political Affairs Committee, a group formed in 1946 by Dr Jagan, Mrs Jagan, Ashton Chase and Jocelyn Hubbard. These were the same people who, along with others, founded the People's Progressive party in 1950. It was then that the *Political Action Bulletin* became *Thunder*, which still is the official organ for the PPP.

21   Jan Carew, *Streets of Eternity* (self-published, Georgetown, Guyana, 1952).

22   Canje is a rural district in the county of Berbice in Guyana.

23   *The Last Barbarian* (Secker and Warburg, London, 1961).

24   Jorge Amado was born in Bahia, Brazil. His novels about social injustice and class struggle have been translated from Portuguese into English, for example, *The Violent Land* (1945), and *Tereza Batista* (1975).

25   *Rivers of This Night* is unpublished.

26   A. J. Seymour (1914–89) was a distinguished Guyanese poet, editor and man of letters. As founder and editor of the literary magazine *Kyk-Over-Al* from 1945 to 1961, Seymour played a crucial role in promoting Caribbean literature. Twenty-eight issues of *Kyk-Over-Al* appeared between 1945 and 1961. Between 1961 and 1984 there was only one issue, no. 29 in 1981. Then *Kyk-Over-Al* was revived by Ian McDonald and A. J. Seymour and

has appeared regularly since 1984. It is now edited by Ian McDonald. Cf. Chapter 9, note 2.

27   Cy Grant is a Trinidadian writer who is better known as a singer and musician.

28   The Potaro is a tributary of the Essequibo river in Guyana. It runs through a part of the Guyanese hinterland where 'porkmockers' or prospectors mine gold and other precious metals.

29   *Black Midas* (Secker and Warburg, London, 1958).

30   Sylvia Wynter, who was born in Jamaica in 1928, was married to Jan Carew in the 1960s. She is a novelist (*The Hills of Hebron*, 1962) and critic, and now teaches in the US.

31   A Jamaican writer, Victor Reid (1913–87) visited Africa in 1960, having already written the successful novel *The Leopard* (Heinemann, London, 1958) which is set in Kenya and focuses on the Mau-Mau uprising of the 1950s. His writing encompasses Jamaican history, politics and identity. His novel *New Day* is famous as the first West Indian novel completely written in Jamaican English. Reid also published children's books, journalism and a biography of Norman Manley. See Chapter 6, note 14.

32   Jan Carew, *Moscow is Not my Mecca* (Secker and Warburg, London, 1964); republished as *A Green Winter* (Stein and Day, New York, 1965).

33   Cf. Salkey's comments in Chapter 4 on second-stage Caribbean writers being rejected by publishers.

34   See Index for Roy Heath. Agricola is a village on the east bank of the Demerara river in Guyana.

35   Jan Carew, *Grenada: The Hour Will Strike Again* (The International Organisation of Journalists, Prague, 1985).

36   See Index for comments on Latin American literature or culture by Salkey, Phillips and Heath.

37   See Chapter 1, note 12.

38   V. S. Naipaul, *Miguel Street* (André Deutsch, London, 1959).

39   Cf. Cyril Dabydeen's discussion of 'here' and 'there' in Chapter 9.

40   Ernest Hemingway (1899–1961) was born in Oak Park, Illinois, and was a novelist, short-story writer and journalist. He was awarded the Nobel Prize for Literature in 1954. He also served as a correspondent during the Spanish Civil War and in the Second World War. Only a few of his works are set in Africa, for example *The Green Hills of Africa* (1935).

41   E. M. Forster (1879–1970) was a British author, famous especially for his novel *A Passage to India*, which is set in India during the time of the British Raj when political agitation for Independence was beginning. *A Passage to India* is a minor classic of English literature, but is not as highly regarded in India or the third world.

42   Mulk Raj Anand was born in India in 1905 and studied in England during the 1920s. He is one of the best-known of the older Indian novelists writing in English. His novels include *Untouchable* (1935); *Coolie* (1936); and *Private Life of an Indian Prince* (1948).

CHAPTER 6

Samuel Selvon: The open society or its enemies?

Born in San Fernando, Trinidad, in 1923, Samuel Selvon was educated at Naparima College in south Trinidad. During the Second World War, he worked in the Royal Naval Reserve, and later on the Trinidad Guardian, *first as a reporter then as a sub-editor. In 1950, he emigrated to England, where he found employment in India House, in London. His first novel,* A Brighter Sun, *appeared in 1952, and his second,* An Island is a World, *in 1954. During this period, Selvon contracted tuberculosis, but was cured after an operation. In 1954, he won a Guggenheim Fellowship that took him to the McDowell Writers' Colony in New Hampshire for one year. Soon afterwards, he began writing full-time, and has so far produced eight other novels, together with short stories, poems, plays and other works. Selvon writes mainly about Trinidad and about West Indian immigrants living in London. His fiction is notable for its comic and ironic insights, and for its original and highly skilful use of Creole as a narrative medium. In 1975, Selvon emigrated from England to Calgary, Canada. He died in Trinidad on 16 April 1994. (This interview was recorded in Toronto on 18 March 1986.)*

Q: Can you briefly sketch your family background.

A: We were a family of seven, and I was born in San Fernando, the largest town in the southern part of Trinidad. My father and mother were very loving people, and when I wrote my first novel, *A Brighter Sun*,[1] I dedicated it to my mother and father. They allowed me complete freedom as a child. My mother's mother was Indian and her father was Scottish.

Q: It seems unusual that a Scotsman should marry an Indian woman in Trinidad at that time.

A: It was a *bona fide* marriage as far as I know, unless it was otherwise and kept from me. But there were records of the marriage. My middle name, Dickson, comes from my mother's father. My mother grew up among people in the village, and had lots of friends among them. I remember occasions when Indian families would pass along selling melongenes, tomatoes or whatever. They would come into the yard, and my mother would converse with them in Hindi.

Q: Was her father rich?

A: Her father was an overseer on a coconut plantation, so they must have

been comparatively well-off. When I was a child, we were fairly well-off –
I would say middle-class – but that did not last very long. By the time
I finished elementary school and went to high school, I had to quit after
Form Six and go out to work.

Q: What did your father do?

A: My father was a dry-goods-man. He worked in a dry-goods mer-
chant's shop on the High Street in San Fernando. He was as pure an Indian
as you can get – a Madrassi.

Q: But so far as your own childhood is concerned, you grew up in a mixed
environment? Was that true of the school too?

A: Yes, the school was completely mixed. I was creolized from a very
early age. When I say 'creolized', I mean the Caribbean sense of the term.
It identifies with the people.

Q: Maybe you can define the term more fully later, but I understand that
you did not have a particularly Indian, or exclusively ethnic upbringing. It
was of a mixed nature.

A: Yes.

Q: What about your early literary interests? When did you first think of
becoming a writer? Were there teachers who influenced you?

A: I had one or two teachers who encouraged me a great deal. I am still
talking about the elementary-school level. I was pretty good at writing
compositions, but at that age, the fact that I would have developed into a
professional writer never occurred to me.

Q: What about high school?

A: In high school the flair for English and writing compositions continued. I think English was my best subject. But I was more interested in the
scouting movement. I mention that, you know, not because it influenced
me, but much of my time between the ages of about 8 to 14 was concerned
with the scout movement. I was a cub, scout, King's scout. I earned badges.
I went in for jamboree competitions, flags and so on. Scouting encouraged
a sense of independence in me.

Q: What role did religion play in your life at that time? I assume you were
baptized and attended the Canadian Presbyterian church?

A: Yes, I attended church, but I don't think religion played a big role.

Q: So, up to the time you left Naparima College (aged 17) there was no
particular interest in writing as such?

A: No. Writing came much later, when I outgrew scouting and I enlisted
in the local branch of the navy about 1942 or 1943.

Q: What was the navy like?

A: It was a branch of the (British) Royal Navy, a reserve. They had set up
a station in Port of Spain, and had built submarine-detectors around the
island. Convoys came to take oil up to Europe, and the Port of Spain station
patrolled their route between Trinidad, Venezuela, Grenada, and places like

that. It was during those war years, that I started to reflect and become more mature in my thinking. I began to write poetry and prose. Then, in 1945, when the war was over, I had to find a job. I wanted a job as a wireless operator hoping to work on a ship and get out of Trinidad. But eventually I took the job of a wireless operator with the local newspaper the *Trinidad Guardian*.[2] While on this job I took more of an interest in writing. Some of my poetry was broadcast on the BBC's *Caribbean Voices*[3] programme. That really made me feel I was able to write. Some short articles were published and spurred me on. Eventually, I got completely out of the wireless operator job, and became a reporter for the *Trinidad Guardian*. After about six months as a cub reporter, I got an offer to work on the editorial desk, and I preferred that. I did some editorials, and generally started to get a better feeling for the fluency of words. Between 1945 and 1950 several of my short stories and poems were published locally or broadcast by the BBC in London. I also published stories in *Bim*,[4] in Barbados, and in *The West Indian Review* edited by Esther Chapman[5] in Jamaica.

Q: Did you know anyone else around you who was writing at that time?
A: Through my newspaper work, I had the opportunity to sub-edit a weekly magazine which used both verse and prose. Through that medium, I met people like Errol Hill[6] who is now a playwright, but used to write poetry too. I knew George Lamming slightly. I got to know Alfred Mendes who used to meet a group interested in writing – Cecil Gray, Joseph Penko, Barnabas Ramon Fortune.[7] We would meet and talk about poetry, or we might have a beer together, and sit around and talk. I don't think we did this with the feeling that it was going to help us. It was just that these guys were also writing, and we would compare and talk about each other's work.

Q: Were there any class differences in the group? Did the fact that you were Indian make any difference?
A: Not at all. I never came across any of that in my lifetime in Trinidad. There was the usual school boy 'coolie' and 'nigger' in school: making up rhymes, 'Charlie, Charlie, chinkey-eyed', that sort of thing. But I felt no discrimination while growing up, not in the navy or on the newspaper. There was nothing that identified me. I don't know if this is in part because I had become so completely creolized and assimilated. I never exhibited Indianized ways.

Q: Did you have particular Indian friends, or did you attend Indian events?
A: On my father's side of the family, there were relatives in the country districts. As a child I would go there for holidays. They were Indian, of course, and I would eat the rice and curry, and the fruit growing in the yard. Then they would send me home. But I was more interested in going to films

in the town than in spending weekends with them. In other words, it did not matter to me that they were Indian or not.

Q: Did you watch Indian films or listen to Indian music?

A: No, we didn't have Indian music. But we had a piano. We used to play 'Drink to Me Only with Thine Eyes' and that sort of thing. It was imitative and came from my father and mother. They would use English colonial phrases which I heard as a child, and maybe was slightly influenced by. We sat down at table, ate with knife and fork, and said grace before meals.

Q: You are considered as a writer who represents West Indian character accurately. You capture the pure West Indian idiom of behaviour, language, speech, etc. It might be interesting to identify elements in your background that enabled you to represent this West Indian character so accurately.

A: What was important were the years when I was working for the newspaper. I read a lot of philosophy in trying to discover myself, and pondering on questions in the way, I suppose, Tiger does in *A Brighter Sun*. I got some books on the craft of writing, and I actually started to build a little library, not many books, maybe a dozen.

Q: Do you remember the authors of those books?

A: I remember *The Story of Philosophy* by Will Durant.[8] That started me off. I read that book several times because, at that age, I couldn't understand what I read, and I had to go back and read it time and time again. I read Richard Jefferies[9] who wrote about the English countryside. This is perhaps the influence of school reading, growing up on English poetry. You must remember that I went through all those West Indian readers with their little bits of Shakespeare and Keats and so on. I love some of those things: 'The poetry of earth is never dead'; 'I shot an arrow into the air'. That is probably where it started.

Q: Did you form any lasting relationships in Trinidad, before you went to England?

A: I had girlfriends, and not all of them were Indian. There was never any question in my mind about belonging to India. In a way, it was a form of childish bravado that you did not belong to a clique, that you were not Indianized. It was a big thing if you were one of the boys, creolized. I saw both things. I saw the Indian tendency, but we never wanted to admit that part of ourselves.

Q: The fact is, though, that you knew a good deal about Indian life. *A Brighter Sun* reveals intimate details about estate living, the life of the labouring class of Indians that would be foreign to most non-Indian Trinidadians.

A: I remember every Christmas time, the scout troop would go into the little country villages round about. We would sing songs for the people on the estates or sugar plantations. I saw it then. Although I am talking about San Fernando as a town, sugar cane grew literally into the town. You stepped out of the main street, and two blocks away there would be a field of sugar cane. So I saw that sort of life. It was right around us.

Q: What circumstances made you decide to go to England? George Lamming said you sailed on the same ship.

A: That was complete coincidence. I didn't know Lamming was going on that boat. I think he was much more serious than I was about the fact that he was going to be a poet and a writer. Although I had experience as a journalist and wanted to be a writer, I don't think my hopes were as deeply rooted as his. When I got to England, if I could not make out as a writer, I felt I could do something else. But to get back to the period when I worked for the newspaper – I had been married for some time and separated. I was married to a girl from Guyana.

Q: How did you meet her?

A: She was visiting Trinidad. It was a hasty marriage. I was working as the sole supporter of my family. I think I resented that, and said to myself: 'Look, this is my life. I am not going to spend it supporting my parents. I'll get married and pull out like everybody else.' That wasn't the real reason, but it was one of the factors why I married. It was not a very mature decision. The marriage lasted a long time before my wife returned to Guyana. Later, she joined me in England, and we lived together as a family for some years. Then we separated again and divorced. But getting back again to the Trinidad period – I had had the early success of my poems and stories being published, and things looked good. But for the same reason that my early marriage did not work – I wanted something more out of life – I wanted to get out of the island. I was too young to buy a car, and settle down to a life of complacency, with the boys at beach parties. I could see that kind of life which, as you know, is carried on so well in the Caribbean, and I said: 'No, I'm getting out of this.' This basically is the reason why I left.

Q: Tell me about when you arrived in England and how your first book came out. Was there help from friends?

A: There was, to some extent. I had made a few friends among English journalists who worked with me on the newspaper in Trinidad. They knew I was going to England, and gave me the addresses of a few people.

Q: *A Brighter Sun* could not have appeared long after your arrival in England?

A: No. I wrote pretty fast during 1950 to 1951. During that time I had a few short stories accepted by English magazines. I also did one or two things for English magazines on a freelance basis, while working as a clerk with the Indian government, at India House in London. At first they would not accept me because I had not come from India. I told them I was of East Indian origin. Eventually, they gave me the job. I wrote *A Brighter Sun* during the time I was working for the Indian High Commission. As a civil servant, I could not publish anything without having it vetted by a civil service official. So they wanted to vet my novel. The way I got around that was by saying I had brought the manuscript with me from Trinidad. So no one vetted it. *A Brighter Sun* was born out of a short story called 'The Baby' which is a little section in the novel. When I had written that story in Trinidad, the idea of a novel had not crossed my mind. Now, in England, I used all my memories of where I lived during my earliest years. I lived imaginatively on the island again. I saw all the things which happened while I was there. They were still vivid and fresh in my mind – the people, the places, the sea, the building of roads. It was not very difficult to get it all down. I submitted the manuscript to a publisher who was recommended to me by one of the people whose addresses I had brought with me from Trinidad, a writer by the name of Maurice Richardson. He showed it to Collins, and they liked it very much, but were slightly hesitant. Then he showed it to Allan Wingate and they took it like a shot. About a week after I sent the manuscript in, they telephoned to say they wanted to publish it.

Q: What sort of reviews did the novel get?

A: It got excellent reviews, and was published in America by the Viking Press. The reviews in the US were very good too: 'A wonderful book. We look forward to Selvon's next novel.' Things like that. I started to work on the second book right away. That was *An Island is a World*,[10] published two years later. I had been ill between 1953 and 1954, and spent almost one year in hospital with tuberculosis. I had an operation. I really became much healthier after the operation, although I was as thin as a rake. Luckily, I built myself up and put on weight after the illness.

Q: Did you go back to India House?

A: Yes. I had had *An Island is a World* published by then. Then I applied for a Guggenheim Fellowship. When I got it, I made up my mind. I decided to chuck everything else and write, knowing that the Guggenheim would support me for one year. The main thing was continuous writing, and since then, although I have done odd jobs in between, in the main, I have stuck to my decision. This is what I consider my most prolific period, the 1950s and 1960s with *An Island is a World* and *The Lonely Londoners*.[11]

Q: What sort of reception did *The Lonely Londoners* get? It was the first of your books with the whole narrative in Creole. Can you remember why you decided to do that?

A: While I was in the States on the Guggenheim Fellowship, I got another Fellowship to spend as much time as I wanted in a writer's colony in New Hampshire, the McDowell Colony for writers. I was hoping to do an historical piece about Raleigh's quest for El Dorado. It was a hodgepodge kind of thing, and I never really made much headway with it. But while I was there, away from the scene of London – this is one of the situations where distance lends perception – I realized that the book I wanted to write was *The Lonely Londoners*. I didn't know what shape it would take. I wrote maybe three or four paragraphs, and when I returned to London some months later, I got to work on it. I was going to write it in Standard English, with the characters speaking in Creole. But for some reason I would write a page or two, then I would scrap it, and think about it again. Somehow it seemed that the creation which I had in mind was not working out at all in Standard English. I said to myself: 'Look, why not just write the whole book using this Caribbean language?' I say 'Caribbean language' but, as you probably know, it is based on the Trinidadian form of the Caribbean language. You know what the Jamaican dialect is like. I decided that the Trinidadian one was the best of all Caribbean languages for me, because it was the one most closely aligned to English. It does not have derivations from African languages like the Jamaican language has.[12]

Q: It is also the one you know best.

A: It is just about the only one I know. In the book I do have Jamaican characters, but I don't treat them in Jamaican Creole. The Trinidad form of language worked so well that, even from the beginning, I felt I was creating something. In six months the complete novel was finished. There was no day when I did not continue writing, until it evolved to a natural conclusion. It just seemed one of those creations where you feel that the language and content mesh to make one whole. One could not do without the other. The strength of the book is that it all works together. For instance, there are some paragraphs which start in straightforward Standard English, such as towards the end of the book when I describe the London landscape.

Q: Yes. Your characters were living in an alien landscape and atmosphere. Your description catches that reality of how different the London atmosphere was from their Caribbean customs and experience.

A: What is also true is that I had reached a section which had to be summed up in sombre prose. That is one of my favourite sections, where Moses is summing up his whole life, and saying the days have gone by, and the boys are coming into his room as if to confession. One is finished with the kiff-kiff[13] laughter, and is completely aware of the situation of Moses. The language of *The Lonely Londoners* was applauded all over the country.

Q: It is a real innovation. *New Day*[14] came out in 1949 in a form of Jamaican Creole that is remote and stylized, not as realistic or usable a form of English as yours. Were the characters actual people you knew, or were they made up from traits of people around you?

A: They are collections of traits taken from real people.

Q: And you lived through or talked about those incidents and experiences?

A: Yes.

Q: Your characters are immigrants facing hardships in an unfamiliar society; yet they joke so much. At the end you do say it is not really joking: there is underlying seriousness too. Did you have that in mind at the very beginning? How did the title come about?

A: I think it came near the conclusion of the book. I didn't start with the title in my mind. The title came in the same way that the book was written. This was what it was going to be called, and I did not give much thought to changing it. Should I call it *The Black Londoners*? There was no question about that. As the book flowed, so the title flowed into it.

Q: The title itself 'The *Lonely* Londoners' is sad, and the main experiences are sad too; yet there is all the laughter.

A: That is a national West Indian characteristic, I think, at least among the people I knew. It has been said that it is used as a sort of protection, a defence mechanism against tribulation and hardship. You laugh at it. They've just locked up a friend of yours for walking on the wrong side of the road, or because he was standing and blocking the passage-way. What do you do? You try to make a joke of it. But every joke is made out of the facts of a tragic situation.

Q: I agree that is one of the principal ways in which the book makes its appeal – through a mixture of comedy and tragedy. But for the first time in a full-length novel, you are writing about West Indian characters living outside of the West Indies. Is this not an important departure? Of course, you may not have thought of it in those terms.

A: Not really. I do believe that if I had not made that trip to America, and had stayed in England, it might have worked out differently. I'm not sure. As I said, distance did give me perspective.

Q: What about your literary connections with Lamming or other people? Did they influence your thinking or writing?

A: George went his way and I went mine. Then *A Brighter Sun* was published, and I met George again. He said what a wonderful book it was. He said he was working on a novel too. We would meet occasionally at the BBC and maybe go along to see someone to arrange a programme, or read a short story or a poem. In that way, our paths would sometimes cross. But, apart from that, during all my years in England, my associations with other writers have been quite casual.

Q: This brings us to about 1956 or 1957. By then you were writing as an established author. Did you consider another book in Creole because *The Lonely Londoners* was so successful? In the next book, *Turn Again Tiger*,[15] you went back to the Tiger story.

A: You see, *Turn Again Tiger* was the sequel in the back of my mind; but I did not work on it immediately. What I think happened is that in the same way that leaving England and going to the US made me think of *The Lonely Londoners*, perhaps, when writing that novel, my mind was set to think about the sequel *Turn Again Tiger*.

Q: But you did not actually go back to Trinidad?

A: No. I spent thirteen years in England before going back to Trinidad.

Q: You were also writing short stories, because *Ways of Sunlight*[16] came out about this time.

A: Shortly after *The Lonely Londoners*, a national newspaper suggested that I do a series of short stories. I then wrote most of those London-set short stories. I had done one or two before and had them published in the *New Statesman* and other magazines. But what set the scene for the book of short stories was the novel. It was not as if the short stories came first. It was after this kind of language had been exposed in *The Lonely Londoners* that people became interested.

Q: Would it be true to say that your literary reputation even today relies heavily on the appeal and staying power of this language?

A: It had an effect on everything I have written since then. It seemed to me that with the acceptance of the language, that everything else – my background, my culture, the place where I came from – were also accepted. It became much more fortifying as an important element, not only in the writing, but in the way I started to think of myself as a person from the Caribbean.

Q: How did you select the name 'Moses' for the narrator in *The Lonely Londoners*?

A: I think you know that 'Moses' is a fairly common name in Trinidad. To be quite honest, I did not think of the connotations the name brings to people's minds. There is probably a lot in the book from that stream of unconsciousness, while writing it. I told you how it was written. Two or three of my books have been written like that, where I was not even completely conscious of what was happening.

Q: By the end of the 1950s, it seems, you were beginning to write less and less about Caribbean settings, and more and more about Caribbean people living in foreign (chiefly English) settings. Did you feel cut off, exiled, at a disadvantage?

A: In a strange way, I feel closer to Trinidad living away from it. After those first thirteen years in England, I have been back every two years or so, irregularly. I go back if and when I am called. I have never been back on my own steam. The times I have been back I noticed many of the evils I fled from. But there are more people in Trinidad nowadays who are themselves conscious of these things.

Q: Does your writing have anything to do with the new level of con-sciousness or awareness? It was not there when you first left Trinidad.

A: My own life started to change after the last war. Everything changed. The third world came into existence. All these nations became independent.

World events changed. It was the beginning of a literary tradition in the Caribbean, with a surge of writers. It must have affected people in Trinidad. Bad habits take a long time to die, and the things I wrote about before I left Trinidad in 1950 still exist. Anyone from the Caribbean will tell you that Caribbean politics is corrupt. I feel that while there may be elements of truth in that, people are becoming aware of the fact that these things should not exist. That is encouraging. Now I would not say that this has happened through my writings. It may have happened through my writings and through the works of other Caribbean writers. Trinidadians can say what they like, but our writing must have had an effect on people at large, whether they like me as a writer, or Naipaul, or Michael Anthony.[17] The fact is that the island has produced so many creative writers. This is a remarkable accomplishment for an island of that size. There are only a little over one million people living in Trinidad. When I first went back to Trinidad, after thirteen years in England, people flung themselves at me, and asked how I could go to England and write language like that in *The Lonely Londoners*. It made foreigners think that we people in Trinidad did not know how to speak proper English. This antagonism existed for some time. Now, ironically, it has changed. What is happening in recent years is that Creole is being exploited in New York and elsewhere. Raconteurs now tell stories in the language that I used in my work.

Q: What were some of the evils that you saw in Trinidad?

A: I consider complacency to be an evil in a young man. At the age I was I could not settle down.

Q: That seems rather sad: to feel that you have to leave your country, but to use your country and countrymen in your writing. It's like you're exploiting them. If you run away from these negative [Trinidadian] influences, it means you are safe from them. Yet you write about people [Trinidadians] who have to endure them. Should you not go back and try to overcome them?

A: Yes, but a writer needs perspective. What I am saying is similar to what Lamming has said about our people as West Indians: they only started to identify themselves as such when they moved outside the Caribbean. There is this feeling that this is the place you belong to. When you get away from it, people do not know who you are. You have to put yourself on the map by saying you belong to an island. You say you belong to a series of islands known as the Caribbean or the West Indies. You don't start by saying: 'I come from Antigua or Tobago.' Someone will ask you where that is.

Q: Is the English-speaking Caribbean one entity? Federation seems a dead idea nowadays.

A: What happens when you go abroad to a place like London is that you are completely isolated, and therefore you have to herd together. The people in England do not say we are ten Trinidadians or Jamaicans or Antiguans. They say there is a bunch of black people from the Caribbean. They lump you together, so you find in yourself a feeling that never existed in the Caribbean, because when you are in the Caribbean, you are isolated in your own island. There is no place where all the peoples from the Caribbean can meet.

Q: The unity you talk about is a sense of solidarity felt outside the West Indies, where West Indians are a minority in a large and indifferent community. Is it not dangerous to have this kind of external solidarity which does not exist within the West Indies?

A: Yes, one does find that outside the Caribbean area, there are many exiled peoples who are trying to formulate their destiny. But they are outside the islands. I agree with you there. Yet this is how it is brought about. There is more feeling of solidarity outside the Caribbean. One thing which might help solidarity within the islands is the University of the West Indies which is situated in Jamaica, Barbados and Trinidad.

Q: You are generally thought of as a writer who represents positive aspects of the West Indies, and you are contrasted sharply with a writer like Naipaul who is regarded as pessimistic. Yet, it seems to me that the evils you mention – complacency, political corruption – are similar to those mentioned by Naipaul. Why this difference in response to the two of you?

A: I don't know what it is. I can only say that I think Naipaul is perhaps the greatest writer the Caribbean has produced. I am not talking about content or value, because someone may bring in Harris or maybe Lamming – I am talking about world acceptance. I have tried to point out Caribbean shortcomings. I have not been as blatant as Naipaul has been. It may be a question of attitude or how it is approached. I use a great deal of humour and sympathy in my work. Those are aspects which attract me, and which, I think, I write about best. But that is not the only angle from which people could be handled. You see a guy who robs his mother and stabs her in the street and your anger will be different. I might say: 'Did he hate his mother?' You might say: 'That son of a bitch has killed his mother right in the street!' Writers are products of what they come out of. When you look at Naipaul's background and mine, we are so completely different. Perhaps if I had gone to university in Oxford, I might have been a completely different writer.

Q: I think the West Indies is all the richer for having such diversity.

A: Yes, indeed.

Q: The majority of people in the English-speaking Caribbean are of African descent. You come from Indian indenture stock. Do you feel any obligation to the Indian population in Trinidad and Guyana? After all, in Guyana, for more than twenty years, Indians have not had political power or influence that is remotely commensurate with their percentage of the population. It is roughly similar in Trinidad.

A: The last time I was in Trinidad, I heard that there were more Indians than blacks in Trinidad.

Q: Neil Bissoondath, the nephew of V. S. Naipaul, has written a volume of short stories, *Digging up the Mountains*,[18] which project the view that the best hope for many Indians in the West Indies is to emigrate. I do not think he envisions any large-scale emigration in thousands, but his stories suggest that people whose ancestors left India, under indenture, to make a home for themselves in the Caribbean, now find the region so inhospitable and threatening, that they are strongly impelled to move on somewhere else. Does that not contradict your theory of Caribbean unity?

A: It does not contradict it at all. I feel that a statement like that, from people who are second-generation is wrong. This is what I said earlier about background. You can see elements of Naipaul's writing in *A House for Mr Biswas*.[19] I could not write a book like that. That has not been my experience of the Indian family. We experienced different things. It is a great novel, a great book of the Commonwealth. If Neil Bissoondath could make a statement like that, he must never have been as completely Caribbean as I consider myself.

Q: That is true. He does not belong to our pre-Independence generation.

A: Not only not to our generation. His statement shows that nothing could come out of his gut which could really be called Caribbean. I criticize too, but I have always professed that this is where I belong.

Q: I wonder to what extent Bissoondath's writing may be the wave of the future, and yours may be becoming obsolete.

A: I hope not. I think he's in the minority. Most Indians in Trinidad are completely westernized. There is no question of that. This whole question was put to political proof in 1949, I think, when East Indians were offered revocation of the old indentured labour laws. The idea was that Indian people should be allowed to go back to India if they wanted. I touch on this in *An Island is a World*, and I should really have expanded on it. There were only a handful who chose Indian rather than Trinidadian or British passports, and decided to go back to India.

Q: I agree that the future of Indo-Caribbean people lies squarely in the Caribbean. What Bissoondath is saying is that many Indians now fear for their jobs, properties, families and lives, and are driven to emigrate. I think it is correct and timely for him to point this out because of the injustices – even self-inflicted ones – endured particularly by Indians in Guyana and Trinidad, but perhaps by other sections of the population as well.

A: With that I would agree, particularly in Guyana. I have talked to black people in Trinidad about this. It is time for a change. They say we should have an East Indian Prime Minister for five years, then change to a black

Prime Minister. Maybe that is how history should be. It is time for the People's National Movement (PNM)[20] to exit gracefully, because no government should last as long as this one has.

Q: I recently read a book by Noor Kumar Mahabir[21] from Trinidad. He recorded accounts of old indentured labourers who had come in one of the last ships from India in 1917 or thereabouts. The accounts say that when the ship left Calcutta and stopped in Natal, one woman asked: 'What kind of people are those? Blacks?' She had never seen African people before. To take someone like her and put her in an environment with other people who are primarily of African origin is to invite trouble. I know you told Ken Ramchand[22] that critics are always observing race relations in your work, when the subject is not in your mind at all. But it is important, and it is in your work.

A: It is important, but it is in my work only as an observation. I quite agree with what you have just said. I know there are some Indian writers in Trinidad who are doing research on this sort of thing, and I am all for that, in the same way that I am all for blacks tracing their African roots. I sometimes wonder why I am not one way or the other. I make myself out to be some citizen of the world who leans neither one way nor the other. I come from roots like this. I grew up this way. That is what I feel is our hope in the Caribbean. This is what I love particularly about people from Trinidad who are like this. There are a lot of others who grew up like me, and are not really tugged by any racial inclinations or religious feelings. We are really open. You might say that we are to insecure people. But it is a kind of insecurity which opens and broadens our minds.

Notes

1   See Chapter 1, note 12.
2   The *Trinidad Guardian* is the main daily newspaper in Trinidad.
3   See Chapter 4, note 2 for *Caribbean Voices*.
4   *Bim* is the pioneering literary journal centred in Barbados. It first appeared in 1942; since then it has actively promoted the growth of West Indian literature in many ways, principally by providing an outlet for the writing of fledgling authors. Edward Brathwaite was a former editor. The name of the journal is closely associated with Frank Collymore, who was one of its founders. See Index for Frank Collymore. Cf. Chapter 8, note 1.
5   Esther Chapman was an Englishwoman who lived in Jamaica from the interwar years. She edited the *West Indian Review*, a journal of the arts which flourished only briefly. She also wrote novels, including *Study in Bronze* (1928) and *Two Much Summer* (1953).
6   Errol Hill is currently professor of Drama at Dartmouth College, New Hampshire. He has worked as an actor, director and producer and is a pioneer in the establishment of a West Indian theatre. He has written several plays including *The Ping-Pong* (1958) and *Man Better Man* (1964).
     See Index for George Lamming.

7   Alfred Mendes is the author of two novels, *Pitch Lake* (Duckworth, London, 1934) and *Black Fauns* (Duckworth, London, 1935).
Cecil Gray, Joseph Penko and Barnabas Ramón Fortune are Trinidadian poets whose work is published mainly in anthologies.

8   Will Durant, *The Story of Philosophy* (E. Benn, London, 1948).

9   Richard Jefferies (1848–87) was an English writer whose observations of nature also contained a mixture of poetry and philosophy.

10 S. Selvon, *An Island is a World* (Allan Wingate, London, 1954).

11 S. Selvon, *The Lonely Londoners* (Allan Wingate, London, 1956).

12 Forms of Creole or West Indian speech are influenced mainly by British and West African linguistic practices. But the speech in each West Indian territory reflects differences in vocabulary, intonation, rhythm, accent, etc.

13 'Kiff-kiff' is Trinidadian slang for light-hearted triviality. It is probably related to English 'kif' or 'kef', meaning a state of dreamy tranquillity.

14 Vic Reid, *New Day* (Alfred Knopf, New York, 1949). Cf. Chapter 5, note 31.

15 S. Selvon, *Turn Again Tiger* (MacGibbon and Kee, London, 1958).

16 S. Selvon, *Ways of Sunlight* (MacGibbon and Kee, London, 1957).

17 Michael Anthony was born in 1932, in Mayaro, Trinidad. He is a novelist and short story-writer. His novels include *The Games Were Coming* (1963); *The Year in San Fernando* (1965); and *Green Days by the River* (1967).

18 Neil Bissoondath, *Digging up the Mountains* (Macmillan of Canada, Toronto, 1985).

19 See Chapter 1, note 12.

20 The People's National Movement is the political party founded by Dr Eric Williams and others in 1955. It won national elections in Trinidad and Tobago in 1956 and stayed in power for thirty years. It was finally replaced in 1987, although it won power again in 1991. Cf. Chapter 2, note 22.

21 Noor Kumar Mahabir is a Trinidadian schoolteacher and researcher into Indo-Caribbean history and culture. He has published many articles and booklets on the subject including *The Still Cry* (Calalou Publications, New York, 1985).

22 Kenneth Ramchand is a literary critic and professor of English at the University of the West Indies in Trinidad and Tobago. His interview with Selvon appeared in *Canadian Literature*, No. 95 (Winter, 1982), pp. 56–64.

CHAPTER 7

Roy A. K. Heath:
Continuing colonialism

Roy Heath was born in Guyana in 1926. He was educated at Central High School, and worked briefly in the civil service, before emigrating to England in 1950. He studied modern languages at the University of London, then became a French teacher in secondary schools in London. His teaching career ended only with retirement in 1989. While teaching, Heath had also studied law, and was called both to the English bar in 1964, and the Guyana bar in 1973; but he never practised law. His first novel, The Murderer, *appeared in 1974. Since then he has written several other novels, and a volume of autobiography,* Shadows Round the Moon *(1990). His fiction is notable for its study of urban, Afro-Guyanese society, which is best seen in his trilogy of novels dealing with one family –* From the Heat of the Day, One Generation, *and* Genetha. The Murderer *won the Guardian Fiction Prize in 1978, and Heath's most recent novel,* The Shadow Bride, *the Guyana Fiction Prize in 1989. (This interview was recorded in London on 20 April 1990.)*

Q: With your background of teaching in London schools, what do you think of E. R. Brathwaite's *To Sir With Love*?[1]

A: I don't like to comment on the books of other writers.

Q: Whereas the experiences, of a black school-teacher are accurately recorded in *To Sir With Love*, I would have thought that the book's attitudes to racial discrimination were unrealistic.

A: It is a book with some good features. Although I have lived here in England longer than I have lived in Guyana, I am not keen on writing about my experiences here because I am still an immigrant. My consciousness was formed in Guyana. I feel that in writing about this country I would be expending energy that could be better used in contribution to Guyanese literature.

Q: It is interesting how all that Guyanese experience or knowledge which you brought from 1950 and stored up for twenty-odd years suddenly finds expression in fiction. Your first book did not appear until you were 48 years old. It is not like Dickens who lived in London and wrote about life in London. Are you aware of any special difficulties or advantages in writing with this Proustian sense of recall?

A: It may seem strange that I remember all these things, but it is not only a question of remembering them because they occurred years ago: it is the power of evocation, of things remembered from long ago, from childhood, which have a strange mesmeric power. People think that most of my books are about the 1920s and 1930s. In fact, this isn't so. The trilogy – *From the Heat of the Day, One Generation, Genetha* – was really one book. *A Man Come Home* was set in the 1960s; *The Murderer* and *Kwaku*[2] were set in the 1970s. I have started a new novel which is set in the 1980s. So you can see my attachment is with Guyana; it is not necessarily with a long-remembered past. I am prepared to write about black experience here. Indeed I have; but not in fiction. To me fiction has something very special about it; and I must write about the place that I love. I have never professed to like England.

Q: How different might your writing have been, had you remained in Guyana?

A: Guyana, like Switzerland, is a very small country, and these two countries have one thing in common: they produce emigrants. One-third of the Swiss live abroad for the same reason that drives many Guyanese abroad: their consciousness is highly developed, and they are unable to engage this consciousness in a country with a very small population that is, in effect, parochial in outlook. I think it is not an accident, for instance, that the Swiss have produced some of the most remarkable psychologists – Jean Piaget, Carl Gustav Jung.[3] Their consciousness is so highly developed that something has to give: they either have to seek an outlet to their talents abroad, or achieve exceptional attainment among their countrymen at home.

Q: Why should small countries like Guyana and Switzerland have people with a more highly-developed consciousness than people in larger countries, like France or Germany?

A: That is an historical question which I would not venture to answer. I can suggest lines of thought that might lead to an answer. For instance, Guyana has a particular history within the Caribbean, with some very odd things that are crucial in Guyanese minds. One is the presence of a great forest [the Amazon] that covers most of the country. Another is the fact that our experience of death was remarkable from the time we went to the Caribbean as slaves (in the seventeenth century) up to 1947 when malaria was eradicated.[4] To have had death all around us must have had an overriding influence. It has had an effect on the Mexicans, for instance, one that is more demonstrable: they are more preoccupied with skeletons and myths of death in their celebrations. Now this is only a suggestion – there is no doubt that Guyanese have a highly-developed consciousness; you only have to look at the works of Wilson Harris and Edgar Mittelholzer[5] to see that they are very interested in inner states of mind.

Q: More so than other Caribbean writers?

A: It appears so.

Q: Quite often people talk about the West Indies or the Caribbean collectively, and there are certainly common factors of Caribbean experience, such as slavery, the sugar industry, and the ethnic make up of the population. In the case of the English-speaking territories there is the same language, and similar institutions of law, government and culture. In talking about Guyana, do you separate it from the West Indies in any way? How similar and how different is Guyana from the rest of the West Indies? You've mentioned the interior – the vast hinterland of the Amazon forest. Does the presence of this large forest encourage a kind of interior self-examination which is lacking in writing from the Caribbean islands?

A: I prefer to say this self-examination is particular to the Guyanese experience. After all, there is no immense forest which covers two-thirds of the country in any part of the Caribbean. When I was coming to England by ship in 1950, I met some Martiniquans who were going to fight for the French in Indo-China. At that time my French was sketchy; but there was a manifest identity between the Martiniquans and myself. No one can define culture. You can speak of certain aspects of culture such as language or religion, but not one of them is crucial. There was a certain identity of psychology between the Martiniquans and me. Therefore, there is a cultural identity throughout the Caribbean including Guyana, although geographically Guyana is not in the Caribbean at all. Jamaica has a particular experience. So does Trinidad. Each island has a particular experience. It is like two people who belong to the same family, but are quite different in certain ways.

Q: Most writers start publishing before the age of 48. There are famous exceptions. I believe Conrad[6] started quite late – in his forties, no doubt for special reasons – the time he spent at sea, or the effort it took him to master English. Why did you start late?

A: I had been writing short stories and poetry since my early twenties, and I did publish some pieces in Guyana, and with the BBC. But writing in a big way only began at the age of 40, as a result of a deliberate decision to sit down and discipline myself and write something long. I was so alarmed that I had done nothing in life that I simply decided I should do what I always thought I could do. I am a hedonist. I love pleasure, and I was having a great deal of fun.

Q: One of the classic English writers, John Milton,[7] set out at an early age to write a great poem. He read, and studied, travelled, and prepared with great deliberation for many years. The result eventually was *Paradise Lost*. What I understand from you is that at the age of 40 you suddenly decided to write long fiction. There was no similar sense of commitment or vocation?

A: My life was so full that I didn't have the time to sit and write something big. I took a similar decision to Milton's, only later. When I was young there was no question of choosing to write rather than enjoy myself.

Q: Is the creation of fiction, therefore, a hardship in the sense that it prevents you from enjoying yourself?

A: No, it is a great pleasure too. There is a scale of pleasures, and I didn't want to grow old and then look back and say I never had fun. To me it is essential that one should enjoy oneself. Some people get married very young when they have not sowed their wild oats, and this can lead to difficulties.

Q: Did you have difficulty getting your work published?

A: Yes. When I first submitted the trilogy as one long novel, it was not accepted. Then, I wrote a shorter novel which was published as *A Man Come Home*.

Q: Between 1978 and 1984 you produced six novels – an exceptionally fast rate of publication.

A: People say that I am a prolific writer, but I am not. It is simply that the trilogy had already been written before *The Murderer* was published. When *The Murderer* won the Guardian prize, publication became relatively easy, although my publishers still wouldn't publish the trilogy as one book. It was 220 000 words long. Of the six books I have written, two are very long – the trilogy, and *The Shadow Bride*.[8]

Q: You still think of the trilogy as one book?

A: It is one book. I wrote it as one book. But Longmans claimed that they could not publish a novel of that length by an unknown writer. At the time, they were mainly educational publishers.

Q: Why did you not seek out other publishers?

A: The reason for publishing my first book with Longman is that I used to go to a friend's place every Saturday, and I met someone there who was an editor at Longmans. When she heard that I was writing a novel she asked to see it. That is how I was published. I knew nothing about publishers or agents.

Q: Then you moved over to Allison and Busby.

A: Yes. Being educational publishers, Longmans sent people to sell their books in schools, whereas the so-called trade publishers sent people to bookshops. It was a different thing altogether. Longmans weren't keen on publishing original work.

Q: You remained with Allison and Busby until they went out of business. Now you are with Collins. Have you experienced any discrimination or prejudice from publishers on account of your race or type of writing?

A: I do not say there isn't a prejudice against my type of writing. All I am saying is that things have gone smoothly for me. I think the reason is that I won the Guardian fiction prize in 1978. Therefore it was worthwhile for the publishing establishment in this country to publish my work. I know exactly the problems that Black writers have. There are a lot of good manuscripts by such writers that cannot find a publisher. There is an excellent little press called the Peepal Tree Press,[9] which has done what you would expect Caribbean publishers to have done before: they have published books which won Guyana Literature prizes. I think these books are very important.

Q: Would it not be better for all such books to be published in Guyana or the Caribbean?

A: I made this point in my speech accepting the Guyana Literature Prize for *The Shadow Bride* last December (1989).[10] I said I looked forward to the time when I could publish successfully and lucratively in Guyana, but there is a problem in sales and earnings. Still, I am prepared to publish in Guyana from time to time without being remunerated. My play *Inez Combray* was entered in a drama competition and earned £100, which was very useful at the time. So although I have a duty to publish in Guyana, from time to time, without remuneration, when it comes to publishing my work generally, I have to live.

Q: You mention other literary genres like criticism and plays, but I assume you prefer to write fiction.

A: No, I prefer to write plays.

Q: Yet you have been far more productive in fiction.

A: Yes, because I cannot write at arm's length for a theatre. I have to be with the theatre. I didn't even see *Inez Combray* performed, which I find a bit distressing. My fiction contains a lot of dialogue. I function as a dramatist. I have never been keen on writing fiction.

Q: I agree that one of the distinguishing features of your fiction is dramatic and authentic dialogue.

A: That exemplifies my theory that an individual is not separate. The individual is part of the collection of experiences, part of the opportunities that are there. Since I am not in Guyana, I find it difficult to write for a theatre that is thousands of miles away. But I am a dramatist, so I have to give up drama, as drama, to write for a theatre here. In other words, I write drama through fiction that is going to be read here and everywhere, whereas if I wrote a play it would be performed here only, and that would not please me.

Q: You feel quite strongly that your best audience is a Guyanese one?

A: Yes. Not that I am particularly encouraged by Guyanese audiences. Nor is there a mass of Guyanese asking me to write for them. It is simply that, through birth, I am attached by the umbilical cord to Guyana. I appreciated receiving the Guyana Literature Prize.

Q: Yet the prize is not a necessary sign of Guyanese reading your books.

A: I agree. But the day after I was awarded the prize, I was recognized in the street in Georgetown. Here, in England, one is a cipher. English people themselves are ciphers here. This is a society of alienation. Very often you don't even know your neighbours. I come from a different society. The fact that a Guyanese could hail me and say 'I have seen your picture in the paper. Congrats!' pleases me no end. Even if an Englishman were to do that – and I am recognized here occasionally – it won't please me in the same way as someone walking down High Street in Georgetown. That was thrilling. One belongs to one's people. People like V. S. Naipaul[11] deny it. Yet the very violence of his denial is an indication that he belongs.

Q: Derek Walcott[12] writes plays, very successfully, and he does it from a distance.

A: Yes, but he had a long experience with the theatre in Trinidad. Perhaps if I had written plays in Guyana, I might have continued to write them here. I know that if I went back to Guyana I would start writing plays at once: I wouldn't write novels. I might write short stories.

Q: As you know, Caryl Phillips[13] grew up in England, but he has built a house in St Kitts, his birthplace, and spends a few months there each year. Have you any plans to go back to Guyana? Do you have relatives there?

A: Yes, I have a lot of relations – nieces, nephews and so on. I go back every two years. It is not simply to see the development of the country, and observe changes, such as concrete-built houses, etc. I could go back and live there tomorrow if I didn't have a family here.

Q: People have said that your early books about yard society are very realistic. I think these books could be usefully compared with the writing of Roger Mais,[14] especially with his first three novels, which are about the slums of Jamaica, offering a powerful depiction of the raw conditions in which the poorest Jamaicans live. I think Mais had a strong Christian conscience. He was also politically active, and was a member of Norman Manley's People's National Party.[15] In *A Man Come Home* (1974) Bird has a mysterious connection with 'fairmaids'.[16] At least that is the story we are told. 'Fairmaids' are creatures of folklore, legend or superstition, but you blend their activities with the raw, concrete actuality of a writer like Mais. Doesn't folklore or legend detract from the reality?

A: I think it is for the reader to judge. He/she is the critic. It is not for me to say.

Q: But you do have this interest in folklore?

A: Yes, folklore is a part of life. It is only in industrial societies that this part of life has little function. I come from a society where, when people disappear, it is believed that they will come back, after they have spent some time under the water with the water people. I cannot see anything contradictory or puzzling there. In *A Man Come Home*, by the way, I didn't say that Bird was connected with 'fairmaids'. That was his explanation.

I see that as something very enriching. But I refuse to judge my own books. I will not defend them either. I will defend what I have said in polemical writing, not fiction.

Q: Surely this is playing with words. As a creative writer, whether you do it consciously of sub-consciously, there must be a selective process impelling you to express your thoughts in one way rather than another?

A: The process is one thing; the work is another. Fiction can only be judged through an emotional reaction to it. Take someone like Dostoevsky: he detested Jews, and shared in the general Russian hatred of them. That's something to be deplored. If I were asked to write a critique of Dostoevsky's work, I would deplore the fact that he hated Jews. I would also say that he is the greatest European novelist, in my opinion. Look at the contributions made to criticism in Europe since the sixteenth century. Sigmund Freud has made contributions; there has also been socialist realism, Marxism and so on. Look what Freud says about why Hamlet didn't want to kill his uncle. I don't believe that at all. But some of the psychological criticism Freud makes is illuminating. You can see that criticism changes or develops. But the basic way of judging art never does, because there is only one way to judge art – through one's emotional reaction. A critical faculty may be employed in creating a work of art, but you have to arrive at the right blend for it to be justifiably regarded as a work of art.

Q: Of course, you have written many such works. You have been praised among other things, for the fact that your language expresses character exactly. Those of us who know the West Indies are able to recognize familiar landscapes, speech patterns, psychological postures, and social situations in your books. I wonder if there is a source of philosophical influence for these aspects of your work. Mittelholzer, for example, had strong views about politics, psychology, philosophy, religion, sex, and other matters which derived from his reading and early domestic influence. Do you see yourself as continuing in Mittelholzer's tradition? What is your relationship to Mittelholzer?

A: None. Whatever relationship there is stems from the fact that we have the same roots. I first read a book of Mittelholzer's only about four years ago. For that matter, I have never read a book of Naipaul's either. I am doing my best to get hold of Mittelholzer's *The Life and Death of Sylvia*.[17]

Q: Your Genetha is similar to Mittelholzer's Sylvia.

A: I once went into a bookshop and took up a book of Naipaul's. I looked at the first few lines, which read 'I have a Portuguese aunt, and Indian aunt, a Negro aunt', or something like that. When I came home I had to take out the same sentence, practically word for word, from the book I was writing at the time.

Q: So it was a conscious decision not to read Naipaul or Mittelholzer?

A: No. I am not a reader. The first time I did any reading apart from school tests, was shortly before I left Guyana, when Martin Carter[18] and I became interested in Marxism and got hold of a book called *A Treasury of Russian Literature*. What it had to do with Marxism I don't know, but it had some beautiful things, including three short stories by Tolstoy. I was also impressed by selections from Dostoevsky. So when I came to write I knew very little about literature. After I published my first book, I was so thrilled by the experience of publication that I decided to read, and I read Dostoevsky in particular – *The Brothers Karamazov* and *Crime and Punishment*. The important thing was that I was writing about a very small environment in the Caribbean. I wanted to read Caribbean literature, but I thought – and the experience I had with the Naipaul sentence confirmed this – Trinidad had an Indian population and a black population; I was writing about the same environment; I didn't want to be influenced in any way. It was a part of the whole experience of not being a reader. To this day I am not a reader.

Q: But you read French authors for your degree.

A: Yes, I have a comprehensive view of French literature which doesn't seem to have any great influence on me.

Q: I would, with respect, wish to question that. What about the realism of Balzac, or the psychology of Stendhal?[19]

A: Everything I read must have contributed, I suppose; this is true. But there are certain very primitive things in the organization of my work. Look at the trilogy. If I had to rewrite it, the structure would be better, I think. Look at *A Man Come Home* – it has a chaotic structure. Yet I've read French novelists whose structure was equally bad, and the French produced some of the best-shaped novels. So there may have been some influence from the French. But in considering influences, I immediately think of a man who wrote for *The Daily Argosy*[20] in Guyana. His pen-name was Uncle Stapie, and he wrote comic pieces. He would say, for instance, 'I am not talking about a gentleman who lives in a house in Charlotte Street', or 'I am not saying it is between Regent Street and Church Street.' I was very young, but I found those pieces very amusing and imitated them in school. I also think of the local barber shop, where I heard many stories and anecdotes. I do not think that the novel is a suitable art form for Guyana. The novel emerged in Europe in the seventeenth century and belongs to a commercial society. I may be wrong, but I feel that drama and the short story are more suitable for us. So the very fact that I am writing in a highly sophisticated form must mean that I got something from the books I had read in my studies. I remember something called *The Roman de Renart*[21] which was an excellent contribution to trickster literature. I was very impressed by it. I suppose when I disclaimed literary influences, I meant that I was not influenced by books that I read of my own accord, but rather for my studies.

Q: Doris Lessing[22] has said that the great nineteenth-century Russian novels reminded her of the African societies she was writing about in her early books.

A: That is absolutely true. When I read a description by Dostoevsky of what we would call a rum shop, it could be in Georgetown, Guyana. In one page Dostoevsky would evoke St Petersburg in such a powerful manner that you feel you are there. Lessing is right about Russian writers generally. Take Leskov's *Lady Macbeth of the Mtensk District*[23] I wish a Guyanese had written that. I am not saying it is Guyanese literature; but it is the Guyanese experience – the old man married to a young woman, the young woman having a lover, the grotesque side of the cat that looks like a person. Another thing is that Guyanese who write tend to be sophisticated, and that often leaves gaps in the experiences that they report. You must go to the countryside where people put aromatic vinegar over the door to keep 'Ol Higue'[24] away. That is everyday life in Guyana. Writers from Georgetown don't know that.

Q: Is Guyanese urban experience therefore less authentic?

A: No, it is authentic because it is the urban experience. But it leaves out a large area of Guyanese life. It is in the urban parts of a country that the distinctive culture dies. The countryside is the guardian of culture. You only have to look at pictures of cities all over the world and see how similar they are.

Q: What has nineteenth-century Russia got in common with third-world societies in Africa and the Caribbean? Is it mainly the feudalistic mores of hierarchy and colonialism?

A: It is not simply hierarchy. The experience is connived at by everybody in Guyana, including servants who come to visit you and go through the back door.

Q: We agree about our Caribbean background of repression, force, cunning, and an environment that has evolved out of slavery, indenture, and a whole legacy of colonial fragmentation. Which literary form do you think is best able to capture and reproduce this experience? You mention drama as your preferred form and you mention the suitability of the short story. You also regard the structure of *A Man Come Home* as chaotic. If I may say so, I find much of your fiction not chaotic, but loosely structured – open-ended. Lamming acknowledges the influence of an oral tradition in his own work. His great novel *In the Castle of My Skin*[25] is very loose-jointed in structure.

A: I am going to read *In the Castle of My Skin* – I have only recently retired, and I have the time. Not only that, but now that I have a large body of fiction behind me, I can afford to say that I am not going to be influenced by what I read. Before there was a danger of being swamped.

Q: But what about the form and the shortness of the form? The oral

tradition consists of folk tales, sententious sayings, stories, anecdotes, remarks and comments, all incorporated in a rather loose, episodic form.
You've already mentioned the Uncle Stapie pieces in *The Daily Argosy*, and
the barber-shop stories and anecdotes. Did you pick up any material like
that when you were a boy in Guyana?

A: I went to work in Pouderoyen[26] first, in the countryside, over the
Demerara river from Georgetown, and I worked there for two very productive years – in the sense of what it taught me. I came into contact with the
Indian community and the Crosby courts[27] where I probably got most of my
material about Indian life. The courts were conducted by Mr Umar to whom
I dedicated one of my books (*The Shadow Bride*). There was comedy and
tragedy. There were people whose dowry hadn't been paid, and others who
came to complain that someone's goat had butted down their fence.

Q: Lamming writes almost entirely of Afro-Caribbean experience, which
is his own, and Naipaul of Indo-Caribbean subjects. By and large this
pattern holds true for most West Indian novelists. Mittelholzer, who comes
from your own background which is coloured, urban and middle-class,
deals mainly with people from that group except in *Corentyne Thunder*[28]
which deals with Indian peasants on a sugar plantation. I was amazed in *The
Shadow Bride*, by the genuine, insider's knowledge of ordinary details of
Indian life in Guyana. I come from that life and can vouch for the accuracy
of those details.

A: That thrills me. That is not cerebral. That can only come from someone
who has this experience from the inside first. My best friend was an East
Indian, George Narayan, whose mother had a 'cook shop'[29] in Lombard
Street, in Georgetown. To get into it you had to go through a long corridor.
Nobody knew the cook shop existed except the beggars who ate there. The
food was dirt-cheap. George's great-grandfather was always there, like a
fixture, or pillar in the middle of the cook shop where the beggars had their
benches. He sat there with his hookah and Sanskrit texts.[30] That was all that
man ever did. So I saw three generations of George's family, as I grew up
with him, and this was another powerful experience of the Indian community. Perhaps it was enough to write six novels. But I never embark on
a project until I am fairly well prepared.

Q: There is much detailed description or commentary in *The Shadow
Bride* of Indian philosophy, theology, music, food, clothes, and everything
else. Such detail can only come from preparation. It is the result of study,
reflection and assimilation over a period of time.

A: But if you study and reflect on what you do not have, it will not work.
You must have that nucleus of real, lived experience, and it must have
occurred at a vital time in your life. This is true for me at least. When people
talk of my authenticity, it is largely because I refuse to do something on
material with which I am not thoroughly familiar. I don't mean familiar in

just knowing about it. I mean familiar in another way. For instance, I am thoroughly familiar with English society in one way, but I am not thoroughly familiar in another way. That is why I won't write fiction about it.

Q: Again, the contrast is between a cerebral approach, and one that incorporates both cerebral and emotional elements. Taking into account our history of fragmentation and separation, of white slave-masters and black slaves, of racial persecution, oppression, resistance and all that, how were you able to reach a broad Guyanese point of view by embracing aspects of social experience generally regarded as alien or hostile to your own?

A: I think it comes largely from my friendship with George Narayan. Although I shouldn't say so, I despise Creole middle-class experience, which is so negative that it is almost unbelievable. I have a feeling that there was a reaction in the sense that I could welcome the experience with George more readily. This is also related to the fact that my father was dead. If my father had been alive, coming from the section of Guyanese society that I did, I might not have been as free to move about. Certainly, I would not have been able to go home to our servants. I would have been taught more easily a class prejudice which would have thwarted what you might call a natural desire to mix. My mother really could not control it. The remarks she made were typical of people from her group. But she loved George; he had the run of our house.

Q: In the 1950s Lamming, Naipaul, Mittelholzer, and Selvon[31] wrote for a foreign audience, and had either to explain local West Indian terms or anglicize them. There was a perceptible gap between their subject and their audience. But you use terms like 'cocobeh', 'jamoon', 'senseh' fowl and 'camoodie'[32] etc., naturally. There is not the same gap between the experience you are relating and the audience you are relating it to. You do not have to translate.

A: I am not writing for an English audience. That is why I find it so simple to do. My bread comes from the English audience, but I am not writing for them. I am writing for a Guyanese or Caribbean audience.

Q: I sense a contradiction there. Let us get at it through your publishing history. Could you tell me the sequence of events after Longman published your first novel, *A Man Come Home* in 1974? What exactly happened when the Armstrong trilogy was not accepted as one book?

A: A review came out in *The Times* calling *A Man Come Home* a masterpiece. At the same time Longmans, to whom I had submitted the manuscript of *The Murderer*, sent me a telegram saying: 'Wonderful review. We will publish *The Murderer*.' It was a bad period in publishing, however: Penguin was sacking people, and Longmans then withdrew *The Murderer*, offering me compensation. Following that, I hawked *The Murderer* around for over two years. The man at Heinemann had wanted to publish, and to strengthen his case, had sent the manuscript to outside readers who wrote extraordinary things about the book. Armed with those two readers' reports I went to Allison and Busby who published the novel. And when *The Murderer* won the Guardian fiction prize I became a publishable novelist, because publishers knew they could sell my work.

Q: But you were still not accepted by a mainstream British publisher.

A: That's right. The Longman book was a one-off thing.

Q: You had to rely on a radical publisher connected with feminist or black resistance and the political left.

A: Yes. I didn't want to leave Allison and Busby. I saw myself probably falling into a situation like T. S. Eliot who made Faber.[33] Allison and Busby valued my work, and since they were a small publishing house, I got to know them well. But by then Collins had been publishing my books in paperback under their imprint Flamingo, which was described as their flagship imprint. So when I submitted new work they were willing to publish it in hardback.

Q: I believe that Selvon and Mittelholzer and the earlier writers wanted very much to write the kind of books you are writing, mentioning 'camoodie' and 'cocobeh' naturally, without explanation, but history was against them. The time was not ripe for that type of writing. At the same time, perhaps you could not write as you are doing now, if they had not written as they did before you.

A: You are quite right. In fact, isn't that why Naipaul said that he began to write about his experiences in England?

Q: Naipaul is a special case. He seems embittered by his Caribbean experience; but, as you hinted earlier, he is an unmistakable product of it. However, I think you described *A Man Come Home* as an 'anthem for the living and the dead'. Why an anthem? Who are the 'living and the dead'?

A: I never explain my fiction. You must forgive me. If you were asking me about my lectures or essays, I would discuss them, but when it comes to explaining my fiction, it must either stand or fall. You may criticize it as much as you like, but don't ask me to say anything about it.

Q: You evidently like the word 'Guyana', and although you try to link it with the larger Caribbean, it seems that you are solidly Guyanese.

A: I am intensely Guyanese. But we belong both to a local and a wider culture. An Englishman comes from England and a wider European culture. A Frenchman is first French, but also European. I am Guyanese and I write for Guyanese. But if anyone suggests that I am writing for them, I don't mind. If I look at a photograph of somewhere in St Kitts, it does something for me. If I look at a place in Central America or Brazil, it also does something for me. In the United States of America it does not. There is a continental connection between the Caribbean and Latin America.

Q: Is the connection wholly geographical, or partly cultural and historical?

A: There is a mysterious connection with geography, and part of it is also psychological.[34]

Q: You mentioned a Marxist interest earlier. A lot of people, especially artists from the third world – former colonies – have strong political convictions which are expressed in their writings. I mentioned Mais, but there are other West Indians who write with a political motive, about the poor living conditions of our people, that is to say, to show the wicked effects of oppression with a view to remedying them. Marxism was felt to be a great antidote to problems during the anti-colonial struggle in the middle decades of this century. What happened to the Marxist interest that you and Martin Carter had?

A: You see it in *The Shadow Bride*. One of the main points about the book is that however much he tried, or however big the hospital he set up from his own funds, Dr Singh[35] would have done very little because the problem is a political one.

Q: In that case, what do you think about the recent history of events in Guyana with the effective emasculation, for over twenty-five years, of Cheddi Jagan,[36] our most widely-known Marxist politician? How did the present situation of chaos, hardship and impoverishment come about in Guyana?

A: There are two things to be said. One is that it is part of the whole third-world experience. Then it is a question of borrowing a lot of money when it was cheap. You can't pay it back because you either did not have the expertise to run the undertaking for which it was borrowed, or you were riddled with corruption. The money was frittered away, and there is not much to show for it. Actually there is a great deal to show in Guyana in some ways: roads and a bridge across the Demerara which we had been trying to build for donkey's years. There are nurseries, at least in Georgetown, which are far more impressive than nurseries here. Women, if you notice, were the last people to abandon Burnham[37] because, in many ways, there were things done for them. Having said that, we suffer from the third-world sickness of imperial domination. You cannot have a one-party system without massive corruption, because party members have special privileges. The one-party system leads not only to corruption, but to inefficiency.[38] In the short term, the one-party system may be capable of doing things that others cannot do, but as a permanent arrangement over about ten years or more it is disastrous.

Q: What do you see in the future for Guyana?

A: There is a great danger that a number of the so-called third-world countries – I don't like that term – will become colonies again. Some of them are already becoming or asking to become colonies.

Q: Who will be the new imperial masters?

A: The people with the money. Europe and the US have the money. The irony will be that Europe and America will actually be called in to solve the problems in these countries when the problems have arisen, in the first place, because of the actions of Europe and America.

Q: What implications will this have for race relations in the world? In the old nineteenth-century world of empires, whites governed blacks. The blacks rejected racial discrimination and colonial oppression and overthrew white rule. Are blacks really likely to ask to be ruled again by the whites?

A: That is the double irony of the situation. Having left us with an administration that was geared to their own imperial interests, and having left us without substantial industries, Europe and America then lent us money so that we now find ourselves permanently in debt to them. The only way out of it is for us all to get together *en masse* and refuse to play ball.

Q: You have the example of China which has carried on independently of the great imperial powers.

A: China is different. It has more than one billion people. China cannot be beaten in war because of the logistics of attacking her. The countries that have successfully become Communist have had large populations and all the resources. The other countries which became Communist were protected by these countries. In other words, if you don't have massive resources, the imperial powers are going to throttle you. They attacked Russia physically and tried to strangle it economically, but Russia had all the possible resources and a very big population.

Q: For all that, there are some good signs in the world today, signs of change in South Africa, for instance.

A: That is the tail-end of colonial domination. It is a good sign in a way. In any case, one should not be too sanguine about South Africa. Look at Mandela[39] who has just been let out of prison. He is being praised to the skies by everybody as the great saviour of South Africa. No wonder today he will breathe fire, tomorrow he might speak moderately, and the next day he will breathe fire again. If you take into account what he said before he went into prison you will see clearly that he is a moderate. Can a moderate get that country out of the mess it is in and get the blacks liberated? Perhaps pressure from below will oblige him to continue breathing fire.

Q: Your view of the world is a bleak one: that the old imperialistic structure of colonial domination still persists, nowadays, in the form of multinational corporations rather than imperial governments. In other words, the basic structure of oppression remains the same.

A: It is not bleak: it is a realistic view. You must always have hope because it is essential to keep you afloat; but you have to be realistic. If you are either optimistic or pessimistic you are going to make mistakes. You want a cool head to be able to stand back and see what is going on. The only advantage the optimist has is that he is likely to live longer.

Q: Are you realistic in your writing?

A: It is realism in a different sense. In fiction you are not solving problems: you are giving a view of the world as people see it. In other words, you act as a mediator, by saying this is the world in which we live. As a polemicist I can suggest solutions to actual problems. I love that. I think some of my best writing has been in work of that kind, for example, the Mittelholzer lectures that I gave in Guyana.

Q: In art, however, you are rendering experience as objectively as you can.

A: If a dictator brings tragedy and starvation to his people, and a democracy does exactly the same, the experience is the same for the people who suffer. Politics is a part of human experience. A fiction writer should bring in everything. In *The Shadow Bride* I made it perfectly plain that one might admire Dr Singh; but there is another statement about him being admired because he does nothing: he changes nothing. Mother Teresa[40] got a Nobel prize for doing great work among poor people in India. There is a lady called Sister Michelle, a Philippino, who does exactly that and more. She believes so much in the eradication of poverty, that she gave her enormous estate to the poor and helped them to run it. Yet we don't hear about her. We hear about Mother Teresa who is obviously a very fine person; but her action changes absolutely nothing. The only way we can change things is by political action. Sister Michelle gave her property to the poor and tried to impart the education and expertise to enable them to run the estate. Her example is dangerous!

Q: But isn't Sister Michelle's action just as pointless in as much as it will bring satisfaction to only a few people? Mother Teresa also brought satisfaction to some poor people in the streets of Calcutta.

A: The difference between Mother Teresa and Sister Michelle is that Sister Michelle created an economic organization, admittedly on a scale that only an individual can achieve. People like Mother Teresa and Dr Singh may have brought limited happiness to a few people. The thing is for the children of these people and their children's children to continue to benefit. In other words, you need a model for everybody to see. This is, qualitatively, a different achievement from Mother Teresa's or Dr Singh's. Mother Teresa is being kind; but she doesn't change the situation. What Sister Michelle has done is to offer a model for changing the situation.

Q: What we need is a lot of Sister Michelles in the world today.

A: Of course, that is not possible.

Notes

1 E. R. Brathwaite, *To Sir With Love* (The Bodley Head, London, 1959). For biographical details, see Chapter 5, note 12.

2 Of Heath's novels, *A Man Come Home* was published, in London, by Longman Caribbean, in 1974, while the others were also published in London by Allison and Busby as follows: *The Murderer* (1978); *From the Heat of the Day* (1979); *Genetha* (1981); *One Generation* (1981); and *Kwaku* (1981). The action of the trilogy is set in Georgetown, Guyana and concerns members of one family – the Armstrongs. Heath's novels study the inner lives of urban, middle-class, usually Creole Guyanese, and concentrate, with equal ease, on men as well as women, and on abnormal as well as normal states of mind.

3 Jean Piaget (1896–1980) is famous for his investigation into the thought processes of children, while Carl Gustav Jung (1875–1961) is more famous as the founder of analytic psychology.

4 The Dutch, as the first colonial power in Guyana, introduced West African slaves into the territory in the early seventeenth century. The high mortality rate in the sugar plantations, where the slaves worked, was due both to the brutality of slavery and to malaria. Malaria was an even greater scourge after 1838 when Indians replaced African slaves as workers on the sugar plantations. Between 1937 and 1946 the population on the sugar plantations increased at the rate of 414 per year. After the eradication of malaria, this increase became 1960 per year. Malaria was a great scourge because of the low-lying coastal swamplands which provided a breeding-ground for the mosquitoes that carried the disease. The eradication of malaria is attributed to a programme of spraying the swamplands with DDT initiated by Dr Giglioli, who was employed by the Sugar Producers Association, the governing body for the sugar plantations.

5 See Index for Harris and Mittelholzer. Harris's first novel, *Palace of the Peacock* (Faber, London, 1960), explores psychological, philosophical and mythical subjects within a Guyanese setting. Several of Harris's later novels continue this exploration. Mittelholzer's novels also combine psychological studies with evocations of Guyanese history and myth. His description of mental and psychological deviation in *The Life and Death of Sylvia* (Secker and Warburg, London, 1953), for instance, has parallels with Heath's study of Galton Flood's fantasies and dreams in *The Murderer*, and with Genetha's self-destructive outlook in *Genetha*. Cf. Chapter 4, notes 1 and 3, and Introduction, note 7.

6 Joseph Conrad (1857–1924) was born in Poland. Although Conrad is regarded as a classic English writer, his first novel, *Almayer's Folly*, was not published until 1895 when he was 39 years old.

7 As early as 1640, John Milton (1608–74) had conceived the idea of his great epic poem, *Paradise Lost*, the first draft of which was not completed until 1665.

8 Roy A. K. Heath, *The Shadow Bride* (Flamingo, London, 1988).

9 Peepal Tree Press, located in Leeds, England, was initiated and is still managed by Jeremy Poynting. Although it began publishing mainly Indo-Caribbean texts, it has now branched out into other areas of literature.

10 The first Guyana Prize for Literature was awarded in 1987, when the prize for fiction was won by Wilson Harris for his novel *Carnival*.

In *The Shadow Bride* Heath leaves his familiar urban, Creole or Afro-Guyanese territory to enter Indo-Guyanese life and customs, which he renders with equal authority and conviction.

11 See Index under V. S. Naipaul.

12 See Index under Derek Walcott.

13 See Index for Caryl Phillips.

14 For Roger Mais, see Chapter 4, note 19.

15 For Norman Manley and the People's National Party, see Chapter 4, notes 20 and 21.
16 'Fairmaid' is a female figure in Guyanese folklore. She has similar characteristics to a mermaid.
17 See note 5 above. Heath's *Genetha* provides an even closer parallel to Mittelholzer's heroine Sylvia, who is plagued by mysterious, sadistic and masochistic instincts and dies tragically, just as Genetha is driven into prostitution by forces she does not understand.
18 For Martin Carter, see Chapter 5, note 12.
19 See, for example, the first one-third of Balzac's *Human Comedy*, and Stendhal's *The Red and the Black*.
20 *The Daily Argosy*, now defunct, was one of three daily newspapers in Guyana in the 1940s and 1950s. 'Uncle Stapie Pun de People' was a weekly column written by the editor, L. Evelyn Moe: it offered social commentary, analysis and criticism.
21 *Le Roman de Renart* (History of Reynard the Fox) is a poetic form related to the French *fabliau*, which flourished in northern France between the twelfth and fourteenth centuries. The poems satirized prevailing events or institutions and exposed human weaknesses. Cf. Caryl Phillips's comments on his reaction to Shakespeare's *Othello* in Chapter 14.
22 Doris Lessing, *Going Home* (Panther Books, London, 1968), p. 19.
23 Nicholai Semenovich Leskov (1831–1895) was a Russian novelist and short story-writer. *Lady Macbeth of the Mtensk District*, his best-known story, was first published in 1865.
24 'Ol' Higue' is a legend of African origin, about an old woman who is reputed to suck blood, especially from young children. There are several variations on her method: she is supposed to shed her skin as a disguise and then reclaim it after hiding it away. She is also capable of changing into a ball of fire, and of becoming a speck of light that can enter a key hole. Although 'Ol' Higue' is most often an old woman, this Guyanese form of vampire may nowadays take the form of beautiful women of any age.
25 See Index for Lamming and *In the Castle of My Skin*.
26 Pouderoyen is the Dutch name of a village on the West bank of the Demerara River in Guyana. Place-names in Guyana are mainly Amerindian, Dutch, French and English, illustrating the mixed colonial history of the country. In fact, the District Commissioner's Office where Heath worked may more accurately be described as being in Plantain Walk, within the Vreden-Hoop, West Demerara local authority.
27 James Crosby was a Cambridge-educated English barrister who was appointed Immigration Agent-General to Guyana in 1858. His generous commitment to the welfare of indentured Indian immigrants won their undying faith and admiration, and long after his death, because of the immigrants' faith in him, they continued to refer to the Immigration Agent-General's office was called simply as 'Crosby'. The name 'Crosby court' is loosely applied to the quasi-legal service provided by the District Commissioner's office to Indians who brought their quarrels and disputes to be settled there. In the period that Heath worked in Vreden-Hoop, the 'Crosby Court' was supervised by Mohamed Umar who was an interpreter in the District Commissioner's Office in Vreden-Hoop. As someone fluent in Hindi and Urdu, Mr Umar could understand and adjudicate the disputes brought to him by Indians who spoke these languages.
28 See Chapter 4, note 1.
29 A 'cook shop' in Guyanese parlance was an inexpensive restaurant. Cook shops were usually run by Chinese.
30 The hookah is an Indian pipe in which the smoke is drawn through water. Hookahs would have been smoked only by older Indians in Guyana, and have virtually died out with their generation.
    The Sanskrit texts being read were probably sacred Hindu texts, for example, the *Ramayana* and the *Bhagavad Gita*.
31 See Index for Lamming, Naipaul, Mittelholzer and Selvon.

32   'Cocobeh' is the Creole name for leprosy; 'jamoon' is a local grape-like fruit; 'senseh' fowl is a type of chicken with short feathers of mixed colour; 'camoodie' is the Creole name for a boa-constrictor.

33   T. S. Eliot worked for Faber and Faber, and published with the firm. In Heath's opinion, Eliot's international reputation as a writer was crucial to the success of the firm.

34   See Index for 'magical realism'. Cf. Chapter 4, notes 16 and 17.

35   Dr Singh is a medical doctor and major male protagonist in *The Shadow Bride*. Dr Singh shows great compassion and personal sympathy for the sick and poor among whom he works.

36   See Index for Dr Cheddi Jagan, leader of the People's Progressive Party.

37   See Chapter 1, note 13.

38   The People's National Congress (PNC) has formed the government of Guyana from 1964 to 1992. This not because the PNC officially advocates one-party rule. The PNC has 'won' several elections despite widespread allegations of fraud and vote-rigging.

39   Nelson Mandela is the leader of the African National Congress, the multi-racial political movement that has consistently opposed the racist policies of apartheid in South Africa. Mandela was born in 1918 and joined the ANC in 1944. He was imprisoned for his anti-apartheid activities from 1963 to 1990. After he was freed, Mandela held negotiations with the white South African government, leading to national elections that were won by the ANC. Mandela is currently President of South Africa. The interview was conducted while negotiations were going on.

40   Mother Teresa is a Yugoslav nun who has dedicated her life to working with the poor in Calcutta. Her extraordinary dedication won her acclaim in the West and the Nobel Prize for Peace.

CHAPTER 8 | Austin Clarke: Caribbean-Canadians

Austin Clarke was born in Barbados in 1934. After elementary and secondary education on the island, he left in 1955 for studies at the University of Toronto, in Canada. Clarke has remained in Canada except for brief visits abroad, and a year-long stay in Barbados during 1975. In the 1960s when he began to produce works of fiction, the West Indian immigrant population in Canada was relatively small, compared to the same population in Britain and the US at that time. But Clarke took these immigrants, living mainly in Toronto, as the chief subject of his fiction, and his novels and stories about them have earned him a reputation as the major black or West Indian writer in Canada. So far, Clarke's best work consists of his trilogy of novels: The Meeting Point *(1967);* Storm of Fortune *(1972); and* The Bigger Light *(1975). He has also written reviews and essays, and an autobiographical memoir* Growing up Stupid under the Union Jack *(1975). Clarke has worked from time to time as a lecturer and broadcaster, and served as writer-in-residence at several universities. (This interview was recorded in Toronto on 22 March 1991).*

Q: Can you identify anyone or anything that sparked your writing?

A: Frank Collymore[1] was instrumental in giving a start to many of us, including Derek Walcott, Edward Brathwaite, John Hearne, Edgar Mittelholzer and of course George Lamming.[2] Frank Collymore was my English and French teacher at Combermere School. Later, after I left school and started to write, he taught me a few tricks of the trade, primarily about using the Barbadian language. I used to concentrate on spelling words the way they sound, with lots of apostrophes. He told me that I should use formal English so far as the appearance of words is concerned, but also inject into that formal construction the nuance and rhythm of Barbadian speech. In Canada, after university, I worked as a reporter in northern Ontario, in Timmins and Kirkland Lake, fitting in a number of pages every day. I then worked as a reporter for *The Globe and Mail*,[3] and two weeks before my probation was terminated, I wrote six short stories. They were written in the Barbadian language and I thought they were extremely original, until I was exposed to Sam Selvon. Then I realized they were copies of his style. In 1963, I wrote *The Survivors of the Crossing* and *Amongst Thistles and Thorns*.[4]

Q: You said you wrote those stories, then you found Sam Selvon. *A Brighter Sun* came out in 1952, and Lamming's *In the Castle of My Skin* in 1953.[5] Did you read either of those works before you wrote your stories?

A: I had not read *A Brighter Sun*, but I had read Lamming's book in the sense that I opened the book before I left Barbados. It was too disturbing for me to finish; but I did read it in about 1960 from cover to cover. It was disturbing in the sense that, at that time, I wanted to be a writer; but having read the book, I felt I could never measure up to the power, and the aspect of episodes that he had written about, because there was nothing left for me to write about. It was a very frightening experience. The Selvon book that I'm thinking about is *The Lonely Londoners* (1956).[6] But, I would have heard trickles of works of Selvon, Lamming, John Hearne and especially Walcott[7] on the BBC programme *Caribbean Voices*.[8]

Q: The title of your first novel seems to indicate a place where many Caribbean writers feel they must begin, that is, with the story of survivors of the crossing – the middle passage. Am I right in thinking that your first novel is a way of paying homage to Africans or their descendants who survived the middle passage? Does it identify their strategies of survival?

A: Yes, it is paying homage to a set or group of people in Barbados. It seemed to me that what was important in the society in which I lived, was the hard labour, living for the harvest, the association of the actual harvest with the celebration of harvest in the church. Since I had a pretty solid grounding in English literature, I attempted to relate that – not that I achieved it – to the best in Milton, Shakespeare and some of those English poets who talked about labour and the Biblical 'sweat of thy brow'. The aspect of revolution in the book comes from my association with politics at the trade-union level, my reading of C. L. R. James's excellent *Black Jacobins*,[9] and some of the political independence struggles in Africa and the Caribbean.

Q: The aspect of revolution in the novel comes through episodes dealing with socialism and the trade-union movement. But your 'revolutionaries' are poor, uneducated cane-cutters. Their consciousness seems exceptionally educated. Is there not a disparity between their consciousness and their real circumstances?

A: Yes, because the circumstances were real and more powerful than the apprehension of the persons in the 'movement'. This is something that I was not aware of at the time of growing up. But I remember wondering why certain people in our neighbourhood succeeded and others did not. I remember walking across this beautiful, long road covered in marl and edged by casuarina trees, if not by canes, to this magnificent yard of the plantation, and buying tomatoes and other vegetables cheap. It occurred to me that greater importance was not attached to the people who owned the plantation than to the people who worked in the fields and I wondered what would happen, since we had the power of numbers, if we decided not to work or if we decided to take over the plantation. What makes such actions fail, I think, is the lack of a strategy. They thought that the enthusiasm of the cause did not need a strategy, and this is something that one can apply to the black movement in America, certainly to the Black Panther movement, and to other so-called black uprisings. I am sure it applies to the situation in Trinidad in 1990.[10]

Q: Their 'movement' was instinctive, without a proper intellectual or overall strategy?

A: I think that political scientists and historians, including literary historians, will tell you that even though a socialist revolution is started by parties of the working or lower classes, it soon changes and becomes an intentioned organization by the middle class. The middle class always brings its knowledge of things to give order to the system.

Q: In *Amongst Thistles and Thorns*, you mention the thistles and thorns of 'men', of 'grief', and of 'poverty'. Are these particular aspects of the working class that illustrate the colonial condition in Barbados?

A: What I like most about *Amongst Thistles and Thorns* is its dreamlike quality. Around the time I was thinking of this novel, I was very impressed by two books – Joyce's *Portrait of the Artist as a Young Man*, and Dylan Thomas's *A Child's Christmas in Wales*.[11] The religious undertone in the boy came from my looking at myself and how I was formed up to that time (about 1964 or 1965) as a result of my exposure to religion in Barbados. I don't mean just going to church. I mean religion in the sense of how Africans and Muslims use the term: a 24-hour thing which encompasses your whole life. The boy's religion shows how it is able to chisel you into some kind of formation that makes you more or less consistent with your environment.

Q: May I ask in which particular sect or denomination of the Christian church you were brought up?

A: If I were filling out an application for a job I would put down Church of England. If I was filling out an application of honesty, I would have to say Christian Mission, Church of God, and the church of the Nazarene.[12] Those were the denominations that touched me. My mother would religiously send me to sing in the Anglican cathedral choir; but in the evening, she would insist that I went to the Church of the Nazarene to save my soul.

Q: I expect that the Anglican Church was more staid and proper, and that if you remained in it, you would have missed out on the more emotional and flamboyant aspects of religious worship as practised in the pentecostal/

evangelical sects. I wonder if these more emotional or flamboyant aspects of religious worship strike a specially sympathetic chord in the West Indies. Your insight into West Indian character is unerring, absolutely sure; emotionalism, flamboyance, and a penchant for self-dramatization are cardinal features of it that you highlight in your fiction. A poignant as well as hilarious example of this appears in *Amongst Thistles and Thorns* where ordinary West Indians argue about who is greater – Churchill or Hitler. Since these West Indians are colonial victims of both Churchill and Hitler, is it not perverse for them to debate, with enthusiasm and delight, the relative merits of their victimizers?

A: It is an ironic aspect of our character that we have not been able to accept our colonized state of insufficiency or meaninglessness. It is obviously absurd for a young Barbadian boy to say who is the greatest – Hitler or Churchill. In the West Indies we have, I think, this artistic quality that we are able to rise up out of our skins. As Lamming would say, we could break down the walls of the castles of our skins, and view the world wholesomely. I don't know whether it is just words. We are brought up in a culture of words; for example, the radio and 'old-talk' around the standpipe, and under the street-light at night.[13] People talk and talk; all around you, you heard talk. I remember going around the Bath Corner,[14] standing at the window of this church with my friends, and we would debate who is the greatest preacher in the village. Our means of determining preaching greatness probably had nothing at all to do with content or doctrine: it had to do with the way the world affected us, and how long the preacher would talk.

Q: When I look at your whole work I genuflect to the three Toronto novels which, in my opinion, represent the best rendition of this city in fiction. This is an enormous achievement for someone who is an immigrant. Do you think the quality of this achievement has been recognized by Canadians?

A: No, it has not been recognized. In 1977 I was seeking the Progressive Conservative[15] nomination for the provincial riding of Oakwood, here in Toronto. I did not win the nomination because there were certain dirty tricks played. What came out of the venom of these dirty tricks was that I was not a proper candidate because I was anti-Semitic. I was told this, because I had a Jewish man seducing a West Indian woman in my novel *The Meeting Point*.[16] *The Meeting Point* was written soon after Pierre Berton, [17] who was then a feature-writer on the *Toronto Star*, began writing articles about discrimination. There was a time, mentioned in his articles, when Jewish people could not rent summer cottages. I think there were still some lingering signs around Toronto: 'No Jews, Niggers, and Dogs'. It was first brought home to us who lived in Toronto that there were quotas on the number of Jewish people who could be dentists, etc. This was around 1955 and 1956. I was actively involved in civil rights. I remember reading Baldwin's novel *Another Country*, LeRoi Jones's play *Dutchman and the Slave*, and the writing of people like Ed Bullins.[18] I remember listening to the speeches of Malcolm X, and I said to myself how unfortunate I was in Toronto that I did not have so obvious a cause to write about. Certainly I couldn't write about a physical lynching. I could write about lynching in a metaphorical sense. So I had to write about the exploitation of West Indian immigrants in Toronto. But I don't consider *The Meeting Point* to be of the genre of *Another Country* or *Dutchman and the Slave*. I consider the book to be a love story, and I was very interested to find out afterwards that the aboriginal word for Toronto is 'meeting place'. What I was trying to do in that book is show what happens when people with different points of view meet and have to live together: they could commit murder and rape, or they could accommodate to each other, and I thought that, to some extent, in the book they were forced to accommodate.

Q: In *The Meeting Point* there is a scene in which, during sexual intercourse with his white female partner, the black West Indian male protagonist regards his thrusting into her as a way of redressing the wrongs of colonialism. Does that particular scene not carry a touch of sensationalism about it, or are you using it in a 'responsible' way?

A: As I said, I was reading *Another Country*, and I was active in local politics. I was a reporter for the CBC at the time, and I used to make frequent trips to Harlem and other parts of America. I was quite aware of the sadness surrounding the case of the Scottsboro boys.[19] I was aware that in certain parts of America if you looked at a white woman you could be accused of raping her. I was also reading Frantz Fanon,[20] not the books, but his articles in *Présence Africaine*. All these things were going through my mind, and I was traumatized by Richard Wright's *Native Son*.[21] I do not believe that if a black man who suffers in society is in bed with a white woman he is correcting wrongs. One reason why this cannot be the case is that the black man would then have to disregard his contribution to the act, and he would have to disregard the more negative aspects of engaging in the act for that purpose. But the scene has a better meaning. You can extract the physical aspect from the act and regard the intercourse as the metaphorical, or symbolical ability of the black man to move inside of the white power structure. But this is to stretch the point – no pun intended. By this metaphor, if the man is approaching, in the most unwelcomed way, and seeking entrance into the white power structure, I think the mere fact of his entrancing may be interpreted as correcting the wrongs of the past which is anyway impossible.

Q: It is a psychological entry into an oppressive structure?

A: I am sure that psychiatrists and psychologists are able to put the sexual act on that level. That is all it is.

Q: The writers and texts you have mentioned so far are seminal. I wonder if they had anything to do with aspects of the second book in the trilogy, *Storm of Fortune*,[22] in which you make the point about black people bringing in a warmer, sunnier attitude to this cold city of Toronto, with its rigid structures of thinking and conduct? We think of Senghor and Négritude.[23] In his poem 'New York'[24] Senghor says 'New York! I say to New York, let the black flood flow into your blood, cleaning the rust from your steel articulations, like an oil of life.' Isn't it precisely the looser, more flexible attitudes of 'black blood' that provoke discrimination in Toronto? With all the exploitation and discrimination that black people suffer in Toronto, how can you claim they have a positive influence?

A: How could I make a claim that our presence has more or less softened, if not civilized this iron-willed society? I was in the American South in 1972 and saw two white men in a telephone truck drinking beer and eating southern fried chicken which was bought and cooked by blacks. Then, at the big dance on the campus, the band was a black blues band. This is the phenomenon: how can a group which oppresses blacks participate in aspects of 'black' culture, and yet after that event, forget what pleasure or cultural enhancement they have received, and revert to their anti-black attitudes? Even if the effect is transitory, insofar as their treatment of us is concerned, the impact is there. In other words, their lives cannot be the same afterwards.

Q: In *The Bigger Light*[25] the tone is more relaxed; there is less violence; and Sam Burman is looking after the child Estelle has had by him. Can we regard the third volume of the trilogy as a more positive look at the fate of the black community in Toronto?

A: *The Bigger Light* chronologically involves, to some extent, the third generation of immigrants to whom certain lessons and aspects of wisdom must have been handed down from the first generation to the second, and now to them. They are in a better position to understand the system. Their improvisation has become more sophisticated. What improvisation does to the psyche is very devastating in the sense that it makes hollow men of us: Boysie with all his accomplishments is reacting as any ordinary immigrant, piling up trophies around him – the car, clothes, music – acquisitions which suggest success in this society. But success has a very dear price. I'm not trying to make an argument that we should remain in a primitive state. I'm not even saying that what Boysie has done is better than trying to be involved in the system in such a way that you have to be always protesting. I am saying that the longer we remain in this society, the more we ought to be able to cope with its nuances. What I find interesting about Boysie is that the dismantling of his protest was replaced by the dismantling of his manhood to some extent.

Q: The West Indian community in England was established a decade or two before our community in Toronto. In the writing of Caryl Phillips,[26] we see West Indians who have settled down and have produced children who have grown up in England. Yet Phillips's older West Indian characters are always talking about going back home. After thirty years of settlement in Britain these characters do not feel integrated. Your West Indian characters in Toronto appear to be ahead of Phillips's characters in terms of integration. If we compare your account of a wedding in Toronto with Lamming's story 'Wedding in the Spring',[27] there is a more overt political treatment in your story, that is to say, you expose police brutality in a way that expects this problem to be corrected. In Lamming's story, the attitudes and problems appear to be more deep-seated. The black sister shows warm, family solidarity in the end, to overcome divisions of race and culture between herself and the Englishwoman her brother is going to marry. But this is a personal gesture that will not affect her fellow immigrants in a general way. Perhaps because Canada is an immigrant society, it is easier for other immigrants to fit in; it is largely a matter of regulating the political process; whereas in the insular, more deeply-rooted culture of Britain, outsiders are less welcome.

A: I think you have just answered the question. Acceptance in England is impossible by anybody who is not born there into the right class. Canadian society is to a larger extent classless, with lower standards for achieving; and I think it therefore offers more hope of acceptance. As an inhabitant of Toronto, I think it offers more hope, and because of the influx of more West Indians like ourselves, it offers a greater protectiveness than English society could ever offer an immigrant. It may be true that the social life in England for an immigrant is more exciting than it is here; but nowadays in Toronto you do not have to mix with Canadians: you may find your life ordered by people who are as much strangers as you are to the society. Also, West Indians in Canada have not fallen into that syndrome so common to those of us who have gone to Britain: that we are going to the mother country, and that if we are scolded, it is a more biting and significant chastisement. In this society there is no one to scold us: we are all immigrants, and even if we are scolded, we could always go back home. It must be more difficult for a Barbadian or Guyanese living in England to go home, so far as the amount of money it needs to buy the ticket: he is more exiled in England than the West Indian in Toronto.

Q: You have used the subject of West Indians in Toronto to produce some excellent short stories. The use of the Barbados Creole combines with a sophisticated sense of form to create a strong impact. Yet you use some of these stories again as episodes in novels. What is the relationship between your short stories and novels?

A: There was a time when I realized that I wanted to be known as a writer, and I was persistently being regarded as a broadcaster and a political activist. I therefore let the activism be expressed in writing. I realized that a market for these short stories was the CBC radio programme *Anthology*. So I would be writing a novel and I would select a part and rework it as a short story, but use it in its original form in the novel. It was purely a matter of making money. I am not suggesting, of course, that there is anything wrong with that so far as the literature is concerned. This leads me to digress and mention my very good friend Andrew Salkey.[28] We have been writing to each other, on average, four letters a month since 1965. When spending a lot of time writing and not seeing quick results, I would be buoyed up considerably by Andrew, who shared my disillusionment and political anxieties as I shared his. If you read that correspondence from 1965 until a week ago, March 1991, I think you would be exposed to the development of Caribbean literature in England, the US, and Canada, in a way that you would not have known had you not read this correspondence. In addition to all the other persons that I have mentioned who influenced me, I think his is the greatest psychological influence.

Q: Did you write stories specifically for the volume *When He Was Free and Young and Used to Wear Silks*,[29] or did the idea of collecting these stories come later? What does the title mean?

A: The title came as a result of doodling one night. It was meaningless really, in the sense that I did not deliberately set out to write it. It also reflects a time of life when I was exposed to jazz. The title story is free-wheeling, like a kind of jazz improvisation; but it is serious in the sense that it deals with a very important aspect of my life, most of which was spent drinking in the Pilot Tavern which used to be at the corner of Bloor and Yonge in Toronto, when I was close to all of the up-and-coming artists – writers, actors, sculptors and painters in this city, if not this country. It revolves around a woman who had a devastating effect on me. She was the wife of a sculptor called Tom Handy.[30] It also describes the worldliness and the waywardness of us as a group, and takes into consideration some of the works that some of the painters were doing. What propelled me in that direction was the success that a short story of mine gained when it won a national competition. This was 'Four Stations in His Circle'.[31] The second collection of stories, *When Women Rule*,[32] was written when I was not particularly successful so far as the acceptance of my work was concerned. It occurred to me that from my early days in Barbados, I was surrounded by women who were perhaps more powerful and intelligent that I had been disposed to accept, and that they really controlled things; hence the title 'When Women Rule'. There is one story in that collection, 'The Discipline', that I particularly like. The idea came after a lawyer friend mentioned the tragic case of a West Indian man who had chastised his son.

When the boy went to school his teacher saw this bruise and labelled it assault. The father was confounded and bewildered when he was prosecuted. But the stories are connected by the theme that, to a varying extent, there is in the background of masculine achievement, a woman figure who pulls the strings.

Q: In 'The Discipline' the West Indian father who chastised his son is confounded by the Canadian legal system. He carries out what in his culture is considered normal parental discipline; but he has come as an immigrant to a culture that interprets his action in a completely different way, and has the power to enforce their interpretation by imprisoning him. His description of himself is moving: 'I was a dried fallen leaf that had to be raked away to keep the lawn pleasant and clean. Or a piece of banana skin kicked out of the way with a well-timed movement of the foot' (p. 143). Canadian society has no use for him; he is merely garbage.

A: That story was written around the time of Bob Marley's[33] death. I had not been exposed to Bob Marley as much as I wish I had been; so when he died I felt great sadness because I had been negligent in applauding him when he was alive. In one sitting I listened to all of his songs to recapture what I had lost. That was used in the story as a means of expressing the great loss that this man suffered: loss of the relationship of father and son, of his own freedom, of the child; the disorientation of going into this alien, cruel, lifeless (court) room where things are said about him that he cannot comprehend; and then, when it is all done, and he understands what has happened and wants to speak, his voice says it's finished. There is also this watch his lawyer is wearing around her neck, bringing in the metaphor of the grandfather clock: tick, tock, tick. In a substantial amount of my work there is always music. In *The Meeting Point* it was the Sixth Symphony of Beethoven. In *Storm of Fortune* there was another piece of Beethoven, and also quite a lot of trying to express in words what John Coltrane[34] was expressing in his notes on the saxophone; and then in *The Bigger Light* there's a more appealing music that is easier to listen to, because the conflicts might have been dissipated or accepted.

Q: Some women observe sexism in your stories.

A: In West Indian culture the woman is at the centre of things. If, as West Indian men, we have a number of women to choose from, we must admit that we are never in command of the situation: the woman is always in command and she too, has the power of choice. Although West Indian women traditionally did not hold important jobs, or did not become prime ministers, the influence they exercised over men was still superior to anything as cosmetic as a woman in a job of political importance. Women were in charge of the home. They provided the succour, psychological and otherwise, of the children. They got together in groups and sustained the extended family for us. They nurtured us and gave us an understanding of how to live.

Q: Your explanation is helpful to West Indian readers, but other readers who do not know the social and cultural background may conclude that in your stories, including 'Griff',[35] where Griff murders his wife, the dice appear loaded against women. In the last story of *Nine Men Who Laughed*, 'How He Does It', it is hard to believe that a professional, Canadian woman would be duped so successfully by a man pretending to be a lawyer, and hiding his marriage from her. She believes him when he says: 'I told you I don't have a wife' (p. 225). The man's successful manipulation of the woman may be regarded as sexist.

A: It is possible that the young woman lover may in fact be so ambitious that she is willing to doubt her best instincts. So far as the wife is concerned, that is a real case. I would meet these two persons, the man and woman, West Indians all of whom went to school together; and there came a time when it was meaningless to confront this chap and ask him whether in fact he was a lawyer. It was no longer important because we all knew; but we weren't quite sure how he made his money. After a while, the wife came to believe and live the lie. So far as 'Griff' is concerned, that was my attempt to describe the psychology of a gambler. In that story too the wife was aware of the destructiveness in the character of the husband; but she was painted with a veneer of English gentility, part of which meant that you do not wash your linen in public. She understood that she had a certain, strange loyalty to this man, and that he had to be presented, so far as her reaction to his idiosyncrasies was concerned, in a positive manner.

Q: Some people believe that you wrote *The Prime Minister*[36] out of bitterness about your experience in Barbados during your visit in 1975. Can you clarify that? Is the novel a wild fling at Caribbean corruption?

A: No, it's not. That book was written with some hostility towards the situation that I myself was in. What is published is two-thirds of the manuscript. I was urged and agreed, against my better judgement, to cut out what I would call the fattening of the book, and leave it bare, to appear to be a kind of pseudo-detective story. It is true that there's a certain amount of anger in the book, but it is not directed towards the system in Barbados. The anger is towards myself for having made the decision to go back, and feeling that my contribution would be worthwhile. As most people understand, you can never go back. The river had become broader, which meant that the banks, which could be protective, were eroded. There was hardly any demarcation between where the river ended and where the bank began. Though the book was edited wrongly, it had a kind of success because it deals with the rape of society by the people who run the society, by their new awareness, and by the infusion of tourists. The 'woman' sections were done separately, so that if you read them in sequence, they would make a short story which would delineate the psyche of the woman who is really the better aspect of Barbados.

Q: You call *Growing Up Stupid Under the Union Jack*[37] a memoir, not an autobiography. What's the distinction?

A: I thought the structure could more easily fit the term memoir. It wasn't a biography in the sense that it did not reflect a chronological development of my situation. A memoir, I thought, was a better term in that I could deal with events which could be repeated over the years, and I could go forward and back in time without damaging the coherence of the narrative.

Q: You are less limited by the structure. Your technique in *Growing Up Stupid Under the Union Jack*, as indeed in all of your fiction, reveals formidable powers of observation. I note, for instance, that there is a passage on dogs which lasts for a whole page-and-a-half in *Growing Up Stupid*. Those of us from a Caribbean background would savour and relish that passage as rich, juicy and healthy, where a Canadian or foreign reader might not. Since you live and publish in Canada, what was the reception of that book like? You mentioned, for instance, that when you saw a boy kiss a dog in Canada, it made you vomit. We treat dogs differently in the West Indies.

A: The book was read by the publisher Jack McClelland[38] who said that it was a perfectly written book and exceptionally beautiful, but it would not make any money. He decided to publish it because of the literary quality. Canadian readers may fall in love with the language and may find some titillation, but are unlikely to get to the heart of it. West Indians read it, I suppose, as they would the Bible, that is to say, a page at a time, and it sends some kind of shocks into them, forcing them to remember.

Q: That business about the overseas exam and the whole atmosphere of competing, and physically fortifying yourself for this grand enterprise! Then you've got a very perceptive piece on cricket when you get advice from the older spectators who are experts of the game through experience. So many of our great men were cricketers – Constantine, Worrell, Sobers.[39]

A: There is too in our background what you could call a symbiosis between brains and sport, in particular, cricket. In my years at school, in Barbados, all the fellows who did well in classics were good cricketers. The same thing doesn't hold in this country, meaning also America, where sportsmen are relegated to the bottom of educational achievement. But going back to the passage about dogs, in Barbados, I don't know whether it is because of the economic or social situation in certain families, but a dog was never kept as a companion: it was kept as a watchdog, to a great extent. A dog knew its place. It was reprehensible to us that a dog, as an animal, could be treated in such a way that you elevated the relationship between yourself and the dog to that between yourself and a person.

Q: The title 'Proud Empires'[40] is taken from the hymn that begins with the line 'The day thou gavest, Lord, is ended', and I interpret the hymn to say that proud empires, like all man-made structures, will pass away; but God's throne is eternal. Where is the irony in *Proud Empires* if the liberation from those empires is going to leave people in the same mess?

A: Nkrumah[41] said years ago that it is better to govern yourself badly than to be governed by a colonial power. I think *Proud Empires* works on two levels: it suggests that the destruction of the old colonial system will come about because of its inherent inhumanity: it also suggests that the people who take over in the new system will be sowing the seeds of their own destruction, because they haven't got a real, new model with which to replace the old one. They could only continue in the way they know. Not that I think it's impossible to have a new model. It is because of the retention of certain dispositions that came during the old colonial system that there is nothing the present rulers can do. That was one of the reasons why the protagonist, this bright young scholar from Barbados decided, through the advice of his uncle who had experienced some of that abroad, not to go to England to study, but to go to a new place. But he was met by a Canadianized version of the same English colonial disposition.

Q: Is there no hope of change from the old colonial pattern – neo-colonialism?[42]

A: Looking at the situation as it exists in Barbados there is no real spirit of change. The novel could not have broken away from real life to such an extent by suggesting that even though this boy had come through that system, and had witnessed all the skeletons and scandals, his new aware-ness acquired in Canada and also in Barbados could change the situation radically. That would be too idealistic.

Q: *Proud Empires* describes a colonial situation; for Barbados has not attained Independence, as it has in *The Prime Minister*; but the corruption there has a taste of post-colonial Barbados. You wrote the novel well after *The Prime Minister*, and it is a work of fiction, not a factual, social docu-ment. But I detect a parallel between the use of (post-colonial) material in a pre-colonial context. This may not be chronologically exact, but quite suitable imaginatively and artistically.

A: In *Proud Empires* I was trying to show that in Barbados there are certain ideas, situations, and persons who are forgotten or not dealt with in the scheme of things. I chose this woman, the mother, who lived a quiet, to some extent, an irrelevant life. She did not impose her personality too strenuously upon her husband or her son. But I felt her life had to be as important as that of the politician, or the policeman, or the tailor, and even her son. The son's education at the college was at best a superficial in-doctrination of ways which taught him how to behave. It did not prepare him for life in his country, nor did it prepare him for life outside his country.

Even though he went abroad he knew, and I knew, he had to come back. But the real education he received was two-pronged. Part of it was given in the tailor's shop where he was thrown up against a romanticization of black world history which was not really understood by the man who was giving the education. It was important that the man had these symbols, these little things in his shop. But what the mother was giving him was a sense of himself.

Q: There is a strong Biblical influence on your style. There are certain passages in *Growing Up Stupid* with a declamatory and prophetic ring which comes straight from the King James Version of the Bible. Then there is that passage in *Amongst Thistles and Thorns* with the mother reading the Bible to fend off evil and to protect her family from harm. What influence did the Bible have on your actual writing technique? You have already mentioned its influence on your religious consciousness.

A: It was not only religious: it was a religious literary consciousness. There was no book in our house but the Bible. Added to that, my mother was functionally illiterate. I know now that people who cannot read have very strong convictions about things, and tend to be very intelligently loquacious; but my mother apparently understood the importance of the ability to read in two ways: she insisted on giving me the best education available in Barbados, and would insist that I read to her. I could not read the Bible by rote, or just mouth the words: I had to repeat certain things in order that she might understand them. That plus going to church gave me a kind of respect not only for the Bible but for the printed word. Not being able on her own to peruse the Bible, she had to develop certain powers of retention of what she had heard me read to her. Her language then was imbued with an obvious biblical quality, in addition to the Barbadian quality; and I think that I may have absorbed that to the extent that, when I approached language, it was not only with Barbadian idiosyncrasies of speech, but with the ponderousness of the language of the King James version.

Q: A critic has described the episodic nature of your novels as a negative quality, in the way your narrative breaks off, raising expectations of a certain episode, character or issue, then dropping it before going on again. The form of your writing seems to me deliberately loose, rather like Selvon's.[43]

A: My attitude to the form of the novel is that I am more concerned with atmosphere and story, than with the structuring of character or plot. I never consider building plot in the sense of putting one block on the other to create tension or suspense. I prefer to do that through characters and atmosphere and language, because I feel that life is not, and can never be so structured. Certainly life cannot, symbolically, be anything but a circle: you begin, and when you end, you come back to a point approaching where you began. When I am writing a novel, plot has to be understood and imagined; structure also has to be imagined in the interaction of characters operating in the unity of the whole situation – the atmosphere.

Q: Your insight into West Indians is like Selvon's. You know their limitations and strengths, their joys and sorrows, and of course, their speech. Your evocation of atmosphere is flawless in the way you reproduce West Indian camaraderie, boisterousness and ribaldry blended dexterously into their experience of victimization, discrimination or oppression. I suppose it is no accident that the greatest Barbadian novel – *In the Castle of My Skin* – has no plot as such. Like your writing, it is all character and atmosphere, although Lamming also adds other ingredients including history and poetry.

A: Our idea of life in Barbados should be reflected in a novel or in any piece of writing dealing with the experience we lived through in Barbados. In other words, Lamming could not have written *In the Castle of My Skin* in the same way as Naipaul wrote *A House for Mr Biswas*. I would go so far as to say that *Biswas* reflects a Trinidadian mentality and *Castle* reflects a Barbadian mentality, and that Barbados is spinally different from Trinidad.

Q: As well as the sureness of your touch in regard to character and atmosphere, your writing has another vital quality: your language is earthy, vigorous and robust. It is used with great relish. Its fluency in meaning matches the fluidity of form that you have already described. It makes your work uniquely West Indian or Caribbean. But you have lived away from the Caribbean for some time now, and are likely to continue living away in the future. What happens when that language is stored up in your memory for so long? Is it the better for it? Does it lose authenticity?

A: I don't know how I've been able to do it, but I have retained voices and sounds from all those years, and even now I could repeat snatches of conversations in which I have taken part long ago, conversations with my mother, teachers or friends in the village. One reason for that perhaps is that I was very good at studying English as a school subject with parsing, précis, verbs, subjects and predicates, and other features of grammar. I feel that my mastery of formal English brought about my love and mastery of the language we spoke, by showing me the value of the choice of words and the effect of placing them in one position rather than another. By being able to freely mix formal structures with colloquialisms, I know how to make a sentence or idea more dramatic and expressive.

Q: Your language has rich literary properties. But our political and economic situation ensures that we are in exile.[44] Therefore we don't have an audience that will appreciate and buy your books. *Growing Up Stupid* is a good example. As you said, Jack McClelland published it knowing it would not sell. You can't expect publishers to do that too often.

A: I've seen indications that the books are now being taught in high schools and some colleges and universities. Even if the first generation of readers of these books do not really understand them, it is hoped that the generation following will. People who were born here of West Indian background, even though they may not know the West Indies, at least because of the situation in which they find themselves, would be forced to identify with this literature which is more *theirs* in the strict sense of identity than the literature written say by Margaret Atwood and Morley Callaghan.[45]

Q: In one way you're a Canadian writer. You have to be talked about in the same breath as Margaret Atwood, Morley Callaghan, Robertson Davies[45] and the rest. Within that classification there's Margaret Laurence's Manawaka trilogy which is a distinguished work. Hagar Shipley in *The Stone Angel*,[46] the first of the three novels, is perhaps the grandest character in all Canadian literature. There are also Robertson Davies's books *Fifth Business, The Manticore* and *World of Wonders*[47] which together comprise his Deptford trilogy. Both Margaret Laurence and Robertson Davies are studied in universities all over the country. Their books are reprinted, whereas your trilogy has never been reprinted. Why? Margaret Atwood, Morley Callaghan and Hugh Garner[48] have all written about Toronto, but neither they nor any other writer has produced as comprehensive and as vivid a portrait of Toronto as you have done. Callaghan doesn't even mention the city by name because he did not believe that in the 1920s and 1930s it had an identity different from other North American cities.

A: Years ago, I was concerned about this, but I feel that the work is there. If I felt any stronger than that I would stop writing and wait for the applause that should come to these books. If I do not accept the classification of Canadian writer, and accept the classification of West Indian writer, how do you evaluate the neglect of this West Indian trilogy written about West Indians in Canada? The explanation is political and anthropological. Literature in this country is determined by factors that are very often arbitrary – more political and sociological. It seems that as the society grows in its multicultural aspect, it ungrows in so far as creative tolerance of our presence is concerned. The problem is important because there has never been in this country a book written by a West Indian or black that was accepted in the sense of being placed among others to represent the variegated fabric of the community. I think the explanation for that is very simple. Even though there are posturings of acceptance and understanding, there really is no serious attempt to recognize, even in a negative sense, that the West Indian is by now a part of the fabric of the society.

Q: Your work can have a direct bearing on this: it clearly belongs to Caribbean literary expression in Canada. You don't fully belong to the group of Lamming, Selvon, Naipaul, Carew[49] and others who relied largely on their memories of the Caribbean to establish their reputation. You fit in with Dionne Brand and Marlene Nourbese Philip[50] except that you have seniority over them. More properly, you fit in with Rosa Guy and Paule Marshall[51] who are able to use their North American experience or have married it to their Caribbean past.

A: I have made two excursions back to the Caribbean with *The Prime Minister* and *Proud Empires*. I don't think I will do that again, because it would be pointless since I have grown away not only in distance, but in attitude from Barbados. At the moment, I am concerned with determining or defining an identity for the Caribbean man who has lived in Toronto for some time, in such a way that he will no longer consider himself an immigrant, an outsider, or a minority person; but would come to understand that his presence here, and the ease with which he continues to live here, is caused by the solid foundation that he got from the West Indies. In other words, what I am going to do next is to draw a character who despises and disregards the national controversy around federalism and a national cultural identity involving the two solitudes, a character who because he has lived here for so long – it might be ten years or three decades – is able to see that this is where he belongs.

Notes

1 Francis Appleton Collymore is remembered as a poet, editor and promoter of West Indian literature. He was born in Barbados, where he taught at Combermere School. In 1942, he was one of the founders of *Bim* magazine, which he also edited for many years. Through his work as a school-teacher and editor, he encountered promising writers, whom he encouraged. *Kyk-Over-Al* and *Bim* are the two longest-running, and most influential literary magazines in the English-speaking Caribbean. Cf. Chapter 5, note 26, and Chapter 6, note 4.

2 See Index for these authors.

3 *The Globe and Mail* is a daily newspaper published in Toronto and advertised as 'Canada's national newspaper'.

4 Austin Clarke, *the Survivors of the Crossing* (Heinemann, London, 1964), *Amongst Thistles and Thorns* (Heinemann, London, 1965).

5 See Bibliography under Selvon and Lamming.

6 See Bibliography under Selvon.

7 See Index for Selvon, Lamming, Hearne, Walcott.

8 For *Caribbean Voices*, see Chapter 4, note 2.

9 For *The Black Jacobins*, see Chapter 2, note 17.

10 The Black Panther movement was a revolutionary black movement in the US during the 1960s, in the period of struggle for civil rights and other basic liberties. In Trinidad, in 1990, a Muslim revolutionary movement called the Jamaat-al-Muslimeen, led by Yaseen Abu Baker staged a coup and detained members of the Government, who were later released in return for an amnesty for those involved in the coup. The coup members were imprisoned, but released after two years when the amnesty was upheld by the Supreme court of Trinidad and Tobago.

11 James Joyce's *A Portrait of the Artist as a Young Man* (1916), and Dylan Thomas's

A Child's Christmas in Wales (1954) are texts about a growing boy; Joyce's novel is regarded as a classic work because of its stream-of-consciousness technique and theory of art. Both texts are set in a provincial atmosphere and are somewhat autobiographical, but *A Portrait of the Artist* also evokes the actual consciousness of the hero in his growing awareness of the world.

12   Clarke mentions a few of the American Evangelical sects which have become very popular in the Caribbean. These are only some of the sects that form the Evangelical movement mentioned by Lamming in 'Concepts of the Caribbean' (Chapter 1 above). See Index under Evangelical sects.

13   In many rural districts of the Caribbean, water was supplied by artesian wells connected to pipes installed in different locations, usually by the roadside. These 'standpipes' served as centres of the community, since everyone came there to get water. Hence the 'old talk' or gossip, and other communal activities that developed around standpipes.

14   Bath Corner was in the district of Dayrells Road in Barbados. It was the location of public baths for men and women.

15   With his background in the civil rights movement, it is curious that Clarke would become a candidate for a Conservative Party. The election was for a seat in the Parliament of the province of Ontario. Clarke did not run again.

16   Austin Clarke, *The Meeting Point* (Heinemann, London, 1967). In this novel, Sam Burman is a wealthy Jewish lawyer living in Forest Hill, one of the more affluent neighbourhoods in Toronto. Burman employs a black Barbadian woman, Estelle, as his domestic, and later seduces Estelle's sister, who becomes pregnant.

17   Pierre Berton is a distinguished Canadian journalist, newspaper columnist and author. He is also a broadcaster and man of letters. His books include *The Last Spike: The Great Railway 1881–1885* (McClelland and Stewart, Toronto, 1971) – about the building of the Canadian Pacific Railway; and *The Arctic Grail* (McClelland and Stewart, Toronto, 1988) – about the quest for the North West Passage and the North Pole from 1818 to 1911.

18   Ed Bullins is a black American writer and one of the most original and prolific playwrights of the American Black Theatre movement. Like LeRoi Jones, he expresses rage against white racism in his work, which achieved great popularity in the 1960s. LeRoi Jones is now known as Imamu Amiri Baraka. His *Dutchman and The Slave* won the Obie award for the best American play of the 1963–64 season. James Baldwin's novel *Another Country* was first published in 1962. It is set in the Greenwich village/Harlem district of New York City, and is inspired by similar rage against racial injustice. Cf. Chapter 11, note 27.

19   In 1931, nine black men were jailed in Scottsboro, Alabama, for allegedly raping two white girls on a train. In fact, following a fight between white and black youths, the white youths, who were thrown off the train, made up the rape story. In the first trial, eight of the black accused were sentenced to death, and one to life imprisonment. Although the Supreme Court reversed this decision, a new trial again produced convictions, and nine death sentences. These convictions were again reversed by the Supreme Court. In a further trial, four of the men were convicted and the others dismissed. Apart from its illustration of naked racial discrimination in the American South in the 1930s, the Scottsboro case is important in legal history because of the decisions of the Supreme Court.

20   Frantz Fanon (1925–61) was born on the French Caribbean island of Martinique. He specialized in psychiatry, while studying medicine in France. In *Black Skin, White Masks* (1952), he records his observations of psycho-sociological and racial problems in the Caribbean. During the French–Algerian war, Fanon worked in Algeria and supported the Algerians. His book *The Wretched of the Earth* (1961) was widely considered as a handbook for colonized people throughout the world in the 1960s and 1970s. Clarke read

Fanon's work in the form of essays which were published in the Paris journal of black culture *Présence Africaine*. These essays were later republished in book form.

21 Richard Wright (1908–60) is the first major contemporary black American novelist, whose *Native Son* (1940), set in Chicago, describes the plight of a black man, Bigger Thomas, who accidentally murders the daughter of his white employer, and later his own girlfriend. Bigger is subsequently executed. The novel is influenced by Marxism to the extent that an attempt is made to show Bigger Thomas's problems as a direct product of a racist society.

22 Austin Clarke, *Storm of Fortune* (Heinemann, London, 1972).

23 'Négritude' was a literary and philosophical movement which originated in the Caribbean but was developed in Paris, in the 1930s, by poets such as Leopold Sédar Senghor, from Senegal, Aimé Césaire from Martinique, and Léon Damas from Guyana. Its core idea was to resist domination by European values and reassert black values. Cf. Chapter 8, note 23.

24 See 'New York', in Gerald Moore and Ulli Beier (eds), *The Penguin Book of Modern African Poetry* (Penguin, Harmondsworth, England, 1984), pp. 235–7.

25 Austin Clarke, *The Bigger Light* (Heinemann, London, 1975).

26 For Caryl Phillips, see Index.

27 For Clarke's account of a wedding, see *Storm of Fortune* pp. 243–53.

For Lamming's story, see George Lamming, 'A Wedding in Spring', in Andrew Salkey (ed.), *West Indian Stories* (Faber and Faber, London, 1971), pp. 28–41.

28 This is another example of Andrew Salkey's role as a promoter of West Indian literature. Clarke's is one of many literary friendships in which Salkey played a supportive and sustaining role. For Salkey, see Index.

29 Austin Clarke, *When He Was Free and Young and Used to Wear Silks* (Little, Brown and Company, Toronto, 1973).

30 American sculptor married to the sister of the Canadian actor Michael Sarazin.

31 For 'Four Stations in his Circle' see Austin Clarke, *When He Was Free and Young and Used to Wear Silks*, pp. 33–48.

32 Austin Clarke, *When Women Rule* (McClelland and Stewart, Toronto, 1985).

33 Bob Marley (1945–81) was a Jamaican singer, guitarist, songwriter and band-leader who became a superstar in the 1970s through his exciting style of reggae, which blended rock, rhythm and blues, soul and Jamaican folk rhythms. His group was called the Wailers. He died of cancer.

34 John Coltrane (1926–67) was one of the greatest saxophonists of all. An African-American, he was born in North Carolina and played in the US Navy band in Hawaii. In the 1950s he played with such jazz greats as Dizzy Gillespie, Miles Davis and Thelonius Monk.

35 For 'Griff', see *When He Was Free and Young and Used to Wear Silks*, pp. 77–103.

36 Austin Clarke, *Prime Minister* (General Publishing Company, Ontario, 1977).

37 Austin Clarke, *Growing Up Stupid Under the Union Jack* (McClelland and Stewart, Toronto, 1980).

38 Jack McClelland is a Canadian publisher whose firm McClelland and Stewart republished many out-of-print Canadian texts, and published new authors to promote Canadian literature during the 1960s and 1970s. McClelland and Stewart continues to be a major Canadian publishing company.

39 Sir Learie Constantine (1902–71) was born in Trinidad and became famous as a test cricketer before becoming a writer, politician and diplomat. Later still, he became Lord Constantine, Baron of Maraval and Nelson.

Sir Frank Worrell (1924–67) was born in Barbados, and played cricket for Barbados, Jamaica and the West Indies. He was the first black to become a full-fledged captain of the West Indies cricket team. He died of leukemia.

Sir Garfield Sobers was born in Barbados and played cricket for Barbados and the West Indies. He is probably the most complete cricketer ever. He was also captain of the West Indies team.

40   Austin Clarke, *Proud Empires*, the last verse of the hymn (No. 556 in *The Book of Praise* (Presbyterian Church of Canada, Toronto, 1972) runs:

So be it, Lord! Thy throne shall never,
Like earth's proud empires pass away;
Thy kingdom stands and grows forever,
Till all thy creatures own thy sway.

41   Kwame Nkrumah (1909–72) became the first President of Ghana (formerly the Gold Coast) after it gained Independence from Britain in 1957. Nkrumah studied in the US, but returned to the Gold Coast in 1947. He was imprisoned for political activities in 1950, but won elections in 1952. After 1957, as President of the first free, English-speaking country in West Africa, Nkrumah's writings and opinions were highly respected on such subjects as colonialism, decolonization and neo-colonialism. Nkrumah's government was overthrown while he was on a visit to China in 1966. He died in Rumania while having treatment for cancer.

42   Neo-colonialism signifies the continuation of colonial rule in a different guise from formal colonialism. After Independence, economic and cultural relationships between Britain and its former colonies remained virtually unchanged. This permitted the former colonial relationship to continue. Neo-colonialism could only thrive with the cooperation of local, non-whites who assumed power and influence after the British left. Cf. the final pages of Chapter 7.

43   The plots in Selvon's novels tend to be flexible and loose-jointed. *The Lonely Londoners*, for example, is basically a collection of independent episodes in which the same characters reappear.

44   Emigration from the Caribbean has increased since Independence because of political corruption, economic hardship, inadequate social services and sheer physical insecurity. The situation varies from territory to territory, but the general picture is one that encourages those who are able to emigrate to do so. Unfortunately, emigrants tend to come from the more educated and skilled groups, which increases hardship, and, in turn, emigration. Cf. Chapter 4, note 41.

45   Margaret Atwood is probably the most prolific and versatile contemporary Canadian writer. She writes poetry, novels, short stories and essays in addition to carrying out numerous social engagements. Morley Callaghan (1903–90) is one of Canada's most respected novelists. In his long career, Callaghan has been famous for non-fiction and broadcasting as well. Atwood and Callaghan are typical writers in the mainstream of anglophone Canadian culture. Robertson Davies is another distinguished mainstream Canadian novelist. Clarke differs from Atwood, Callaghan and Davies in ethnic and cultural terms. Yet he writes about people who live in the same urban milieu as these writers.

46   Margaret Laurence (1926–85) is also a mainstream anglophone Canadian novelist who wrote three novels set in the fictional prairie town of Manawaka: *The Stone Angel* (McClelland and Stewart, Toronto, 1964); *A Jest of God* (McClelland and Stewart, Toronto, 1966); and *The Diviners* (Alfred Knopf, New York, 1974).

47   Robertson Davies's trilogy appeared as follows: *Fifth Business* (1970); *The Manticore* (1972); and *World of Wonders* (1975).

48   Several of Atwood's novels are set in Toronto, for example, *Lady Oracle* (1976) and *Life Before Man* (1979).

Some of Callaghan's novels are also set in Toronto, although the city is not named: for example, *Such is My Beloved* (1934) and *More Joy in Heaven* (1937).

Hugh Garner's *Cabbagetown* (1950) is set in Toronto during the Depression.

49 See Index for Lamming, Selvon, Naipaul and Carew.

50 For Dionne Brand, see Chapter 10; for Marlene Nourbese Philip, see Chapter 9, note 24.

51 For Rosa Guy and Paule Marshall, see Introduction, note 4.

CHAPTER 9

Cyril Dabydeen: Here and there

Cyril Dabydeen was born in Guyana in 1945. His early poetry won awards before he emigrated to Canada in 1970. In Canada, Dabydeen completed postgraduate studies in English at Queen's University, before settling in Ottawa. Dabydeen's writing first appeared in Canada in small literary magazines, but it now consists of several collections of poetry, two collections of stories, three novels and two anthologies which he has edited. His collections of poetry include Goatsong *(1977) and* This Planet Earth *(1979). His stories are collected in* Still Close to the Island *(1985) and* To Monkey Jungle *(1988). Two novels,* The Wizard Swami *and* Dark Swirl *both appeared in 1989. The anthologies are mainly of immigrant Canadian writing:* A Shapely Fire *(1989) and* Another Way to Dance *(1990). Dabydeen's writing successfully captures the mixed feelings and ambivalent attitudes of displaced and marginalized people living in exile. He has won many awards, including appointment as poet laureate of the city of Ottawa from 1984 to 1987. (This interview was recorded in Ottawa on 16 March 1991.)*

Q: Did you do any writing in Guyana?

A: Yes, I wrote a good deal of poetry. In 1964, I won the Sandbach Parker gold medal for poetry.[1] A couple of years later, I won the first A. J. Seymour Lyric Poetry prize.[2]

Q: How did you get the idea of writing in your head at all?

A: I used to visit the British Council library and the public library in New Amsterdam.[3] Also, the name of Mittelholzer[4] was fairly well-known. He was from New Amsterdam which is just four miles from where we lived in Canje. So there's some sense of a historical and literary tradition. I also religiously read all the back issues of *Kyk-Over-Al*[5] in the public library. This was the 1960s in Guyana, a time of ferment when we were forging new identities, moving away from self-contempt.

Q: You are very productive – about a dozen books already. Mittelholzer was also very productive – 25 books in a very short career. It's very interesting to hear you say that Mittelholzer was an inspiration. Who were some of the aspiring poets, or writers like yourself at that time?

A: There was Cecile Norbriega and Wordsworth McAndrew;[6] A. J.

Seymour was a nurturing figure to some of us. His own sensitivity and warmth as a human being was what I cherished, and because he was a figure very much in the local media, we looked up to him. He was helpful and wrote the introduction to my *Poems in Recession*.[7] The few times we went to Georgetown, we'd meet him. But it was more of a deferential type of a relationship.

Q: Between the early 1960s and 1970 when you emigrated to Canada, was there any other influence on your work?

A: Martin Carter[8] was a seminal influence. There was a newspaper called the *Berbice Times* that published his work. I was in Teacher's College, but because we were living in a country area, we didn't have access to what was going on in Georgetown, and the University of the West Indies. We didn't have exposure except for the instances that Seymour now and again provided.

Q: Why did you come to Canada?

A: It was fully imbued in us that to become successful writers we had to go abroad. There was also the example of Naipaul, Lamming and the others in London, and Austin Clarke in Canada.[9] Whenever these men came to the Caribbean, they were front-page news. I also listened to the BBC programme *Caribbean Voices*.[10] I was aware of what was going on abroad in the middle and late sixties, and I knew I had to leave Guyana. I also wanted to come to university. I felt you only grew as a writer if you had access to university education. I came to Lakehead University, in northern Ontario, and one of the things that struck me was the University library with current periodicals and magazines. Through these I came to know what was going on in Australia, America, Canada and Britain. Those were things I never had access to in Guyana where I was overwhelmed by the heavy metaphorical writing of the early poems of Derek Walcott.[11] In Canada people were writing a more accessible type of poetry, and I began to change my own heavy, dense metaphors.

Q: What specifically were the new styles of writing which you encountered in Canada which altered your own approach to writing?

A: I attended poetry and literary readings, for instance, with B. P. Nichol,[12] the sound poet. It was exciting to hear him read, and chant, and hum his poetry. I also remember reading a lot of Leonard Cohen.[13] It was from the total lack of pretentiousness in his style, and reading him night and day for a short period of time, that I think some of the poems in *This Planet Earth*[14] came into being. I also took a course in creative writing and was exposed to the work of American poets like Theodore Roethke, Robert Lowell, Peter Redgrove, and British poets like Ted Hughes. I also read Sylvia Plath,[15] and later did an MA thesis on her.

Q: When did you settle in Ottawa?

A: I went to Queen's University, after Lakehead, to do a postgraduate course. I lived in Kingston[16] for a few years. Then in 1975 I came to Ottawa.

I had the choice of living in Toronto too. But I had come from Guyana to Lakehead, and Kingston and just couldn't get used to Toronto with its mechanized society, the jangling of the subway trains, and people in a constant hurry. That's perhaps why my star as a writer hasn't risen as high as that of some of my colleagues. I am not close to publishers, or to literary parties and the network that is in Toronto.

Q: Still, you've received several honours and awards, the most important being poet laureate of the City of Ottawa from 1984 to 1987. How did that happen?

A: The criteria were to have a number of books published and be known in the community. I had to read before the audience of City Council.

Q: Is it possible for you to imagine the kind of writing you might have been doing now, if you had not left Guyana at all?

A: There were no publishing houses in Guyana relative to what we have in North America. I know *Kyk-Over-Al*[17] started all over again; but even that would have been very limiting. I would also have missed an expansion of my thought and imagination had I not come to North America. Then there is the advantage of being away from where you are born when writing about it. When I look back at the Caribbean or Guyana, from this perspective, I can see things in a more detached way than I would have been able to do had I stayed there. Having said that, one is aware of losing a sense of how the society is evolving in an immediate way. But I have gone back from time to time, and I keep abreast with what is going on.

Q: So you think there are both gains and losses?

A: But the gains override the losses. And also one should not forget that all my formative years were spent in the Caribbean. I left there when I was in my twenties, and the residue of those memories is still in my consciousness.

Q: One of the two anthologies you have edited is sub-titled *Changing the Literary Landscape*.[18] In drawing attention to the writing of immigrants like yourself, through your anthologies, how are you changing the literary landscape of Canada?

A: In the 1970s and early 1980s, I was involved with a society called The Canadian–Asian Studies Association.[19] It was the Japanese-Canadian novelist, Joy Kogawa,[20] who put me on to it. I used to organise readings for the Association and I crossed the country from Halifax to Vancouver in doing so. This gave me exposure to writers like Rienzi Crusz, the Sri Lankan poet,[21] and some of the Japanese and Chinese-Canadian writers. I also met educators, who would often ask for the works of these writers in book form. At the time, it was very much the mainstream Canadian writers who were getting all the attention. But from the 1970s, you had a new population from third-world countries who were coming into Canada in large numbers. They didn't come here just to improve their standard of living: they came with minds, psyches and imagination which, sooner or later, had to be expressed. My work as an anthologist was one way of exposing these new Canadian writers until they could get their own books published.

Q: These new writers draw attention to the fact that there are other (neglected or unseen) aspects of the Canadian literary landscape?

A: Yes. It is a question of how you define Canada. In terms of physical landscape, Canada is merely rocks, trees and lakes. But if it's also the contribution of our spirits, souls, and the things we all bring who are living here, then it should be redefined as a landscape of mind and spirit. It makes for a country which is not preoccupied with simple economic development, but also with dimensions of spirit. It resists the notion of what has been called the 'Coca-colaization' of society, or the homogeneity caused by the military-industrial complex which controls the economy. New ethnic groups lend dynamism to the society and ultimately greater social and cultural richness.

Q: You should be quite pleased that what used to be pejoratively called 'ethnic writing' in Canada has now come into its own. There are so many of the newer writers nowadays, among women alone Dionne Brand,[22] Claire Harris,[23] Marlene Nourbese Philip[24] from the Caribbean, and male south-Asian or Caribbean writers, like Moyez Vassanji,[25] Rohinton Mistry,[26] Neil Bissoondath,[27] Arnold Itwaru[28] and yourself.

A: I thought this was going to happen inevitably. Most of the writers you mention are from the Toronto area, and Toronto is currently, according to UNESCO, the most multicultural city in the world. But all parts of the country are beginning to see this manifestation of diversity of spirit. This is how the literary landscape has changed.

Q: I presume all these writers are affected by this concept of 'here and there'? Can you define 'here and there' and say why you think it is important for new Canadian writers?

A: If you've spent your early years in a third-world country, and have come here as an immigrant, you just can't deny the existence of that former part of your psyche. I often use the swing of a pendulum to reflect what happens to the imagination: I could be sitting here in Ottawa, but at any moment my mind can go back there. Images and echoes come from there – Guyana or the Caribbean – then you're here again. A certain kind of symbiosis takes place between 'here and there'; it takes place continually, I feel: and it is reflected in any creative or imaginative work that you produce.

Q: There is a continuous mixing of recollections from your place of origin and your current experiences here where you are now?

A: Continuously. It has to do with the power and recall of imagery. Something may trigger off the imagination, and set off echoes; it may be something from there, for instance; then by chiselling away at it, the amorphousness begins to get less, and the poem, or story, or novel begins to take better shape. The novel *Dark Swirl*,[29] for instance, is the product of imagery from the Guyanese legend of the Massacouraman,[30] and the explorations of Gerald Durrell, the British naturalist whose book *Three Singles to Adventure*[31] contains animal stories set in the Guyanese forest. Perhaps it's the elemental quality of these stories which came back to me and which I began to explore in an imaginative way in Canada. At the same time, I became interested in depth psychology: so the novel came out of my recollections of the elemental world of the tropics of South America, with its legend of the Massacouraman, and my interest in depth psychology.

Q: I can see that these concepts of 'here and there' may be playing in your mind constantly; but where does the question of an audience come in when you are here in Canada and you write a novel like *Dark Swirl*?

A: That is a question one wrestles with all the time. In *Dark Swirl* the dialogue was written in Standard English, but my publisher in England felt it might be more authentic to use Guyanese Creole. I was thinking in terms of a North American readership, and that's why the dialogue in the original draft of the novel was not in Creole. Audience does create a problem, and I am still wrestling with it.

Q: When Selvon, Lamming and Naipaul[32] went to England in the 1950s, they found that their Caribbean language was a great drawing card. It was, different, exotic, colourful – a new manifestation of the English language that was welcomed by English critics, if not by a wide English readership. In those terms, why should you feel compelled to deny yourself the resources of this fantastic richness that we have in our Caribbean language?

A: One has to think of the literary work as an end in itself. If it does not communicate, what is the point of writing?

Q: In 1956 Selvon wrote *The Lonely Londoners*[33] completely in Creole. Mind you, it was a doctored language – he had an English audience in mind. But he thought that the nature of experience that he was trying to communicate could not have been communicated as effectively in any other way. Perhaps you can never have a one hundred per cent communication of actual experience. But *The Lonely Londoners* was successful. Now, you seem very concerned about whether your audience will receive what you are trying to communicate to them, especially when you're writing about Caribbean subjects. I wonder whether more full-blooded use of Creole would not be preferable with such subjects?

A: As you know, I have Creole in some of my stories.

Q: Yes.

A: There is a poem called 'Sir James Douglas, Father of British Columbia'[34] which I usually read in Creole after first reading it in Standard English; and quite often people will say, 'Why don't you write more poems in that kind of language?' It has greater spirit and feeling for them; but I sometimes suspect that they respond to the exotic quality of the strange sounds. In other words, they respond positively for the wrong reasons. I realize the importance of Creole in accurately reflecting the fracture in the society I came from. It was a colonized society of marginalized people, sugar-cane cutters and rice farmers trying to make ends meet.

Q: Yes. That is exactly what Selvon communicated to his English audience nearly forty years ago, and Austin Clarke[35] is doing the same thing here in Canada.

A: But it still makes me wonder if the Canadian audience fully comprehends the elements which we want to convey. People have also told me that they don't understand the Caribbean language. Maybe it's the same with Scottish dialect, or any other form of regional English. Canadian readers say it takes too much effort on their part. Perhaps it was different for Selvon and others in the 1950s. People haven't got as much time nowadays. It is also possible that in England, in the 1950s, people were more inclined to accept the speech and cultural practices from other parts of the world as part of the experience of empire. It seems to me that in Canada people are more impatient in dealing with things they do not understand. I think this will change. As publishing becomes broader, I think people will become more curious about dialogue with Creole speech.

Q: Some of your poems rely on Caribbean source material and images, unaccompanied by the Caribbean language. You would mention a 'salempenter',[36] for example, or exotic foods; but they are presented in language that doesn't match them.

A: My instinct is towards what I would call the organic quality of the work. The organic elements come from the elemental world which, for me, is still the tropics, the place where we came from. Because I didn't grow up in this society, I cannot easily fall back on its flora and fauna. It's not embedded in my psyche, in the way the tropical, elemental world is. That's why I go back to what I am comfortable with.

Q: Here is one of your Poems, 'A Tame Life',[37] which illustrates the point I am making about the language not entirely matching the subject, and thus producing a somewhat dispersed effect:

How shall I tame them
these things of the night
they keep coming in
going out

a salempenter night
in moonlight
squawking

> – slither
> and crawl
> breaking out
> with emerald
>
> moulting
> chickens running
> wings flapping
>
>   more commotion
> in this coop
> grass bespattered
>   foul dust
>
> I breathe in
>   across a shingled
> shadow, a house coming
>   down with stilts –
>
> a beating
> dragged out.

Salempenter and the shingled house on stilts are Caribbean; but the language of the poem as a whole evokes thoughts, impressions, nuances of feeling that don't quite match these features of the tropical Caribbean. At any rate, one has to make an effort to get them to match. Maybe that is the effect you want. But I feel caught between two stools. I have to struggle a little to bring the salempenter and the shingled houses on stilts from that tropical scene into line with the emotions that are being communicated to me in Standard English.

A: That is the sense of 'here and there' at work. 'How shall I tame them . . .' the poet asks at the beginning. They come into his consciousness. They're there; he just can't exorcise them. The sheer act of writing the poem is an effort towards exorcism.

Q: The interplay between images from 'there' and the reality of 'here' is, in fact, the subject of the poem?

A: Yes. The need for taming suggests that the images from 'there' are wild and demonic, subterannean, and have to be exorcised.

Q: If the poem dramatizes this attempted exorcism, that may be why I am aware of struggle and conflict. If that is your intention, I have to agree that the Caribbean language would tend to reduce the feeling if not of outright conflict, at least of elements in opposition to each other. Of course, all your poems are not like this. In several, your subjects tend to be based on the social observation of everyday incidents: someone comes for a visit and observes something; and the observation is expressed in conversational idiom of Standard English that matches the passing quality of the subject. In 'New York City',[38] for instance, the persona visits a friend who talks about this and that, and about his economic success; and the visit ends. There are many other poems like that which convey a tone of the casual insignificance or ephemeral quality of contemporary life. I think your poems are remarkably adept at reproducing the texture and substance of ordinary, everyday reality for most people. Is your comment that that is all there is to it?

A: I'm not sure if I'm deliberately making a comment on contemporary life being ephemeral. Even though it is very much part of my psyche that life is like that: one is born and eventually dies. The key for me is imagery. It's to capture an image and develop it. If the image is an immediate one of people that you meet in everyday life, that becomes the focus. Some poems also have a narrative appeal, but essentially the poem is what the images suggest. If they suggest ephemerality or the transience of life, then that's what I'm saying.

Q: The poem 'They Call This Planet Earth'[39] tells the story about a girl being raped. It is very much an Ottawa poem with a central-Canadian point of view that mentions the Parliament Buildings and financial cutbacks. There doesn't seem to be much Caribbean content. The poem has the episodic, narrative quality of something you read in the newspaper.

A: That anecdotal element might suggest irony and humour; for the case of the girl being raped may be an illusion, a presentation of the irony of existence, the sense of life having darker forces juxtaposed to more positive ones.

Q: Your poems deal with a wide variety of subjects including love, the universe, exile and the nature of Canadian citizenship. Questions of identity and homelessness preoccupy you in *Goatsong*,[40] and other early poems, especially where you consider the meaning of Canadian citizenship for someone who is a member of a visible minority.

A: The longer I live in Canada, the more I feel that my mind and imagination are trying to be more firmly rooted in the Canadian soil. You'll find this in some of my newer poems. In the older poems there is a linear questioning of one's self, as a member of a visible minority who has been here for ten or fifteen years, and is still not accepted as Canadian, even though he or she might have official status as a citizen of Canada. Now I'm trying to be more firmly rooted, psychically, in Canada. There's a poem I've written about the Capillano suspension bridge where I'm reflecting as an immigrant on the bridge. The persona is more integrated in the Canadian landscape, and no longer sees himself/herself as marginalized. It's more perhaps the duality of existence now.

Q: So from *Goatsong* up, does that duality or conflict between notions of 'here' and 'there' become less and less as the immigrant becomes more integrated into the Canadian landscape? Or does the duality become a concern of general philosophical concern?

A: A general philosophical concern. Having said that, though, I don't want it to appear that in twenty years from now one will become accepted in spite of one's pigmentation or where one comes from. I think Canada will still keep on wrestling with people like myself. Mind you, I think in the middle part of the next century, when you will have a greater presence of people of colour in this country, the questions may not be asked by artists like myself in the same way we're asking them now. In a place like Toronto, for instance, we will feel far more comfortable because we will see more people like ourselves.

Q: What about immigrant children born here? Do they have to wait that long to feel comfortable?

A: Non-white children think they are the mainstream when they are in school, but once they begin to look for jobs, they get a jolt right away, because they are seen as 'outsiders'. Consciously, they are forced to go back into the question of roots. I was told recently by a Toronto councillor that she always assumed that she was Jamaican until she went to Jamaica for the first time in twenty years, and found that she wasn't as Jamaican as she thought she was.

Q: With your heightened awareness of racial problems in this country, and your professional role as a race relations expert, I am surprised that I don't find militancy or political activism in your poems. As you know, Indian people have been thrown on subway tracks in Toronto. They are called 'Pakis', and were beaten up regularly in the 1970s.

A: There is militancy in my poems, I think; but not expressed in a blatant way. This does not mean that the spirit and solidarity with people who have been victimized is not there. That's why I'm in the Ministry of Race Relations. I'm involved, in a professional way, working towards what I call 'institutional change'.

Q: But this tends to produce what I see as a mildness of tone. For instance, in *This Planet Earth* the poem 'Brazil' (p. 28) has a last stanza which says:

and I am confused in Canada
because I can hardly shake a fist
at the wind; I am too tame

Sun do not rob me of this anger

It's as if you do feel the anger; but there is a conscious effort to restrict yourself, and not express the force of your real feelings. Could it be that your concern about audience, or something like that, limits the full-blooded expression of what is really you?

A: No. The anger is expressed in the poem itself: that's where the anger is: it says, 'and I am confused in Canada'; that's part of the anger;

> because I can hardly shake a fist
> at the wind; I am too tame
>
> Sun do not rob me of this anger

The poem coheres the anger. There are two different things – the poem, as a reflection of the anger of the persona, and the individual who writes the poem. The persona is confused because there are forces in Canada which are holding him back. That doesn't mean the anger is not there.

Q: But it's suppressed.

A: Not suppressed; the mere fact that the poem is written down is an expression of the anger. If I hadn't written those words, then the anger would not have been there; but what is also reflected is dissatisfaction with the forces that are imposed on the anger. The poem describes the whole situation as against just giving a banal expression of the anger. That has to do, I think, with the integrity of the poem.

Q: I know that you've expressed criticism against Canada, for example, in 'Lady Icarus'[41] which deals with an immigrant who is led to commit suicide because of immigration problems.

A: That's a poem that clearly condemns the Canadian Immigration system. And much depends on the way the poem is read. I used to read it all over the country and chant it, so that it resonated with the passion of the persona.

Q: You write with the aim of an oral delivery in mind?

A: Oh, yes. Clearly so. The mere fact that the lines are so short suggests that I want the incantatory effect that comes from reading the poem aloud. This is especially true of my earlier poems.

Q: I have heard you read and agree that part of the effect in your poems comes from an oral delivery. I also agree that there is an element of protest in your poems and stories; but its quality still seems relatively subdued or controlled when compared, for instance, with similar writing by Dionne Brand. In one of her poems, Brand complains about being constantly asked whether it is hot enough for her in summer, in Canada. In winter she is also questioned, over and over again, about why she left her 'lovely, sunny country'. She expresses her frustration and disgust in the last line of the poem by saying that if anyone asks her such a question again 'I will claw his face, and cut his tongue.' Many of your poems deal with similar feelings of frustration, for instance, in 'Citizenship',[42] where you object to being asked

'Where do you come from?' over and over again. But your persona's statement of protest is more subdued than Brand's.

A: It is less shrill.

Q: It may be that Brand writes from a position that is overtly Marxist or socialist – at any rate, more activist than yours.

A: My story 'Mammita's Garden Cove'[43] describes the disturbed feelings of an immigrant looking for employment in Toronto. He is frustrated and angry. But perhaps I should agree that it is the silent cry, the anguish of the heart that I am trying to capture.

Q: Since you've written so much more poetry than fiction, do you see yourself primarily as a poet?

A: No. At this stage I'm writing more fiction than poetry, partly because I feel I can communicate to a larger audience in fiction. Fiction gets more attention than poetry in this country, which is not necessarily to say that that's the only reason why I'm turning to fiction now.

Q: Is there a preference for the novel form rather than stories?

A: Fiction is a lot more physical work. A good short story should have the poet's sense of form and the novelist's sense of drama. My training as a poet serves me very well in fiction.

Q: *The Wizard Swami*[44] reminded me of Naipaul's *The Mystic Masseur.*

A: When I wrote the first draft of the novel I was still a teenager, and I was reading a lot of V. S. Naipaul. Devan, the 'Indian swami' is picaresque, a bit of a villain in himself, and yet a man searching for identity. He is marginalized in the village and is yearning for something beyond that; so he ends up eventually in Georgetown.[45]

Q: Naipaul's Pandit Ganesh did a similar thing. Both characters live in the same makeshift world in which they grab at straws.

A: I have some sympathy for Devan: he's a man who is not content with living in his small world of Providence village; he sees an opportunity to get beyond it and takes it; he has ambition and drive, but he fails in the end to escape his origins. The novel is not a strict allegory although Devan starts in a village called Providence and trains a horse called Destiny, then ends up in Providence again.

Q: Far from being allegorical, I see the novel as being very realistic, and Devan himself as an authentic portrait of a rural Indo-Guyanese.

A: Devan is a composite of some of the pandits I knew in my area. Some of them had genuine aspirations toward Hinduism; but because of unemployment and lack of opportunity, a few became alcoholics. Yet people looked up to them, which invited exploitation. But these pandits should be seen as victims of poverty and colonialism. They had no support from India, for instance. That's why the practice of Hinduism in Guyana is fraught with tragedy.

Q: *The Wizard Swami* is similar to David Dabydeen's novel *The*

Intended.[46] It offers a more public view of Guyanese Indian society with the All India League and elections, whereas *The Intended* is more about domestic relations and family matters, such as the common practice of wife-beating. I can make the same comment on your fiction as I did earlier about your poems – that the tone is muted in so far as you describe conflict, and then resolve it in almost a playful manner, or do not resolve it at all. In your story 'Antics of the Insane' in *Still Close to the Island*, for instance, the protagonist kills the chickens in retaliation against his wife, but he happens to work in an asylum anyway; so the reader is left wondering who is mad.

A: That is the humour and irony I spoke of earlier. There is also a certain playfulness; but that's not to say the stories are not serious. The essence of the contemporary short story is character; not so much situation. Everything must enhance character. That's where, in my view, the contemporary short story is moving towards. You may be right in noticing a muted tone in my stories, but that's part and parcel of the way the character perceives the world.

Q: Yes. That is not necessarily a negative criticism; but it may indicate a movement away from Caribbean assertiveness and pungency toward a more moderate and balanced viewpoint that could be called Canadian. In other words, your work may reflect the process of cultural integration you mentioned earlier. As a Canadian writer, with the resources that you do have, and living here as an immigrant, what is the prospect for your writing? Are you always going to interpret between 'here and there'? Or do you see a day when you will be Canadian, when your type of Canadian experience will be validated and accepted in the same way as that of someone born in Vancouver, the Prairies, or Newfoundland?

A: That has to do with the way the society as whole moves and changes. The problem is no longer one of two solitudes.[47] What we really have in Canada is a country of many solitudes, and I don't think a time will come when these solitudes will disappear entirely: there will always be solitudes. What can change, though, is the validation of 'there' in terms of 'here': it can happen through art. As I have said, at the moment, there are problems. Our artists are not fully appreciated: our work is still seen as exotic. *Dark Swirl* was reviewed in the *Ottawa Citizen* and trivialized. The reviewer hadn't a clue about the Caribbean. One review of *The Wizard Swami* said the novel had too many exotic characters: the caption read 'Racehorse Novel with too Many Exotic Characters'. This prompted a phone call from a man who wanted to sell me a racehorse. He had seen the review and wanted to sell me a horse for $25 000.

Q: *The Wizard Swami* is a serious novel about colonial chicanery, mimicry and corruption in the Caribbean. I see what you mean about trivializing your work.

A: But the future is not hopeless. As I have said, Canada will wrestle with our presence for the foreseeable future. Yet, sometimes when I read to an audience, even in places as far away as Alberta, I sense an acceptance or validation that has to do with the act of art itself. I should like to emphasize that it is through the artistic process of reading a poem or short story before an audience, in the very act of the work of art manifesting itself in the reading and reception of it that validation occurs. Nothing, it seems to me, can achieve this as substantially as art. You can find employment for people; but real psychic validation will not occur through that. We have to be aware of those psychic elements which are what will really make survival possible. When we are dead what will remain will be the products of our mind and imagination – our books, art and music: those are the things that could really validate our presence in this country, the fact that we lived here in the 1970s, 1980s, 1990s and beyond.

Notes

1   Sandbach Parker, a large commercial firm in Guyana, established a poetry medal as their contribution to the arts.
2   The prize is named after A. J. Seymour. See Chapter 5, note 26.
3   New Amsterdam is the chief town in the county of Berbice in Guyana.
4   For Edgar Mittelholzer, see Index.
5   *Kyk-Over-Al* was the literary magazine started by A. J. Seymour in 1945. See Chapter 5, note 26.
6   Cecile Nobriega and W. McAndrew are poets whose work appeared mainly in Guyana. McAndrew was also a specialist in Guyanese folklore.
7   Cyril Dabydeen, *Poems in Recession* (Georgetown, Guyana, 1972).
8   For Martin Carter, see Chapter 5, note 12.
9   For Naipaul, Lamming and Clarke, see Index.
10   For *Caribbean Voices*, see Chapter 4, note 2.
11   For Derek Walcott, see Index.
12   B. P. Nichol (1944–90) was an editor, novelist and experimental poet. He was a member of a sound poetry collective known as The Four Horsemen. His signature 'bp Nichol' reflected his break from more traditional styles of writing.
13   Leonard Cohen was born in 1934 and has produced several volumes of poetry, two novels, a collection of songs, plus several recordings of his songs.
14   Cyril Dabydeen, *This Planet Earth* (Borealis Press, Ottawa, 1979).
15   Sylvia Plath (1932–63) was an American poet who settled in England and married the English poet Ted Hughes. Following her suicide, her work was very much in vogue in the 1960s and 1970s.
16   Queen's University is in the town of Kingston, in Ontario.
17   See note 5 above.
18   The anthology is *A Shapely Fire: Changing the Literary Landscape* (Mosaic Press, Oakville, Ontario, 1987). It includes Canadian authors mainly of Caribbean origin.
19   The Canadian–Asian Studies Association is one of several groups or learned societies consisting mainly of university teachers. These societies hold a large, joint conference each year to present academic papers, exchange knowledge and promote research in their field.

20 Joy Kogawa is a poet and the author of *Obasan* (1981) a celebrated novel about Japanese-Canadians who were interned in Canada during the Second World War.

21 Rienzi Crusz is Sri Lankan by birth but has lived in Canada for many years. He is the author of several volumes of poetry.

22 For Dionne Brand, see Chapter 10.

23 Claire Harris was born in Trinidad and emigrated to Canada in 1966. She is a school-teacher, photographer and poet.

24 Marlene Nourbese Philip was born in Tobago in 1947 and moved to Canada in 1968. She studied law before becoming a writer. She is the author of two volumes of poetry, *Thorns* (1983) and *Salmon Courage* (1983) and other books, including *She Tries Her Tongue, 'Her Silence Softly Breaks'* (1989) and *Harriet's Daughter* (1990).

25 Moyez Vassanji was born in Tanzania in 1950. He studied physics at the Massachusetts Institute of Technology. He lives in Toronto where he is an editor and author. He is founder of *The Toronto South Asian Review*, and author of the novels *The Gunny Sack* (1989), *No New Land* (1991), *The Book of Secrets* (1994), and a collection of short stories, *Uhuru Street* (1992).

26 Rohinton Mistry was born in Bombay in 1952. He emigrated to Canada in 1972. He has written a volume of stories, *Tales from Firozsha Baag*, and a novel, *Such a Long Journey* (1991).

27 For Neil Bissoondath, see Chapter 4, note 27.

28 Arnold Itwaru was born in Guyana in 1943, and now lives in Canada. He is a poet, novelist and critic. He is the author of, among other books, *Shattered Songs* (poetry), 1982; *Body Rites* (poetry), 1991; *Shanti* (a novel), 1988 and 1990; and *The Invention of Canada: Literary Text and the Immigrant Imagination* (criticism), 1990.

29 Cyril Dabydeen, *Dark Swirl* (Peepal Tree Press, Leeds, 1989).

30 A 'Massacouraman' is a giant-sized, hairy, man-eating monster which is shaped like a man, and lives in lakes, rivers and creeks in the Guyanese hinterland where 'porknockers' or prospectors work.

31 Gerald Durrell, *Three Singles to Adventure* (Hart and Davis, London, 1954).

32 See Index for each writer.

33 See Bibliography.

34 *This Planet Earth*, pp. 41–2.

35 For Austin Clarke, see Index.

36 Name for a large type of lizard, common in Guyana coastlands. The lizard is also spelt 'salipenter' or 'salepenter'.

37 In Cyril Dabydeen, *Elephants Make Good Stepladders* (Third Eye Publications, London, Canada, 1982), p. 16.

38 *Elephants Make Good Stepladders*, pp. 26–7.

39 *This Planet Earth*, p. 70.

40 Cyril Dabydeen, *Goatsong* (Mosaic Press, Oakville, Canada, 1977).

41 In *Goatsong*, p. 16.

42 In *Goatsong*, p. 33.

43 In Cyril Dabydeen, *Still Close to the Island* (Commoner's Publishing, Ottawa, 1980).

44 Cyril Dabydeen, *The Wizard Swami* (Peepal Tree Press, Leeds, 1989).

45 The novel is set in Guyana. Devan grows up in a rural area, but eventually moves to Georgetown, the capital city.

46 David Dabydeen, *The Intended* (Secker & Warburg, London, 1991).

47 In his novel *Two Solitudes*, Hugh MacLennan describes English and French cultures in Canada as two solitudes which have so far failed to become integrated and produce national unity.

CHAPTER 10

Dionne Brand:
No language is neutral

Dionne Brand was born in Trinidad in 1953. In 1970 she emigrated to Canada, where she still lives. She studied at the University of Toronto, where she has almost completed a PhD in education. She has recently taught at the University of Guelph, in Canada. During the 1970s, she was an activist in the student movement, and the Black Education Project set up to improve educational opportunities for blacks in Toronto. She also worked in the women's movement, and in 1983, went to Grenada to work for the Agency for Rural Transformation. She witnessed the American invasion of Grenada in 1983, but returned to Canada soon afterwards. Her commitment to socialism comes through her work. She has so far produced nine books, which consist mainly of collections of poems; a volume of short stories, Sans Souci *(1988), and a non-fiction work,* Rivers have Sources, Trees have Roots – Speaking of Racism *(1986) which exposes racism in Toronto, and is co-authored by Krisantha Bhaggiyadatta. (This interview was recorded in Toronto on 15 March 1991.)*

Q: Why did you come to Canada?
A: I was 17, just out of high school. At that time everyone was migrating to Canada, as they had gone to England two decades before. I went to school in Toronto, then to the University of Toronto in 1972. I graduate with a BA in English and Philosophy.
Q: Where were you heading?
A: I had decided years ago that I was going to write. English literature was my strong subject. My uncle was a school teacher in Trinidad, and he would look particularly at our English language exercises, grammar, and things like that. He would make us do more school-work, which I enjoyed more than anybody else. More importantly, grandmother told us stories every night.
Q: Where did she get the stories from?
A: Her own past, I suppose. They were 'soucouyant' and 'la diablesse'[1] stories. She told stories about my grandfather, about her family, and what they had done.

Q: Did you read anybody like Naipaul and Selvon[2] before you came to Canada?

A: Selvon was the first Caribbean writer that I read, and he was the second writer who gave any context to where we actually lived. The other book I read was about Toussaint L'Ouverture[3] and the uprising in Haiti. It shook me, because doing history in school in the Caribbean, at the time, you didn't learn those things. Then I began to hear about African-American writers. I remember my uncle had *Giovanni's Room*,[4] but I never attempted to read it. I also read Naipaul's *The Mystic Masseur.*[5]

Q: You had a sense of yourself which we who came earlier from the Caribbean did not have.

A: I think I was lucky to be born at the time I was. I left in 1970 after the uprising in Trinidad. There was a Black Power movement, and even a Black Panther[6] party. Young people were going natural (in hairstyles), and that was a revolutionary statement. I was eager to read African-American books, and to be part of that statement.

Q: With that kind of literary background behind you, I presume you continued your reading in Toronto where more books of that kind would have been available.

A: I remember reading *Brown Girl, Brown Stones*,[7] maybe the first year I got here. Then I found Nicki Giovanni, Sonia Sanchez, Don Lee,[8] the whole range of African-American poets of the sixties. I admired their style, and tried to write like them. I went to Erindale College of the University of Toronto, and on the campus we had an African, Asian and West Indian Students Association. Through that we did a lot of agitation about racism on the campuses, and organized events. I also worked with *Spare* magazine, and began to publish poems in it.

Q: What is the publishing background of *'Fore day Morning*?[9]

A: That book had a lot to do with memories of back home – my grandmother and the place where we lived in Guayaguayare. It also came from a sense of personal loss because I was very close to my grandmother, and when she died it was a great blow. There is also sadness leaving the place where you were born; but our leaving was somehow preordained just by the conditions that we were born into. I often say that we get grown up to go away just like any other cash crop. There is a sadness about the life there not being sufficient.[10]

Q: All of us are exiles and feel a sense of loss over what we left behind; but you must have had expectations in coming here?

A: Yes. The truth is that I came to go to school and go back.

Q: So part of the pain of exile is being trapped here, not being able to go back?

A: Then I didn't want to. Gradually, I had to accept that it didn't seem as if I was going anywhere.

Q: The situation that we came from changes and makes it more and more unlikely that we will go back; it's not entirely out of choice that we keep staying here.

A: I finally decided that I don't live there, and in some ways I don't live here either; so I live between here and there.

Q: You came here young enough to be able to articulate the experience of exile in a different way from Selvon, Naipaul, Lamming[11] and the old-guard writers who had their lives formed in the Caribbean, then went abroad. To some extent, you were formed here as well.

A: I grew up here. Though aged 17, coming out of a Trinidadian house I was about 13; so my growing up happened here.

Q: The older writers had very solid memories of home to fall back on, and they mined those memories in their writing.

A: I wasn't as nostalgic, I think, as some of them might have been. I was new. Here I was being able to make connections with African-Americans. I saw great hope in that. I didn't long for home at all. I longed for a past, a kind of validation of my history, which I thought I could find in a past that was beyond my grandparents.

Q: It was not located in the Caribbean?

A: No. It was located somewhere in the consciousness of a people that had to do with slavery, that other exile.

Q: In *'Fore day Morning* there is vivid evocation of tropical scenery and landscape. You describe St Mary's Estate, which is helpful when a story about it comes up later on in *Sans Souci*.[12] There are nice memories of sucking mangoes, and taking baths under standpipes: those are fresh. Perhaps they have already faded in your mind.

A: I decided that I must leave such memories before I romanticize them too much, even though those are still the memories that I count on for much of my work up to now.

Q: But you put them in the back of your mind?

A: I try to make them real and not nostalgic. That's what I've tried to do with the images as I've used them repeatedly, to keep them new and non-nostalgic.

Q: After *'Fore day Morning* you wrote *Earth Magic*,[13] which has some fine images, but I take it that children's writing was not a line you were going to pursue.

A: No. But when I left university, I worked at a place called the Black Education Project, and saw that there was a real dearth in the school curriculum of materials that had anything to do with black children. The book is an attempt to do something about that.

Q: From *Earth Magic* you go on to *Primitive Offensive*. I see parallels between *Primitive Offensive* and *The Arrivants*.[14] Was Brathwaite an influence?

A: Not much, although I had read his work. Actually, it was Carpentier's *The Lost Steps*, and Harris's *Palace of the Peacock*[15] that helped me with those evocations.

Q: But your one-word lines and rhythms are similar to Brathwaite's, and you deal with identical subjects of loss and chaos. There is the same reach back into African origins, and an attempt to establish a connection with New World experience. You bring in South Africa and the fate of black people in the contemporary world of the 1970s and 1980s.

A: But that is so much the terrain of black poetry. I begin *Primitive Offensive* with an old woman sitting, watching. I think that it is old women and women generally who can see. Because of their position within society, they watch a lot. This old woman is trying to think of what her eyes would have seen the moment the whites approached whatever village on that continent [Africa]. The verses with her in it are much fuller, plumper, more fleshy than the later verses of not knowing what happened, of some huge tearing away which was unbelievable, and therefore without sufficient words to describe it. That's why the lines get narrow and sparse. Also it had a lot to do with the end of the Black Power movement and meeting that silence where many things were undermined. I thought I must be as terse and tight as possible.

Q: The title 'Primitive Offensive' suggests militancy. It is a post-sixties' militancy that mentions Fanon, and catches a sense of the anger and civil strife that swept American cities in the 1960s and 1970s. There is an aura of urban riots, and of the impatience and violence of people who have put up with too much for too long. But the offensive is 'primitive': there are frequent images of body parts – eyes, legs, genitals, armpits, skin, vertebrae, belly, skull, bones, etc.

A: Yes, it was out of nothing. Why do you continue to exist given this history! That is why I say 'prop up my elbows'. Prop them up so I can fight. Also, part of *Primitive Offensive* involves searching for a history. I think there's a line that says there is not an impression even in the clouds of what our history is, what we are, where we come from, or what happened?

Q: The dehumanization and erasing of a people's history?

A: And how I try to find it. I can't find the pieces. I can only find a fingernail here, something else there, small signs that don't add up. But I am desperate, and will use any sign of a past.

Q: Your musical rhymes add poignancy to your blend of loss, groping, and militancy:

> Obatala, Shango, Babalawo
> Oshun,[16]
> Tell him to go to hell,
> Tell him, his southernmost orifice,

Tell him we'll kick his ass,
Obatala, Shango, Babalawo
Oshun.   (p. 48)

But there is quite a change in your next collection of poems, *Winter Epigrams to Ernesto Cardenal in Defense of Claudia.*[17] Your interest in Ernesto Cardenal, the Nicaraguan priest, poet, Marxist and humanist identifies your ideological preferences. Roger McTair's Introduction to *Winter Epigrams* explains the connection with Claudia and Cardenal. The poems in *Winter Epigrams* are witty and ironic and carry a message; they are very readable. But why did you choose that particular form?

A: *Primitive Offensive* took me a year to write, and by the end of it I was totally depressed. *Winter Epigrams* suddenly came to me, and I wrote it in three months. I couldn't stop myself. I think it was relief from *Primitive Offensive* which had left me in such a bad mood. It's almost like seeing a death, followed by the kind of jokes you make afterwards at the wake. I needed renewing too. When I happened upon the epigram, a form that is so tight, pithy, with so much in it, I became fascinated.

Q: In *Winter Epigrams*, you criticize Toronto quite a bit:

i give you winter epigrams
because you are a liar
there is no other season here.
                          (p. 5)

Some of the images associated with winter in Toronto are quite harsh, involving starkness, freezing, wickedness, dirty clothes, depression and disease. The discomfort caused by climate is mentioned over and over again. You find it hard to live here?

A: I think it has a double meaning, that notion of winter. One meaning is the cramped, sparse way in which you have to live in a country such as this, in a large, industrialized, metropolitan city. The only thing I know about my neighbours is what I see across the way.

Q: It is the urban, cloaked-in existence that you dislike?

A: It tightens and cuts away so much of life that I often go to some other place rather than remain here waiting to live. The coldness was the fall guy for that. Just look at people's bodies during the winter, all crunched up; it does have an effect on one. This is the spot where you wait to live; you make plans. Look at the hundreds and hundreds of plans we make every day on the telephone; one is always waiting to live here.

Q: Austin Clarke's[18] characters say that Canadians are too serious; they don't laugh, and it has to do with the weather.

A: Maybe it's only us who come from some place else that can notice it;

but there is a visible, physical change in people, if you see them on the street one winter day, and then you see them on the street again on a summer day: there is an incredible change. In the summer they are perfectly willing to say 'Hello'; but I think that nine months of cold does have an effect on your soul in some way. The tightening-up of the shoulders, the sinking of the head into the coat, the sheer physical discomfort of it must have an effect.

Q: But one has to see this against the background that this place, increasingly, is your home; this is where you are living, and in the 54th epigram you say:

> comrade winter,
> look what you've done,
> I have written epigrams to you,
> e'en poems,
> can it be that . . . ?
> no, no, I am not your lover,
> perhaps . . . your enemy.
>
> (p. 18)

It seems to me that you are struggling with acceptance of this boxed-in type of living which, as you rightly say, restricts and hems you in.

A: I guess it is also what do I need from it? What do I take from that cloaking and anonymity? I have to admit finally that there must be something that I take from it. There must be some relevance, because I'm not here totally against my will. I must acknowledge that. The thing with a poem or set of poems is that if at some point you don't take account of your own contradictions, there is no use writing them.

Q: That acknowledgement is something that goes on throughout your work. At first you acknowledge the newness of Toronto; then at a later stage your approach to the city is more flexible, witty, ironic, even playful, and then perhaps it will change yet again.

A: I insist on living in the present, and taking account of what is actually happening.

Q: I thought I detected certain ideological attitudes in your earlier poetry. I don't mean that they were rigid or dogmatic, but you now seem a little more accepting than in *Primitive Offensive*, where you were intent on recovering the lost dislocation. In *Winter Epigrams* you are facing up to the adversities of life in Toronto; but the honest self-examination and critical sharpness are accompanied by anecdotal spiciness and a tone that is surprisingly good-natured, jocular, more relaxed. I don't know if it's the form of the epigram itself, or a change in your outlook that produces this quite appetizing mixture.

A: It is also significant of a quixotic place that I arrived at after writing

Primitive Offensive. The first half of the epigrams dwell on winter and the shape of living here, while the second half deal with the political or Left situations that I have become involved in, and which I look at with some irony.

Q: You are a spokesperson, I suppose, for downtrodden, third-world victims of international structures of exploitation and injustice – in particular, American imperialism and capitalism. I guess it was a gradual process of your political ideas evolving from being directed against British colonialism, specifically, to being directed against international corporate capitalism. I assume your position was Marxist?

A: Yes, I was a Marxist. I still am, despite various failures. I still believe that the people who do most of the work in the world get very few benefits, and that such inequities need to be overturned in some way. They haven't gone away just because of the present situation in the Soviet Union, or because Poland has adopted a free-market economy. General suffering, starvation, people working for low wages – those things still exist and need redress.

Q: The problems are still there, but a Marxist remedy would have less currency now because of the Soviet experience in the last year or two. More importantly, we have to acknowledge the fact of American power, especially in Caribbean and Latin American countries where it manifests itself in the Monroe doctrine,[19] an old and nakedly imperialistic policy of controlling and bullying smaller nations. When you consider how West Indian leaders have behaved, in that context, what has happened to your ideas? At the time of *Winter Epigrams* Williams[20] was in power in Trinidad, and Burnham[21] in Guyana.

A: When I wrote *Winter Epigrams* I was much more hopeful of the possibilities for people overturning those kinds of systems. I had just seen the end of the fighting in Zimbabwe. The Sandinistas were in power in Nicaragua, and Bishop was in Grenada. The wings of the American eagle hadn't clamped themselves over so much of the world as they have today. I wasn't saying that the Soviet Union had the perfect model to follow. I saw the Marxist proposition as a possibility for overturning certain kinds of capitalist systems that we experienced in Latin America or the Caribbean. How that would look – the shape of it – we could determine as we did it; but I felt that it was quite possible for a whole population to have a vision of equality, to see the possibility of living without being dominated by the kind of patronizing and patriarchal governments that we have in the Caribbean.

Q: When did you go to Grenada?

A: I went in February 1983; the invasion was in October. I went with CUSO (Canadian Universities' Service Overseas). I worked for an agency for rural transformation which looked for money for projects like the Farmer's Union; I also worked for a group called CARIPADA (Caribbean

Peoples' Development Agency) as an information officer, writing reports and publishing a newsletter.

Q: What did this Grenadian experience do to your writing, actually seeing one successful example of breaking away from unjust American domination?

A: Until the invasion I was incredibly hopeful. I kept being hopeful despite the difficult work and conditions. I must say that it was inspiring. But there were difficulties: things didn't move as fast; the telephone didn't work; the tractor didn't get up the hill. Nevertheless, what I thought I saw was a change in people's view of how much control and direction they could give to their own lives. There was some overzealousness in the progress being made, and there were some conflicts; but they don't detract from the whole process of overturning an oppressive colonial structure. I was absolutely flabbergasted by the Grenadian process of bringing in the budget, for example. It was not like in any other parliamentary democracy. Their budget didn't come down until everybody had seen it and said, 'Well, I don't think that's right.' I saw that. I sat in a room and saw old women and men, who said: 'Why are we making so much rum and not sugar?' That was really invigorating.

Q: What did you think of Maurice Bishop[22] himself?

A: He was a breath of fresh air. You know how distant government is in the Caribbean. This didn't happen. I saw people on the street, on the beach – Jackie Creft, Maurice Bishop. I saw people talking to their 'rulers' as if they were ordinary people like themselves. I had never seen that in the Caribbean.

Q: How did it (Bishop's People's Revolutionary Government) fall apart?

A: I think that they worked incredibly hard and worried a lot. The problem with the Marxist or socialist position is that it cannot offer you a lot. It can offer a kind of equality; it cannot offer excess; and also there is a tendency to want what it offers delivered immediately: it cannot offer that. That revolution lasted only four years, 1979–83; and it was trying to correct a five-hundred-year-old problem; plus it had a lot of external forces against it. It was hard for it to hold out. I think they saw that external threat, but they had their own internal demons. They were driven to make it work. The very drive to make it work was what made it backfire. It blurred some visions. They had to prove it could work in the face of all kinds of outside sanctions and aggressions. They were in an impossible situation to begin with, not because of something they could not do within the 110 square miles that was Grenada, or with the population (150 000 people) who wanted to do it. It was because of what it began to mean on the international ideological front: the revolution was much greater than them.

Q: Did they really believe that they existed in a cocoon, where they could run a socialist paradise?

A: I don't think they thought that. They had dreams which threatened American imperialism.

Q: In *Chronicles of the Hostile Sun*[23] you record your impressions of the revolution and its aftermath in Grenada. But there is a pervasive tone of scepticism, questioning, even despair. What happened to the promise of change and redress? The following untitled poem is typical:

> Presently I have a vile disposition
> it does not appreciate great sunsets
> from 'the villa' looking over the carenage,
> old fort and point salines
> not even the afternoon sun
> escapes my criticism.   (p. 29).

That sounds quite bitter. Did Grenada destroy your hope in socialist transformation?

A: That was not a great year. Here I was in Grenada with the possibility of assuaging the past in some way; and it had fallen apart. I thought, what the hell do we have to do to get redress? So in writing *Chronicles of the Hostile Sun* I was incredibly angry and terribly despairing at some points. Mighty ideas are not the same as military might.

Q: The United States has the military capacity, publicity skills, and economic strength to demonize any popular leader and give the rest of the world a good reason for removing that leader by force. Then, if necessary, they can go ahead and do it. That being the case, how can a broad coalition of socialist or well-meaning attitudes help to redress the evident imbalance of a world under American capitalist domination?

A: We don't live in great times now at all. In certain other years I had seen a glimmer of hope in what people were able to accomplish through popular movements. But I am a writer, and therefore my role at any point in the development of these events is to record them.

Q: Your current role as a recorder contrasts with the previous militancy of *Primitive Offensive*. In *Chronicles to the Hostile Sun*, what is the relationship of the writer to a situation of injustice or oppression? The following poem betrays a sense of frustration about this question:

> Someone at a party
> drew me aside to tell me a lie
> about my poems,
> they said 'you write well,
> your use of language is remarkable'
> Well if that was true, hell
> would break loose by now,
> colonies and fascist states would fall,

housework would be banned,
pregnant women would walk naked in the street,
men would stay home at night, cowering.
whoever it was, this trickster,
I wish they'd kept their damn lies
to themselves.   (p. 33)

That seems to indicate that your writing has a direct aim to redress wrongs, and you feel a sense of failure or disappointment when that does not happen.

A: Yes, but the tone is so funny: I recognize my weak spot as a writer. When I started to write I thought that writing was action and I still do; but I've come to a wry kind of look at what I think I do when I write. That's why someone at the party told me a lie about my poems. I hope that these poems do this. I know they do something else; but I put them forward anyway, just in case they do this. I put them forward as weapons. But I understand the failure of those weapons sometimes. I understand the vulnerability involved in that weaponry. But I also know that people don't like where they are now. Tyrants and tricksters can try to keep them at that place; but I feel something comes up. I'm not underestimating the weight, breadth and brutality of the American system; but it has cracks, and we have a responsibility to keep looking for those cracks.

Q: Your poetry may not succeed in redressing wrongs; but it could still serve a useful purpose in raising awareness: keeping us looking for those cracks, just keeping people alert. But what I see as your sense of disillusionment in *Chronicles* raises a particular problem; for there is a moral principle involved when you talk about goodness, justice and dignity being ground down by oppression. In one poem you say:

And rain does not rust bombers
instead it looks for weakness in farm implements
                                    (p. 45)

Since the weather favours the American invasion, it seems that even God is against the weak and oppressed.

A: That day it looked like it. The rain wouldn't come, I had lived through a month of rain, and all of a sudden when the Americans come to invade, there's this wonderful sky: the weather is perfect. To some extent my objective is to reflect even the despair. That's how it felt that day.

Q: It is consistent with your idea of acknowledging the reality: being true to yourself. But there is another aspect of telling the truth about the weak and oppressed. Caribbean communities living abroad usually show a united front when facing the common enemy of a hostile, white host community.

This unity tends to paper over the race, colour, and class divisions that separate us in the Caribbean. Maybe the issues are slightly different in the diaspora, or is it that, living abroad, you lose identification with specific Caribbean issues such as the racial problem between Indians and blacks in Trinidad and Guyana?

A: Someone asked me why there was very little reference in my work to Indians in Trinidad. The only thing I can say is that it was about the time I left Trinidad that, because of the kind of influences I had on me, I became a kind of black Nationalist who saw affinity with African-Americans, and looked for a past in Africa as really central while ignoring the past right there around me. It was silent in my writing. After all I attended Naparima High school which was about eighty per cent Indian. That was an experience that later helped me in my political organizing. It also helped me to do *Rivers have Sources, Trees have Roots – Speaking of Racism*,[24] and have a vision like that, where we interviewed South Asian aboriginals, blacks, and Chinese people.

Q: It seems our colonial divisions were too strong for many of us. Exile, for all its disadvantages, has encouraged multi-racialism and multi-ethnicity among us, and this is obviously better for both of us, for our host communities, and for the world.

A: I went home in 1979 after the United Labour Front (ULF) had taken shape with working-class solidarity between oil-field workers and cane-field workers. I felt that was a really hopeful thing. Then it disintegrated.

Q: There seems to be a gap which long residence abroad is producing in Caribbean writers. Look at someone like George Lamming: he is formed in the colonies, comes abroad, writes books, then goes back to the colonies to continue to work, not necessarily writing. He has never really left. He is unambiguously Caribbean. That's quite different from Caryl Phillips, David Dabydeen,[25] and yourself.

A: I think the long sojourn, which has turned out to be more than a sojourn, has shaped the issues as much as anything else. It shaped the topics and themes in the way that I would approach and comment on them. It has become like that because I now live in the same mental and psychological space as people in El Salvador, Trinidad, Nicaragua, etc., and those become the themes that I pursue apart from the other themes about my grandmother, childhood, or some women I knew in Trinidad. I think that has happened in ways that it would not have happened to the last generation of writers. I'll tell you what else happened to me. I go up to Soufrière in St Vincent and I meet two children playing with little bits of chalk that they find in the gutter outside of their school, and I start to play with them, and they say to me: 'Are you from town?'; and I get totally sad, because I'm not from town, and I can't describe where I'm from. That's the saddest thing that has ever happened to me. I understood that I was outside of their games, and their frame of reference. At that moment I felt I understood more than ever before where I belonged and didn't belong; and I realized that I had lived for fifteen years without those children or their jokes or laughter, as much as I had lived here for fifteen years without here too.

Q: I wonder if groups of Caribbean people in the diaspora aren't being pushed in the way that the African-Americans are. African-Americans, James Baldwin said a long time ago, are different from West Indians because West Indians are a majority in their own place and could govern themselves. African-Americans will always remain a minority in the US just as communities of the Caribbean diaspora will remain minorities in larger cultures. Perhaps all they can hope for is social justice, equal job opportunities and things like that.

A: Perhaps.

Q: If I can turn to your versification briefly, I think your technique is very effective in 'PPS Grenada' where you list familiar items that are personal enough to concretize and reinforce the practicality of the ideological issues you are advancing.

A: That's very deliberate. I try to do that because I think that's the only way you could understand.

Q: You humanize the ideology in quite a natural way. I noticed in *'Fore day Morning* that your poems were fixed and rigid, not entirely perhaps; but the forms seemed to be worked at in a more deliberate, self-conscious way. Here in *Chronicles* they're looser and more flexible: you've developed an idiom. You are writing much more easily and confidently without aiming at special effects, or revealing that you are doing so.

A: By the time I reached *Chronicles*, I realized I could say anything and just keep going, and it would work.

Q: I regard *Chronicles* as probably the pivotal work in your development as a poet. From here on, it seems, your writing does not have to be pre-planned. The result is quite eloquent, at any rate, to a reader who shares your ideological preferences.

A: All of a sudden I realized that I could put anything into verse, unlike earlier when I thought it had to be just so.

Q: That's quite evident. Now you seem to have the confidence to take on almost anything, and present it with movement, rhythm and fluency. You achieve this, for instance, in the untitled and unpunctuated passage in *Chronicles* which runs for one-and-a-half pages (pp. 67–8). It looks like continuous prose, but has no punctuation except for a full stop at the very end. Is that a poem, or prose poetry, or poetic prose? It doesn't matter. It works. Since you've written so much more poetry than prose, I assume you prefer to be known as a poet. This is why I was struck by the great success of your stories in *Sans Souci* which reveal a surprisingly mature control of character, speech idioms and the creation of dramatic situations. 'Blossom,

Priestess of Oya, Goddess of winds, storms and waterfalls' is an excellent story. You have captured Blossom's speech idiom and personality perfectly. Everything about her matches, and the story flows.

A: What I was trying to do with 'Blossom' was to write in the Caribbean language, giving it a seriousness because generally the language tends to be used a lot in humour, as opposed to really describing our life. I wanted to let Blossom go through everything in her life in that language.

Q: You capture the full actuality of her situation within an urban, metropolitan context that is alien to her habits and preferences. Yet she has the strength to come out and do something about it. You describe all that with a certain power and rightness that are totally convincing. That brings us to the subject of women.

A: That story is based on fact: I met this woman running a basement speakeasy in her house, and she had run the speakeasy for years and years. She was a Jamaican woman without a single tooth in the front of her mouth, and she would throw people out who were drunk. Also one day I saw an old man xeroxing something. I thought I'd read over his shoulder and it was all these little potions he was preparing for people. He was an obeah[26] man and that was obeah gone modern tech. It's interesting how our people could come here and adapt things that used to work for them somewhere else so that they work for them here too.

Q: That illustrates Caribbean initiative and ingenuity, a will to resist and survive; but one reason why I revel in a story like 'Blossom' is that I know the language. I wonder how a Canadian audience would react, and what you thought about your audience when you were writing your stories.

A: I've gotten used to so much since my childhood. I've gotten used to Shakespeare and Chaucer. They can get used to it, I thought. The woman has integrity; the language has integrity, and it can be learned and understood; and I just did it. That story came very quickly because a lot of it depends on its flow and rhythm, so that as soon as it started it just kept going.

Q: It does not appear doctored at all. It appears to have come out spontaneously, but again I wonder about a Canadian audience's reaction to the Creole idiom.

A: I've read it to Canadian audiences, and no one walked out. But I stopped getting concerned with the audience that we face here. I decided that all of what I was describing was perfectly human and understandable, and that if people wanted to they'd find out about it.

Q: I revel also in 'St Mary's Estate' (pp. 43–51). You were earlier saying something negative about nostalgia, but these recollections of your childhood are so true to life. 'My grandfather had children and outside women and outside children' (p. 46). The character-sketches, an observation of the landscape, flora, fauna, and activities all ring true. Is it not dangerous artistically, to ignore or depreciate the validity of the circumstances out of which we came?

A: Nostalgia is different from memory. Memory doesn't lie.

Q: In 'Photograph' (pp. 53–78) you talk about the grandmother who raised you. She was a powerful woman almost as self-possessed as Jamaica Kincaid's mother.

A: That also just wrote itself. I got the beginning lines: 'My grandmother has left no trace, no sign of herself' (p. 53). The sound of it just kept going, and I kept writing, every once in a while referring to the photograph, never having a photograph of her, but having a memory which adds up to such a photograph. I remember building the memory and then remembering there was no photograph.

Q: In your stories the women have a certain resilience. The men come and go, like Victor in 'Blossom', but the women go on apparently forever. Is that particularly Caribbean? Was it part of your family? You talk about your mother going abroad and coming back while you stayed with your grand-mother.

A: It's very much what I saw in my family, and what I saw in the other families on MacGillvray Street. When I worked on the black Education Project here in Toronto, I saw so many women with children here, all on their own, working all kinds of shifts, with the children having to stay home by themselves, always in the position of having to figure it all out.

Q: Women do take the brunt of things?

A: Oh God, yes. I saw that all the time. My family is full of women. My grandfather went to the rum shop, while my grandmother had twelve children.

Q: Was your grandmother a dominant figure?

A: She may not have thought so, but she certainly influenced me. When I meet other women writers, be they Caribbean or African-American, that is one of the commonalities that I'm struck by, the presence of women. Can you say that for example of Earl Lovelace's women?[27] He has several women characters but somehow I never find them drawn in their fullness.

Q: I don't see the women in Lovelace's fiction taking on special roles; the men are always doing something usually with bravado and panache.

A: The *subject* in his work is not women, even though they are there.

Q: I should think this is true for West Indian writing in general. Is it not dominated by male writers?

A: It's not just dominated by male writers but dominated by themselves as subject in it, despite the evidence of their own lives. Many people grew up in families like mine. The image of one of my aunts, one kid on her arm, one at her waist and one at her dress-tail was an image that I will always see. I always see that woman walking down Caribe Street in San Fernando and that image will always guide me in some way.

Q: You almost wonder what women here are complaining about.

A: Although that was a sign of resilience and forbearance and strength, it wasn't a sign of power. That's what they were missing. They could forbear, uphold, or be strong; they could try to find ways out of their difficult situation, and control their internal lives; but the power to absolutely burst out of that wasn't there.

Q: Feminists here are calling for a change in traditional power relations. I assume that you regard your writing as feminist.

A: Absolutely.

Q: I know a young woman who is doing research into your writing. It's your feminism that attracts her, and she is going to interpret your writing by applying contemporary feminist theories to it. But you write from direct experience. Are you articulating feminist theory, or what life was for you and others around you?

A: I know how theory tends to feed on itself; but I come from some place, and it's the place that I try to keep close to, both with my Marxism and feminism. What I think I saw in Blossom was that although she had little control over some things around her, she was gradually taking control. She was heading willy-nilly into some way of holding herself together. I see women doing that every day, and I think I've got to write that down.

Q: That's new; it doesn't exist in previous West Indian writing: the kind of women who drink, socialize openly and are completely frank about their sexuality.

A: But I grew up with those women; my aunts were those women. My aunts had big loud laughs. I am not saying that they conquered life, or that life was beautiful for them or anything; but I saw them wrestle with it, and I wanted to describe that wrestling. I saw one woman here, who had a man for whom she became pregnant, but he had once beaten her up so badly that she lost consciousness. She did not call the police, because she would have been arrested and deported. She got up, took the subway and went home. I see incredible things like that, every day, and I want to write about them.

Q: I want to compare your story about the black girl travelling on the train to Montreal and being called 'Nigger Whore' with 'Sketches in Transit . . . Going Home',[28] which describes West Indian immigrants in Canada travelling on a plane going back to visit the West Indies. The second story seems wholly successful, with sharply-etched vignettes of each character and his/her situation, as well as a clear contrast between the reality of that situation and the fantasy-life of each character. It is a tragic contrast that never explicitly mentions racism, or colonialism, or injustice, as the culprit responsible for the contrast; but there is no doubt of this in the reader's mind, while 'Train to Montreal' protests a little too much about racism and discrimination and loses poignancy as a result.

A: You might be right about 'Train to Montreal', but an experience does not always come deeply-shaded.

Q: Obviously the incident bothered you, because you mention it in three separate pieces of your writing.

A: It happened, and I thought, I'm going to write about that man.

Q: It depends on what you want your art to do. After all you're a political activist and feminist as well. For your most recent collection of poems, *No Language is Neutral*,[29] you've taken the title from Derek Walcott's *Midsummer*.[30] In *No Language is Neutral* you write seemingly in long prose paragraphs. You mix Creole with Standard English. You dispense with stanzaic divisions. You seem to be inventing your own form as you go along. You have such control over language that you are able to do anything.

A: Yes, I now have control as in 'PPS Grenada'. I can go in and out of both languages. In *No Language is Neutral* I am also trying to be explicit about my sexuality. Just like writing in Creole, I thought that it had to wait until I could do it really well, because lesbian sexuality is either not represented at all, or very badly represented by heterosexuals. I wanted to express how tender and gentle it was, but I had to wait until I had the words to do it with. My coming out is like my coming out in poetry now. I have found refuge in other lesbian writers like Adrienne Rich,[31] whose 'Twenty-one Love Poems' is a beautiful piece of work on love between women. It took an enormous amount of literature to accomplish our oppression, not just as lesbians, but also as women. We have to produce an enormous amount of literature to do the opposite. Until now, I have looked at black and working-class women's lives. Now I'm dealing explicitly with lesbian sexuality. Black lesbian writers like Cheryl Clarke or Audre Lorde[32] have given daring voice to our experience. It's daring to want to come out in a culture – black culture – that's basically under siege. It's a great responsibility. I can't leave those women out there alone taking on that responsibility; it's time for me to come out in my work, too.

Q: I see militancy in *No Language is Neutral*, for instance, in 'Blues Spiritual for Mammy Prater'[33] where you celebrate the memory of an ex-slave woman whose patience pays off. There is a definite spirit of resistance and defiance in the poem. But it is a sober militancy.

A: Maybe it's more steadfast. Some of the other poems may be forgotten, but I have faith that this one will survive, because this woman sits and survives for one hundred and fifteen years waiting for a photograph.

Q: I think you've come through, both technically and ideologically, to a position of great maturity and poise. You've found a voice that lets you interpret your experience smoothly and openly, without special pleading, anxiousness or self-doubt.

A: I think for me the voice is now unshakable: it can say anything it wants, with certainty.

Notes

1   A 'soucouyant' is a female vampire or 'Ol Higue' (See Chapter 7, note 24) who can turn into a ball of fire at night, and suck the blood of her victims. She sheds her skin at daybreak, and if it is salted she cannot re-enter it without dying.

    'La diablesse' or 'bride of the dead' is a notorious creature of the night, attractively attired in fancy clothes and a hat. At the end of one leg can be seen a Satanic cloven foot. She solicits male company and invites her victims to her home where she can lead them into disaster.

2   See Index for Naipaul and Selvon.

3   François Dominique Toussaint (1743–1803) was an African slave who in 1800 helped to liberate the French Caribbean colony of St Dominique (Haiti today) from French rule. In 1801, Napoleon Bonaparte sent a new army under General Leclerc to retake St Dominique. Through treachery, Toussaint was arrested and imprisoned in France where he died. C. L. R. James's classic *Black Jacobins* is a biography of Toussaint. See Chapter 2, note 17.

4   James Baldwin, *Giovanni's Room* (Dial Press, New York, 1956).

5   V. S. Naipaul, *The Mystic Masseur* (André Deutsch, London, 1957).

6   The Trinidad Black Panther party modelled itself on the American Black Panthers. (See Chapter 8, note 10.) They were part of a Black Power movement whose members formed the National Joint Action Committee and led a demonstration against the trial, in Canada, of Trinidad students who were accused of conspiring to burn down the computer centre at Sir George Williams University, in Montreal. The climax came in April 1970 when three-quarters of the Trinidad and Tobago regiment under Lt Rex La Salle revolted. A state of emergency was declared, and the revolt (or uprising) suppressed when Venezuela and the US sent arms and ammunition to the government of Trinidad and Tobago.

7   See Introduction, note 4.

8   Nikki Giovanni was born Cornelia in Knoxville, Tennessee, in 1945. She is a poet and author who first achieved fame in the 1960s as a black activist and feminist. She has lectured widely in universities in Europe and the US.

    Sonia Sanchez was born in 1934 in Birmingham, Alabama. Black herself, she has been professor of black literature and creative writing in several universities, and is the author of many volumes of poetry and plays.

    Don Lee was born in 1942, in Little Rock, Arkansas. He is a Black poet, essayist and university professor who now writes under the Swahili pen-name of Haki Madhubuti.

9   Dionne Brand, *'Fore day Morning* (Khoisan Artists, Toronto, 1978).

10   Cf. Chapter 8, note 44, and Cyril Dabydeen's notion of 'here and there' in Chapter 9.

11   See Index for Selvon, Lamming and Naipaul.

12   Dionne Brand, *Sans Souci* (Wallace-Williams, Toronto, 1988).

13   Dionne Brand, *Earth Magic* (Kids Can Press, Toronto, 1979).

14   Dionne Brand, *Primitive Offensive* (Williams-Wallace, Toronto, 1982).

    Edward Brathwaite, *The Arrivants – A New World Trilogy* (Oxford University Press, London, 1973). Cf. Chapter 2, note 2.

15   For Carpentier, see Chapter 4, note 16. Carpentier's *The Lost Steps* was published in 1953), and translated into English in 1956.

    For Harris, see Introduction, note 7.

16 Obatala, Shango, Balawo, and Oshun are deities of the pantheon of Yoruba belief practised in Nigeria, and other West African countries. Survivals of Yoruba worship also exist in Trinidad and other parts of the West Indies.

17 Dionne Brand, *Winter Epigrams* (Williams-Wallace, Toronto, 1983).

18 See Austin Clarke's novel *Storm of Fortune*.

19 The Monroe doctrine takes its name from James Monroe (1758–1831), 5th President of the US, who made a policy statement to Congress on 2 December 1823, outlining international spheres of interest. European interests were confined to Europe, and the US regarded itself as the dominant power in the Americas. But this policy did not originate with President Monroe, and it has been reasserted and adapted by several succeeding American Presidents. It can therefore be taken as a broad statement of American foreign policy, which means that small or weak countries, for example, in Latin America and the Caribbean, cannot implement policies of their own if they don't meet the approval of the US.

20 For Dr Eric Williams, see Chapter 2, note 22.

21 For Burnham, see Chapter 1, note 13.

22 Maurice Bishop (1944–83) was leader of the New Jewel Movement, a political party which was formed in 1973, and came to power in Grenada in 1979, after a coup that ousted Eric Gairy's régime. Bishop became Prime Minister in the People's Revolutionary Government that succeeded Gairy, but he was killed by the People's Revolutionary Army on 19 October 1983, following a split in his government. One week later, Grenada was invaded by American troops. Dionne Brand is expressing her admiration of the People's Revolutionary Government.

23 Dionne Brand, *Chronicles of the Hostile Sun* (Williams-Wallace, Toronto, 1984).

24 Dionne Brand, *Rivers Have Sources, Trees Have Roots – Speaking of Racism* (Cross Cultural Community Centre, Toronto, 1986). The book was co-authored with Krisantha Bhaggiyadatta and describes the experience of several racial minorities in Toronto. Brand's association with Indians in Trinidad helped her to get on with her Sri Lankan co-author.

25 See Index for Phillips and Dabydeen.

26 Obeah consists of spiritual and religious practices and ritual which are part of the cultural inheritance that slaves brought from West Africa to the Caribbean between the sixteenth and nineteenth centuries. These practices take different forms in different Caribbean territories, e.g. Voodoo in Haiti.

27 See novels by Earl Lovelace, for example, *The Dragon Can't Dance* (André Deutsch, London, 1979); and *While Gods are Falling* (Collins, London, 1965). Also Cf. Lorna Goodison's comments on women fighting back in Chapter 12.

28 'Train to Montreal', in *Sans Souci*, pp. 15–30; 'Sketches in Transit . . . Going Home', in *Sans Souci*, pp. 131–45.

29 Dionne Brand, *No Language is Neutral* (Coach House Press, Toronto, 1990).

30 Derek Walcott, *Midsummer* (Farrar, Straus, and Giroux, New York, 1984).

31 Adrienne Rich was born in 1929 in Baltimore, Maryland. She is a distinguished feminist poet, writer and academic and the author of numerous volumes of poetry, essays and plays.

32 Cheryl Clarke was born in 1947, in Washington, DC. She is black and the author of several volumes of poetry. She is a member of the collective of *Conditions*, a feminist journal.

   Audre Geraldine Lorde was born in New York City in 1934. She is a black poet, novelist, librarian and university professor with many books to her credit.

33 In *No Language is Neutral*, p. 17.

CHAPTER 11 | Jamaica Kincaid: From Antigua to America

Jamaica Kincaid was born in Antigua in 1949. In 1976 she emigrated to the US where she became a staff writer on The New Yorker *magazine. Some of her contributions to* The New Yorker *form the basis of her first book, a collection of stories,* At the Bottom of the River *(1983). This was followed by the novels* Annie John *(1985) and* Lucy *(1990), and the travel book* A Small Place *(1988). In less than ten years Kincaid's literary reputation has blossomed, until she has come to be regarded as probably the most important West Indian woman writing today. Her fiction uses varied techniques from those of conventional social realism to symbolism, allegory, and the more convoluted techniques of magical realism. Kincaid's main characters tend to be women, and she is regarded as a spokesperson for women. (This interview was recorded in North Bennington, on 16 February 1991.)*

Q: I believe you came to America in 1965. Why here and not England?
A: It wasn't a deliberate choice, but it was one of those accidents in which there was a choice.
Q: Yet in *Annie John*[1] which I regard as a novel, the fictional heroine goes to England. Why did you think, imaginatively, that you had to make the main character go to England and not America?
A: Because that is what people where she came from did. The girl's whole life was very much connected to Europe, and Europe was England; so it would make no sense to suddenly have her go to America. It would be inexplicable unless I meant to explain a lot more than I wanted. The book is true in some way to my own life. But it's also true to other things – to a path that my own life did not take. The path my own life took would require another book.
Q: I don't think before now, that I've encountered any author quite like you in Caribbean literature in English. In the 1950s, there was an expectation that Caribbean literature would record different or exotic customs, colonial phenomena that would interest British publishers. Such literature was then criticized for being mainly of sociological, historical and perhaps political interest. It did not involve deep psychological studies.[2] What I find with your work is that although it deals with the West Indian environment,

and the real day-to-day circumstances of living there, it is primarily about people. No one can say that *Annie John* has no psychology: it is there; and it goes deep and wide.

A: I think that the Caribbean people I knew, Antiguans, are like that. They are deeply psychological people. I had nothing but a public school education in the West Indies. I have no academic credentials whatsoever. The thing that I have is what anyone from my background had – English literature – of which I read a great deal when I was little. I always loved books, but I think that if there is anything different about me, it is that I do not have to, or want to please an English audience, or an English colonial audience. I think the major thing for me was that I came to America; and not England, or Canada; and that it was not required of me to behave in some way. When you are in America you can invent yourself. I was able to figure out a voice for myself that had nothing to do with where I went to school, or with what I was born to, or where I came from. That I came from a colony was of no interest to Americans. That I came from people who were peasants, poor people, was of no interest to anyone: only what I had to say. Nothing about me was important: only what I could do right now.

Q: How different would your achievement have been had you gone to England?

A: It's quite possible it would not have existed at all. I cannot imagine that if I had gone to England, I would have become one-half of the person that I've become. It's just sheer luck on the one hand; and yet that luck must have had behind it, some kind of consciousness, or choice, because people aren't just lucky. You make your luck, as they say. One of the things that I think is an important quality in someone from places such as I am from is anger. You cannot express anger at your historical situation in these places. There isn't anything about us, any reflection about our past that England or places like that used to accept. I think it's an interesting path that V. S. Naipaul cut out for himself. He's a wonderful writer. The tragedy is that he had to learn to loathe what he came from, and to look at it in an untruthful way; but truthful for the people he's grown to love, those he now most admires, and whose civilization, he thinks, is the only one worth inventing. I think that the rest of us were somehow not able to do that, and for some of us it ended in defeat.

Q: Much of what you say about Naipaul's self-hatred has been said by Andrew Salkey about Mittelholzer.[3] Mittelholzer was a sick man. His psychology was wrong.

A: You see it in Naipaul's face – the inner loathing. I imagine him being the sort of person who, when he comes across his reflection, thinks that that cannot be what he looks like, because he must somehow think he looks like an Englishman. I know what I had to leave behind when I began to write, and when I began to look at what I was facing as a writer. I had to come to

terms with where I came from – who I was. I had to face the little I came
from. However benighted or low it was, it was mine; I would be nothing if
I hated it. And when you talk about that psychology, it isn't anything I read;
we are like that: we are complicated and rich in psychological development.
I don't say that out of false pride; it feels true to me.

Q: Fiction can't lie. *Annie John* confirms what you are now saying.

A: Fiction can't lie?

Q: No. Because you would recognize the lie straight away. It wouldn't fit
into the rest of the fiction. In spite of what you say though, *A Small Place*[4]
seems to reproduce many of the insights of *The Middle Passage*[5] which is
still considered to be a destructive book. It is the Naipaul book that set West
Indians most ablaze with anger. And that was 1960. Of course, there are
differences, but the insides of each book are pretty much the same, in the
sense that both *The Middle Passage* and *A Small Place* describe a small
country which has been despoiled by centuries of colonial exploitation,
with the result that it's left with a people who now exploit themselves. The
power of recovery is absent from both books.

A: I read *The Middle Passage* after I had written *A Small Place*. As I have
said, I think Naipaul really is a great writer, and I don't flatter myself to
think that there are any similarities between his book and mine; but I would
say that the difference between Naipaul and myself is that I am not ashamed
either of anything that has happened in the place I come from, or of the
things that have been done by the people I come from. I suppose the most
vivid thing I remember from *The Middle Passage* is how Naipaul despised
the black people getting on the train, going towards Southampton to take the
boat; he even used the shape of a black man's bottom to denounce him. It
was so racial. On the whole, people behave badly if they can get away with
it. I think that it's not entirely your fault if you are conquered. It's one of
those things that could go either way from time to time; and from time to
time, you find yourself in either position as a human being. It seems deeply
wrong, for example, to denounce white people as genetically racist. It seems
to me that they are only behaving the way they behave because they are in
positions of power that enable them to get away with such behaviour. I wish
that people with power could say, 'I'm just not going to do it this way. I'm
going to try to figure out a better way.' By not relying on such criteria as
race, class and wealth, we wouldn't get the inequities which lead to incredible disruption and damage that can never be mended. Then it filters down
to individuals in this destructive way. Someone like Naipaul is very destructive. He does a lot of harm to himself and to us. I may not be as good a
writer, but I feel I have a larger view than he does.

Q: I agree with the claim of a larger vision in *A Small Place*, where I see
you noting terrible inadequacies, deficiencies and deformities with grief,
whereas in *The Middle Passage* they are flung at the reader in some passion.

Truth is there in both cases, I think; but the tone is different. In your case, it's a reluctant acknowledgement of human wrongdoing, whereas in Naipaul's book there is an almost triumphant sense of discovery in nailing the wrong-doer.

A: But these things about wrongdoing have to be said. Yet there is one thing that I have against writers from our part of the world: they are very political: they respond to past hurts, but don't hold the people who live in their homelands accountable enough. There is a great deal to be said against American domination in our part of the world, as there was against Euro-pean domination. It's very painful. Still, we have to hold the people who rule us accountable. They are worse in some ways, because although it hurts to be betrayed by a stranger, when you are betrayed by someone close to you, it's more painful. A country like Trinidad was robbed blind of its oil wealth by its rulers.[6] The kind of violence that now occurs in these places never took place before Independence. We all longed for Independence, believing that if we could be free of colonialism we might have a chance for some kind of interesting life. It's only gotten worse, and we have done it. In a very short period of time life has deteriorated disastrously.

Q: If I were to classify Caribbean writers by age groups, I would see three groups, beginning with De Lisser, James, De Boissière and Claude McKay[7] in the pre-Second World War period; then jumping to the better-known group of postwar writers such as Mittelholzer, Selvon, Lamming, Naipaul,[8] and others; I would place you in a third group of writers who became known in the 1970s or after. But classification by age is not exact because people like Austin Clarke and Earl Lovelace[9] would straddle the second and third groups. It is not age so much that places you in the third group, but Independence. Independence came in the 1960s, and the best writing of the second group – people like Selvon and Lamming – deals with pre-Independence experience. These writers were looking ahead to an expecta-tion of Independence curing the ills of colonialism. I think you have had a chance to look at the post-Independence experience which these writers did not have. Lamming, for instance, was an excellent observer of issues surrounding colonialism and the promise of Independence; but once Independence came, Lamming became silent in fiction. Perhaps other inter-ests preoccupied him. Certainly he has been very active with the labour union movement in the Caribbean in recent years. But Lamming is best remembered for his brilliant analysis of the damaging effects of colonial-ism, and the political strategies[10] that preceded Independence in the Carib-bean. I wonder if those pre-Independence issues stimulated his imagination in a way that post-Independence issues did not.

A: Lamming upbraided me in Miami recently because he was saying some things he admired about Fidel Castro and I found them disturbing. I admire the revolutionary Castro, but that's where I stop. Cuba sells vaccine to Brazil. Cubans have things about them that you can admire. But at what cost? As a writer, I cannot admire them very much. There is the question of freedom that's essential to a writer – freedom to think. When you know about what people who are writing have gone through in Cuba, it is just impossible to say some of the things Lamming was saying about Fidel Castro.[11] So I said that. And it was hard to do so because we were in Miami, and the people who are opposed to Castro in Miami are so hideous, you don't want to agree with them on anything. But I just thought I couldn't let it go, and Lamming gave me a real dressing-down. But it was the way he did it, and the language in which he did it. It was the old language of rebellion. But that is finished, you know – rebelling against the great United States. The rebellion is not against the United States, it is about the things that the powerful United States can do and does do: that is what one is against. Lamming was still fighting that battle of Independence.

Q: When you think of Lamming growing up in Barbados, and dedicating himself to fight colonialism, can you imagine how he felt when Castro ousted Batista?[12] It was a new dawn. How then could Castro do anything wrong? But I realize that power can corrupt.

A: That is what was so disturbing. He read something from his work, and it felt as if it was coming from someone with a closed mind. Lamming's writing is very closed and it's done in nineteenth-century patriarchal language.

Q: I regard *In the Castle of My Skin*[13] as a great novel, a classic work of fiction.

A: It's great! But that language is one of the things I rebelled against. I could not have done so if I had gone to England. I would not have been able to see how to do it. Once I came to America, I could rebel against that voice, and that way of looking at the world; that is the patriarchal nineteenth-century English view which is very grand and wonderful. But I did not have to accept it. I could write in a voice that was my own. I could invent a voice, and have it accepted as mine.

Q: The first feature that defines your writing for me is its dealing with issues typical of the post-Independence generation. A second feature is your voice as a woman.

A: I was interested in your list of writers,[14] and the different generations, and I noticed that there wasn't one woman among them.

Q: I think there are historical reasons bound up in a whole colonial-feudal-patriarchal nexus of the Caribbean that might account for that.

A: Are Paule Marshall and Rosa Guy considered Caribbean?[15]

Q: They illustrate the problems of the classification thrown up by immigration and exile. There is now another category of writers whom we should call diaspora or Fourth Stage writers. This is a third feature that defines your writing – that it comes from the Caribbean diaspora, that is to say, communities of Caribbean immigrants living outside the Caribbean, especially in Britain, Canada and America. These diaspora writers may be distinguished from the earlier writers of exile such as Selvon, Carew, Naipaul, Salkey, etc. in that their formative years are significantly shaped by living abroad. This is not true for Selvon and company, certainly not in their early work, although it may become more true in their later work.

A: I'm not sure that 'diaspora' is the right term for the writers you describe. I consider myself Caribbean. I am a citizen of Antigua, and I live here because it would be hard for me to live there and work. I made myself into a sort of an exile. It wasn't intentional. It's one of those things that I realized I was doing as I was doing it, and when the time came for me to become an American citizen, I didn't. I will never become an American citizen. So I don't consider myself a diaspora writer.

But we don't come from a culture that values us, and we don't know what else to do with ourselves. It would not be at all impossible that if I went to Antigua I could get killed. One of the things I noticed about writers who live there, and one of the reasons why I do not live there, is that you become very involved in politics, and you no longer write. Your creative energies are taken up with the political situation. Merle Hodge[16] is an incredible example of this: she organizes women's groups in Trinidad. This is good; but it will never come to as much as her writing would come to. It will never touch as many people.

Q: Yes, the political interest of your fiction is not uppermost. *Annie John* is a wonderful novel. I found Annie's relationship with her mother very moving and realistic, so I don't think the novel is limited in appeal to women only. I found the mother figure particularly striking. She was no doubt based on your own mother?

A: My mother is a very, very great woman; but her position, history, success, plus her own limitations conspired to keep her where you see her now. Within all of that is a person who is an empire unto herself. I often think of her as a civilization now in its decline. When I knew her as a child, she was in her great reign, her full flowering. But when you meet her now, you can see, as somebody in *The Pirates of Penzance* says, 'the remains of a great woman in her'.[17] She has never really done anything other than have me and three other children.

Q: She's inspired marvellous writing.

A: It's from my mother that I got to love literature. When I was seven years old, she gave me a copy of the *Oxford English Dictionary* for my birthday. She had taught me to read when I was three-and-a-half years old, and she was very proud of me that I liked to read. I used to sit and read the words in the dictionary starting at 'A'. Early on, I neglected things that my mother thought were important and would spend my time reading, and we would have enormous fights over this devotion I had for books. At one point it seems to have had a bad influence on my character because I would steal money to buy books, or I would steal books. I used to have all these books under our house. They were books that no one could see because they were stolen, or I had bought them with money that I had stolen. And my mother had left me with my three brothers. I was supposed to do some work, help clean up the house or something, while she was gone. I started to clean and then I came across a book and I couldn't put it down. When I looked up later, I realized my mother would soon be home, and I had done absolutely nothing. I started to do things and she could see that I had not done anything but had instead been reading a book, and it put her into such a rage that she got all the books that I had. She searched and searched and reached under the house, and took all my books and burned them. She was recently talking to me in this kitchen, and something happened, and I remembered the flames. I don't know if you remember how fire looks in the sun in that climate – a kind of red flame. I had forgotten this story until she was here recently. It must have happened not long before I left home – I remember the great sadness, because books were the only things I knew and loved, and I did not know what would replace them. I didn't know what else to love. It was a significant moment. I'd quite possibly spend the rest of my life trying to write the books that were taken away from me then. I've written four so far.

Q: This story of your mother in its domestic context has the paradoxical quality of a great love story, of love being mixed up with hate. Oscar Wilde, in the 'The Ballad of Reading Gaol',[18] says that each man kills the thing he loves, and each man has to die. That inextricable ambiguous love/hate generates, fortifies and sustains the mother–daughter relationship in *Annie John*.

A: I don't know if it's true for women, or just true for me, but my development as a writer has very much to do with my personal psychology. It dawned on me that in figuring out the relationship between the girl and her mother, and observing the power of the mother, and eventually her waning authority, that it was leading me to a fictional view of the larger relationship between where I come from and England. I must have consciously viewed my personal relationship as a sort of prototype of the larger, social relationship that I witnessed. I can feel myself intellectually going towards this way of looking at these things, which is to say, I'm trying to look at power without the dressing of my mother and me, or mother and daughter. I want to look at just how it is the powerful and powerless exist.

Q: So from that personal relationship between parent and child, you have begun to see the old colonial relationship in terms of parent-power and child-powerlessness. But it also applies to the world at large, because the United States exercises similar kinds of colonial or parent-powers over

Latin America and the Caribbean, for instance, where the Monroe doctrine[19] is still applied by a stern parent keeping unruly children in line. Then there is the Persian Gulf war.

A: Don't get me started. I have strong feelings on that.

Q: We'll leave it out. What about the role of obeah[20] and the supernatural in your work? I come from Guyana where obeah flourished.

A: I remember Guyana as a real centre for obeah. Guyana and Haiti, were places back home that were more powerful for obeah than other places.

Q: As you know, West Africans have a more direct relationship with the spirit world – the world of the ancestors – than Europeans; and much of that survived in the Caribbean despite all the fracture of colonialism over three centuries. The mother in *Annie John* uses obeah. Was Christianity married to it?

A: Yes. My mother was a good example of this. She always did both. Sometimes she was in this world, and sometimes she was in another. She grew up in a household that was quite split. Her mother was a complete pagan, and her father was a Christian. When she lost her brother, her father insisted on medicine, unlike her mother. These people go back and forth because they know others who practised only one system, and succumbed. I myself will take penicillin, but I have no problem with people who believe in both. I grew up knowing a girl who was slapped because she was possessed.

Q: Does the fact of the borders of reality being quite fluid in the world in which you grew up have anything to do with your fictional technique, especially in *At the Bottom of the River*?[21]

A: Yes, I come from a culture that moves back and forth very easily. One culture abandoned them, and the one that conquered them didn't let them in; so they were on the border all the time. From time to time, they found things to embrace in the culture that wouldn't let them in. The culture that abandoned them still offered them the deepest cultural and spiritual nourishment. People who were Christian or embraced the European culture had a great deal of pain. They seemed unfree, uptight. They were always rich, always the most prosperous; but there wasn't too much about them that was joyful. It seemed to come at enormous sacrifice, and many people just abandoned the European or Western idea – most people, actually. One of the things that is so wrong about the West Indies is that we abandoned a lot of ideas from the Western world that wouldn't let us in.

Q: As I have already said, I think *Annie John* is a particularly successful novel. Apart from its profound psychological study of female relationships, of oppression, and of people generally, it ends with as great poignancy as I've found in almost any other novel. How did you work out the technique for the ending of *Annie John*? Was there a particular model that you used to make Annie's journey to catch the boat, and as she walks along, to notice all the familiar landmarks, and reminders of familiar experiences? The drama it creates is overpowering; it wrenches your heart out, and brings tears. Then you leave, perhaps never to return.

A: I have to say that I was quite heartbroken when I was actually leaving Antigua. I was 16. I had no idea that I would write. I'd never wanted to be a writer. I didn't know that people wrote, or that it was possible for a person like me from my background or complexion to ever do such a thing. I remember leaving and feeling that this place, this situation had tried to squeeze the life out of me, and that I was going to live. I didn't know how; the possibilities were extremely narrow; I was going off to be a servant, a caretaker of children, and possibly get an education, possibly become a nurse, possibly something else. But essentially, no one really cared if those things happened. What they cared about was that I help my family. They meant that once I got out I should send money home and support my family.

Q: The leave-taking of the heroine of *Annie John* may be usefully compared with other leave-takings in Caribbean literature, for instance in *In the Castle of My Skin* and Naipaul's *Miguel Street.*[22] Lamming's ending is closer to *Annie John*'s. Typically, Naipaul's is more distanced. But all three leave-takers are young Caribbean people struggling to cope with their inner convulsions of leaving the place and people that shaped them forever.

A: I am interested in telling the truth. When I was a child I had a good memory, which was considered admirable until I began to remember things that no one else wanted to remember; then it became an accusation. Nothing would pass by me. Someone would repeat something we both witnessed, leaving out things that I would fill in. As I got older, it wasn't a joke anymore. People began to say: 'Oh, you remember all those old times stories.' My mother still says that to me. But what I remember is not an old times story: it's the truth. It is ironic that I was also accused of being a liar as a child. I now consider that what I must have been doing was to try and protect my privacy. I was a great liar. But it turns out that I'm the person who remembers what really happened, and who's not afraid to say what really happened. To myself, this is the reality of our life and not just my personal life, but the lives we all live as a society. People do not like it – Antiguans, especially the ones living here will say: 'It's true but did she have to tell everybody?'

Q: It is common for oppressed groups or those who suffer discrimination to feel that their writers are giving away their secrets, and thus making them more vulnerable to their enemies.

A: You can't free yourself unless you know what really happened, unless you can face what really happened. You have to tell the truth.

Q: I see your truth-telling ability demonstrated very effectively in *Lucy*[23] where you expose the typical hypocrisies of white, middle-class American liberals. You capture all the little details: their nuances of feeling and meaning, their ways of saying one thing but doing something quite different. It is incredibly fine observation. This no doubt is the gift that developed from your childhood.

A: I'm glad it turned out that way, because there were so many times when it seemed like a curse that I could not escape. I could not do anything else but observe these things. I was accused also of having a sharp tongue because I was always able to distill a person's character in a few words. At first it was amusing to everybody. Then it became a curse, because I saw too much, and I could sum up too much. If I hadn't become a writer, can you imagine living in a place like that in which you are not allowed to speak?

Q: Could there be others like you probably still living there?

A: I don't think there's so much unique about me. There are people much more intelligent than I was. If there's any difference between me and these people it is that I was not really afraid. And I was not in awe of my family's position in society. I always thought I was an outsider – for all sorts of reasons: I was too tall; I was too thin: I was too flat-chested; I was too bright when I wasn't supposed to be; we were too poor; my mother was a Dominican: I was always outside.

Q: That sounds very colonial. At the same time, you were able to read a lot while growing up. The influence of Milton's *Paradise Lost* is pervasive in *Annie John*. There are so many references to a snake, for instance. There was the actual snake that your mother was carrying without knowing it. Then later she herself was called Satan.

A: I never knew that these things were such an influence on me – these religious images. The story of the snake on the mother's head really did happen to mother. The question is why did I remember it and give it significance within all of those other incidents. I had to memorize and write out parts of *Paradise Lost* as punishment. It is interesting, after four books, that I begin to see a pattern in my work. What's most interesting is how influential some things have been; for instance, the biblical books of Genesis and Revelation were my favourite things to read for a long period of time. Revelation is a pretty terrifying thing for a child to read; but it conveys the idea of a 'paradise lost' never to be regained, and that is a big motif in my work. Some people say I have grown up in a paradise. No one growing up in any of these islands ever thinks it's a paradise. Everybody who can leave, leaves. So it's not this paradise that's a big influence on me. It's not the physical Antigua. It's the paradise of mother in every way: the sort of benign, marvellous, innocent moment you have with the great powerful person who, you then realize, won't let you go. There is something else from *Paradise Lost* that I seem to put in my work: 'Better to reign in hell than to serve in heaven' (Book I, line 263). I completely believe that. But I had no idea that it was so pervasive in my work. There is the rub of something. It seems so interesting that the people who have been most influential in destroying the psychologically whole me, have also given me the language to understand this. That brings me back to the feeling or idea that you just can't denounce or hate people, because you get all sorts of things from all sorts of people. Included in the bad things, you get some good things too.

Q: It is that mixed quality of human experience that you capture so well in your writing – the good with the bad, the strong with the weak, and so on.

A: It's so obvious.

Q: You might say it's obvious, but when I grew up in the Caribbean, things were very sharply divided. It was strong against weak, white against black, city against countryside. You belong to a generation which can see that these divisions are not quite so clear-cut. You have seen post-Independence rulers who are black do even worse than the white colonialists. It's not just white versus black.

A: No. It's human.

Q: I remember Derek Walcott's poem 'A Far Cry from Africa'[24] causing great offence to some West Indians because it expresses sympathy for the child of white, British oppressors who is 'hacked in bed' by Mau-Mau warriors fighting for Kenya's freedom from British colonial rule. But it is possible surely to identify a violation of humane feeling even if it is perpetrated for 'good' reasons. You remember Walcott's lines:

> I who am poisoned with the blood of both
> where shall I turn, divided to the vein
> I who have cursed
> The drunken officer of British rule, how choose
> Between this Africa and the English tongue I love?

A: This is why you have to call Castro to the carpet. It's just wrong, whether it happens in Castro's Cuba or Batista's.

Q: Your attitude brings together both your penchant for the truth and your feeling for the mixed love/hate quality of human experience. There is a crucial part of *Annie John* where the mother calls Annie a 'slut', which is followed by a powerful exchange and Annie's flaming riposte: 'Like mother, like daughter.' Your description afterwards contains many references to chasms, holes and divisions. Your attitude seems to be that wholeness is constantly disrupted by fragmentation. This is a recurring pattern in your work. *At the Bottom of the River*[25] is also full of deep, deep holes and pits of blackness.

A: Yes. Someone told me that there was a psychology class in Columbia University which was using *Annie John* as a literary text.

Q: The dreams in *At the Bottom of the River* are psychologically so

vibrant. They give that book a surrealistic air of reality transformed significantly by the supernatural.

A: Those things are, to me, very Caribbean. I used a very formal English
in *At the Bottom of the River*: it's the language of my school days.
I combined it with a modern form to describe this very real, local thing.

Q: I agree. Take 'Girl', the first piece in *At the Bottom of the River*. It's
amazing how you turn the most mundane everyday details into art. The
story appears as a simple catalogue of everyday happenings in the life of a
Caribbean girl. Yet the sum-total of the catalogue is quite different from its
parts. It is like Picasso taking a piece of disused or old machinery and
placing it by itself in a studio where it is seen in a completely new light,
as a work of art.

A: You recognize every Caribbean mother in that story 'Girl'.

Q: Yes. We all went through those experiences, but you have made them
into art. I can imagine the American or British reader who does not know
those experiences praising you for your invention. In fact, there is not much
invention in the local details of the story. The artistic creativity is in the
combination of the details, the technique of ordering them. This is inspired.
To some extent, I see 'Girl' as an encapsulation of your achievement as a
writer. It foreshadows your record of a Caribbean woman's experience
from her own point of view, and it combines this record with a degree of
psychological penetration that is matched only in very few Caribbean
novels, for example, *A House for Mr Biswas* and *In the Castle of My Skin*.
You remind me of the Irish writer Edna O'Brien[26] whose fiction hit the
literary world of London in the 1960s with similar impact. Was she an
influence?

A: I love Edna O'Brien, but I only read her after I started to write. The
authors that I read before I started to write were mostly eighteenth-century
and nineteenth-century novelists – the Brontës, Jane Austen, Dickens –
colonial literature. When I started to write, I read Virginia Woolf, but not
the twentieth-century classics like Joyce. I read Doris Lessing, and liked her
'Children of Violence' series. I read Edna O'Brien much later because we
had the same editor who gave me her books. The work of hers that I truly
love is a novella called *A Rose in the Heart of New York*.

Q: I find your work, like Edna O'Brien's, vividly and naturally revealing
the innermost secrets of a woman's life unobtrusively, just factually.

A: I didn't know I was doing that. I have no real distance on what I write,
because it's so much an act of self-rescue, self-rehabilitation, self-curiosity:
about my mind, about myself, what I think, what happened to me in the
personal way, in the public way, what things mean. It's so much a personal
act that I have no real understanding of it. So when you describe the
psychology of it, I can't comment.

Q: Your psychological penetration, the almost childlike frankness of your observation and the transparent simplicity of your style produce writing which I think is very similar to James Baldwin's.[27] In some ways, I regard you as a female James Baldwin.

A: I would never dream of thinking that I resemble such an astonishing writer. But the power of these things will have a way. If it's true then somehow the language is beautiful. I've noticed that when it's true, the language is just right.

Q: When you think of how Baldwin opposed that white power structure in the 1950s and 1960s – the courage it took! His prose was so clean and clear. His writing was entirely free of fussiness, like yours. He stated plain truths and they were very compelling.

A: It is poetic beyond belief when you read it.

Q: I think your achievement is similar to his in so far as you both quietly and unobtrusively record compelling truths in language that is deceptively simple. That's how technique masks technique. It appears to be artless, but it is not. Now with four books behind you and being still at the beginning of your career, can you see your work going in a particular direction?

A: I don't know. I suspect things. There's a museum in Boston called the Gardiner Museum. They asked me to come and pick one painting or one object and talk about it. I picked a painting that I suspect isn't very good. It was of a woman who, as archduchess of Austria, with her husband, ruled the Netherlands for Spain at that time. The painting is very much about what she owns. Some of these paintings actually include the duchess with her hand on the head of a black girl or a monkey, just something that was owned. It was a time when Europe behaved the way the rest of the world now behaves: Invade! Conquer! Anyhow what is interesting about her and the things that she used to own – me, for instance – is I now get to tell her a few things about herself. It's all metaphorical, mind you, but I think I'm drifting that way – to now tell the people who used to own me a few things about themselves. They invented a life for me. I cannot do that. I know the danger of invention. I will tell them the truth about themselves.

Notes

1   Jamaica Kincaid, *Annie John* (Farrar, Straus, and Giroux, New York, 1985).
2   Novels by Selvon, for instance, were regarded as mainly 'sociological', whereas some of Mittelholzer's works, or Naipaul's *A House for Mr Biswas* were seen, at least partly, as 'psychological'.
3   See Index under Mittelholzer.
4   Jamaica Kincaid, *A Small Place* (Farrar, Straus, and Giroux, New York, 1988).
5   See Introduction, notes 6 and 11.
6   Revenues from oil, which was discovered in southern Trinidad in the early part of the

twentieth century, helped to make the island the most prosperous of British Caribbean colonies. The sharp rise in international oil-prices in the 1970s increased Trinidadian wealth enormously; but the island's current economic difficulties have been attributed to mismanagement and corruption by the People's National Movement which ruled Trinidad for thirty years, beginning in 1956.

7 See Index under Claude McKay.

8 See Index for Mittelholzer, Selvon, Lamming, Naipaul.

9 See Index for Austin Clarke and Earl Lovelace.

10 Lamming's third and fourth novels, *Of Age and Innocence* (1958) and *Season of Adventure* (1960) consider some of the racial, cultural and economic problems that need to be solved before Independence could succeed.

11 Fidel Castro deposed the Cuban dictator Fulgencio Batista in 1959, since when Castro has ruled Cuba. Kincaid refers to censorship and other restrictions placed by Castro's communist regime on writers in Cuba.

12 Fulgencio Batista (1901–73) was originally an army sergeant. He seized power in Cuba in 1952 and became a dictator before he was overthrown by Castro. Batista died in exile in Portugal.

13 Cf. Clarke's comments on *In the Castle of My Skin* in Chapter 8.

14 The list includes writers from the first three stages of Caribbean literature as outlined in the Introduction. As a post-Independence writer, Kincaid belongs to the third stage, although her account of (white) Americans in *Lucy* betrays uniquely fourth-stage expertise in non-immigrant frontier subjects.

15 See Introduction, note 4, and Chapter 10.

16 Merle Hodge was born in Trinidad in 1944. She attended university in England, then made a visit to Africa. Her novel *Crick Crack Monkey* (1970) is a loving and lyrical evocation of rural Trinidad, with its mixed racial and cultural heritage and uniquely Caribbean blend of warmth and exuberance.

17 From the comic opera *The Pirates of Penzance* (1879) by W. S. Gilbert and Arthur Sullivan.

18 'The Ballad of Reading Goal' was first published in 1898. It was written while Wilde was in Reading Prison.

19 See Chapter 10, note 19.

20 See Chapter 10, note 26.

21 Jamaica Kincaid, *At the Bottom of the River* (Farrar, Straus, and Giroux, New York, 1983).

22 See Bibliography under Lamming and Naipaul.

23 Jamaica Kincaid, *Lucy* (Farrar, Straus, and Giroux, New York, 1990).

24 In Walcott, *In a Green Night* (Jonathan Cape, London, 1962), p. 18.

25 See note 21 above.

26 Edna O'Brien, the Irish novelist, who lives in England, is famous for her authoritative studies of the inner lives of contemporary women in numerous works of fiction, for example, *The Lonely Girl* (1962) and *A Pagan Place* (1970).

27 James Baldwin (1924–88) is the African-American writer who achieved fame in the 1960s with such collections of essays as *Nobody Knows My Name* (1961) and *The Fire Next Time* (1963), which had an apocalyptic quality, lucidly exposing American racism, and predicting dire consequences for the whole of American society. Baldwin also wrote novels, for example, *Go Tell it on the Mountain* (1953); *Giovanni's Room* (1956); and *Another Country* (1962). Cf. Chapter 8, note 18.

CHAPTER 12 | Lorna Goodison: Heartease

Lorna Goodison was born in Kingston, Jamaica, where she attended St Hugh's High School before enrolling in the Jamaica School of Art, and later the School of the Art Student's League in New York. Although trained as an artist, Goodison became interested in writing poetry, and has so far produced three collections of poems: Tamarind Season *(1980);* I am Becoming My Mother *(1986); and* Heartease *(1988). She is also the author of a volume of stories* Baby Mother and the King of Swords *(1990). Goodison's works combine a strong sense of patriotism and deep compassion for the underprivileged with distinctly mystical overtones. She lives in Jamaica, but frequently travels abroad to attend conferences, give readings, or serve as writer-in-residence at universities. (This interview was recorded in Toronto on 1 April 1991.)*

Q: Did you always want to write?
A: At first I did not think of myself as a writer. I thought I was going to be a painter. That's what I studied in Jamaica and in New York.
Q: How did the shift come from painting to writing?
A: Writing just took over and became very insistent and 'colonizing'. I was painting, but I was certainly writing too. I used to write poems and hide them away. Then I started publishing them in the *Sunday Gleaner*,[1] while I was in high school in the sixth form; but I wouldn't put my name to them.
Q: It seems you began like so many other writers in the West Indies without the literary support or artistic structures that more developed societies have.
A: There is no real support system for someone like me.
Q: How did you get *Tamarind Season*[2] published?
A: In the early 1970s, I was a copy-writer for an advertising agency in Jamaica. Sometimes, half-way during the day, I would say 'I'm sick of this (copy-writing), and I would go into my room and lock the door and try to write poems. Everybody at the agency knew that, and one of them who did production work for *Jamaica Journal*,[3] one day said 'They need some poems in *Jamaica Journal*. Why don't you give me some of those poems?'

152

So I did, and he took them to Neville Dawes[4] who was then director of the Institute of Jamaica. He liked the poems and decided to publish them.

Q: It is possible to see your work beginning with social observations and documentation in the first volume, then moving off gradually into more spiritual concerns in your later books. But I would have thought that, all along, even in your first book, there is an instinct for reflection on abstract themes. Maybe both things are true. In other words, while there may be a general development from the concrete toward the abstract in your work, there is also a mixture of both all the way through.

A: There have always been strong currents moving through my work, and at some point one may be a little more in ascendancy, but I think they're always there, even in the work I'm now doing which is more openly 'spiritual'. The more I journey into myself the more I become concerned with everything that affects humanity.

Q: There is a strong sense of universality in your work, whereby you regard yourself as one unit in a large group of units. I wonder where that comes from. Your early work, certainly your stories, talk about the communalism of the society you grew up in: if everyone did not share all they had, at least they knew about each other.

A: Yes. I think this might have to do with the fact that I was born into an enormous family. I grew up with eight siblings and my mother and father. My mother had this curious way that a lot of West Indian women have: that if you have nine children, you can just as easily care for ten, eleven, or twelve. We always had other relatives' children in our house too. It was wonderful; but it also makes me cherish my space and privacy, because I never had it when I was growing up.

Q: In your poem 'The Road of the Dread'[5] you open with a threatening situation of fear and danger: there is a snake and barbed wire; yet the poem ends with a vision of sharing, where you say: this person has this quality, that person has another quality: put the two together and you have union, solidarity and presumably a sense of security.

A: That poem says something about my personal philosophy. You have to be really brave to go into some places, especially those deep inside yourself. It's sort of blind faith that you need. You just don't know exactly what's going to happen, but you do know something: that some people have certain qualities which you need, and if you combine them with your own qualities it will make something positive.

Q: Are there any spiritual or mystical writings, such as those of Blake, for instance, that generated such attitudes?

A: For some reason I was not attracted to Blake; his drawings yes, but not the writing. It's only recently that I've started to read anything that could be called mystical. What happens to me very often is that I experience these things, or I write them. Then afterwards, I will find a source that will explain them to me. So now I think I can understand Blake, because I've written what I have written. I didn't write it because I had read Blake. When I write, sometimes I know the meaning at one level, but sometimes the deeper level doesn't come to me until long after. One day I'll be walking along, and I'll think of a line I've written, and suddenly I'll begin to understand its deeper meaning. I go through a lot of drafts too, and sometimes I think, the poem is finished; but it's not. It is always asking me to go further and further.

Q: I'm impressed by your observation of Jamaica, of the Caribbean landscape itself, the people, the sounds, the words, the rhythms of the people's speech – everything. The evocation of all that is in the 'The Road of the Dread', for instance, while a poem like 'Bridge Views'[6] captures the class distinctions, poverty, violence, the political background. Being West Indian, I recognize the fact that these are people I know; this is how they sound; this is their psychology; this is how they behave; these are their concerns. It all registers as truthful, authentic. In several poems in *Tamarind Season* you seem particularly taken by the mixed nature of Jamaican society. You talk about one strand coming from here, another from there, for instance in 'Ocho Rios' where you celebrate the variety of the Jamaican past, and you end with the ironic line: 'which colonizer is winning in Ocho Rios?'[7] In other words, Ocho Rios (or Jamaica) might have come out of colonial violence, rivalry, and mixing, but now it doesn't belong to any of the former colonial rivals. This idea of the mixed or Creole nature of Caribbean society keeps recurring.

A: It is a mixed society. There are many historical and cultural influences that go together to make up Jamaica.

Q: Some people could see this multi-ethnic and multi-cultural diversity as negative – chaotic, or confusing.

A: It is not that I don't see anything negative about it, but it *is*; it just is. Sometimes I think this is what produces the enormous energy in the Jamaican people. The society is always in the throes of some great change or other; but it produces remarkably creative people.

Q: You record the throes – the class distinctions, poverty, violence, exploitation.

A: They are there, and I don't think any of it should be hidden. That's one thing I feel very strongly about. That is why I have a poem called 'Jamaica 1980'.[8] There were actually over 800 people killed in the election in that year.[9] These are human beings. Somebody should talk about them. Walt Whitman said: 'whoever walks a furlong without sympathy walks to his own funeral drest in his shroud'.[10]

Q: You are not providing solutions to their suffering by writing poetry.

A: No, but I feel that where I can talk about it, I should. I think that after

1980, we should have had some public grieving, some ceremony, or monument to the fact that over 800 people died. We never really did.

Q: You are interested more in the human aspect of this event than in the political, although I realize that you can't divorce them completely. In the poem 'My Late Friend',[11] you show some of the most pernicious effects of colonialism, for example, the psychological and moral deformation produced by a preoccupation with physical characteristics such as skin colour and the shape of one's nose. This is a direct result of colonial experience and the mixing of races. The protagonist in 'My Late Friend' is consumed by self-hatred on account of her physical characteristics; this is perverse; yet you record it with sorrow; you don't reject her.

A: Yes, because it must be awful not to be able to be at peace with something as fundamental as the colour of your skin.

Q: In *Tamarind Season* you have a poem called 'A Jean Rhys Lady' and in *I am Becoming My Mother* you have another poem, 'A Lullaby for Jean Rhys'. Obviously, you consider Jean Rhys[12] important, or you feel strongly about her. But in the first poem the images of claws, flames, drunkenness, representing violent or destructive features are in sharp contrast to the second poem, a lullaby about sleep.

A: 'Lullaby' was just before Jean Rhys's death. It's the same kind of thing that would make me do the 'Jamaica 1980' poem. It's just a dreamer's attempt to make something right in a world over which I have no control. That's the most that writers can do with their writing. I don't have any illusion that I'm making a great impact or changing anything. I see in Earl Lovelace's[13] work too, that he will correct a wrong which he knows you can't do in real life; so you do it in literature.

Q: Except I think he goes a little more self-consciously out to be political. He usually portrays destructive social or political forces which are opposed by the people. His characters are always talking about the people and their potential to overcome. Your writing doesn't have that.

A: I don't want it to have that.

Q: Lovelace has good observations, and he sees the issues squarely; but I think his work is too theoretical and unrealistic. On the other hand, as I have said, I find your writing to be wholly authentic in description, situations, psychology and speech.

A: I think that is one of the highest compliments that anybody could pay a writer. If I go through my work and it doesn't sound authentic, I just don't want anything to do with it.

Q: In your second volume of poems, *I am Becoming My Mother*, I see some political interest in poems like 'Jamaica 1980,' 'For Rosa Parks' and 'The Bedspread'. In more personal poems, when you talk about your son, mother and family, there's a strength of passion that is quite overwhelming.

A: I feel strongly about being a mother, and I feel strongly about my mother; but I think it also has to do with the way I see life. For me it is important to get things in your life in the right order, and I think you begin with loving those closest to you. I couldn't go and love the whole world and be concerned about the fate of a million nameless, faceless people if I weren't able to love my own mother. It's important to recognize and salute the heroic quality of ordinary life.

Q: I think you achieve exactly that in 'For My Mother May I Inherit Half Her Strength'. It is a kind of mini-epic celebrating the heroism and grand achievements of ordinary people. Your mother was a queen in her own right. Jamaica Kincaid[14] calls her mother a queen.

A: When I showed my mother that poem she was very upset. She said I had told the whole world our business, and I felt badly because I meant it as a tribute. But other people in the West Indies said that that was the story of their mother and father. Then I'd travel abroad to read from my work, and people would say 'That's the story of my mother too.' I began with what was closest to me and ended up with something that is, in some ways, universal.

Q: Exactly. Personal details of your own family become a matter of affection felt by everyone for their family. But I am a little puzzled by the phrase 'the paid penance of my poems', which recurs in several poems. If it means that somehow in writing poetry you are undergoing a penance, what are you being punished for?

A: I began by saying that I really didn't think I was going to be a writer. What I didn't say was that I always had a sense that if I really surrendered to writing, it would demand an awful lot of me that I wasn't sure I wanted to give. I would prefer to have had an easy life, where I didn't have to get up in the middle of the night because I had to write these things. I went through a phase when I tried to resist writing; but I wouldn't say I feel that way any more, because I came to a wonderful acceptance of the vocation of poet.

Q: In particular poems in *Heartease*,[15] there is the assertion of a vision of human brotherhood, sisterhood, peace – marvellous things that the poems themselves don't give. Your Jamaica poems come from the ground up, but not some of those in *Heartease*. I wonder if anyone has made the criticism that they are assertive: they come out with statements, but the reader doesn't always get the experience that produced the statements.

A: That's probably quite valid, but I don't know. That's all that came out.

Q: Perhaps the point is that such things can only be asserted. I wonder about the term 'heartease' itself, because you've written several poems about it in this second volume. Is it relief or ease from all of the pain that the human heart goes through?

A: Yes. It's also the name of a place almost at the centre of Jamaica. A lot of my poems are about journeys and journeying, even 'Heartease New

England 1987'. It just seemed terrific to me if, in your journey through life, you could reach a place called Heartease, where you could have a measure of ease that would have come through wisdom gained from being on the road a long time, and experiencing certain things. That is what 'Heartease New England 1987' essentially is: it is a poem about wisdom: if one bird alone cannot measure the distance of the bridge, a group of birds can do it. It is through writing poems, and telling stories that I found what my mission is: why I have been sent into this life. That is what gives me heartease. Sometimes I get closer to it; and at other times I am far away from it.

Q: You mention 'journey' and 'mission'. It's as if God or somebody has sent you on a mission, and as you journey through life, you get satisfaction when you feel you are accomplishing your mission.

A: Two or three times in my life I've felt that. I remember once I was in London, and in the middle of a reading I was struck by the thought: you know something, I'm a *poet*. Every now and again I get a feeling like this.

Q: Several of your poems use the phrase 'get a glimpse of'. In 'The Road of the Dread', when solidarity and insight are attained at the end, you 'catch a glimpse of the end' [of the road]. At that stage, you have found your mission which you describe as follows:

> For my mission this last life is certainly this
> to be the sojourner poet carolling for peace
> calling lost souls to the way of Heartease.
>
> (p. 41)

Your idea of heartease appears to have a mystical component in it. You say you did not read mystical writings, but I thought there was a Trappist[16] influence in your background?

A: It is only now that I'm reading Thomas Merton.[17]

Q: After you wrote these poems?

A: Yes. I think I must have read somewhere that Trappists don't speak. I remember when I was child I always had this romantic notion that I should go into a Trappist monastery. A lot of those poems, certainly the *Heartease* ones, were born of a big silence. I spent a lot of time alone and that's how the poems came out: there was a silence for a long period of time, and then they came up to the surface.

Q: That might distinguish these *Heartease* poems from the early ones. The early ones seem to come out of the hurly-burly of experience, but the *Heartease* ones are more reflective. They contain biblical rhythms, phrases, and straight references. Do they also convey Christian doctrine?

A: Probably yes, because I grew up in the Anglican religion. I went to a very high church, which is close to being Roman Catholic, and I loved the ceremony – the lights and candles. But I wanted some of it to be in me, and that never happened. An Anglican deaconess taught us comparative religion, and that is when I began to take an interest in other religions apart from Christianity. I could see that there was a greater fullness than what I was being exposed to. That's why I like Thomas Merton: he sees God in everybody's religion. That's the kind of religion I think I subscribe to: some world religion that is not a religion; it's a religion of the lovers of God as Sufis[18] would call it.

Q: Did you read any Sufi writers?

A: Only recently. I also have a friend who is a Sufi.

Q: Ali Darwish?

A: Yes. He is a short-story writer, and had some influence on my short stories.

Q: Again there is the pattern in which you express things that are in you, and then later you find that the writings of other people fit in with or confirm what you said.

A: Yes, that is in fact what happens. I wonder what will happen now that I've read these other people.

Q: That would be interesting to see in the future. The strands of thought in your poems are distinctly mystical. One strand, as already mentioned, is that of universal human solidarity; another is the journey toward heartease which could be another name for God. In 'Some Nights I Don't Sleep', you end with the lines:

> for some night is not for sleep
> is to use collective light
> as laser beams
> to clear the home stretch
> to Heartease.

(p. 26)

The persona in the poem is a seeker on a spiritual journey. He/she has an urgent desire to find an all-embracing truth. I think that's mystical: this yearning in an individual to seek unity with a larger reality, but not to go through conventional means of reasoned inquiry; it is to make that intuitive jump or link. In the beginning you said you relied on faith. I believe that's what true mystics rely on.

A: I think you have expressed exactly what it is I feel. It is just that I didn't know for a long time what it is or why. I've always had this extraordinary desire for something which I could not articulate, and I didn't know where to find it.

Q: I wonder if we can also see that desire in your stories in *Baby Mother and the King of Swords*.[19] The King of Swords appears both in your poems and in your stories. Who is the King of Swords?

A: In tarot cards the King of Swords is an attractive figure who beckons to you with one hand, while he keeps his other hand hidden behind him with a sword in it; and when you get really close and begin to trust him, he takes out the sword and wounds you. Some people can be drawn to what destroys them over and over again.

Q: I am interested in this idea of not being able to avoid self-destruction, especially since these stories are written from the point of view of a girl growing up. I assume this is the experience of your own girlhood, not necessarily your own life story.

A: Yes, and through osmosis in listening to other women.

Q: Your stories reproduce all the colour and texture of life in Jamaica around about the 1950s; but I want to focus on this self-destructive instinct in women because it appears in much West Indian writing. The women in your stories, for example, 'I Come Through' and 'By Love Possessed',[20] suffer a great deal. They seem to expect it and, perversely, may even love it.

A: I don't think they love it. I don't think they know how to avoid it. That's a different thing. They just have no concept of how to avoid it. I think maybe this coming generation will probably know. We are a people who are not too long out of slavery or brutish post-slavery conditions. In fact post-emancipation conditions were not much better than slavery. We have to evolve ways of coping with the peculiar make-up of our society. Love and marriage are basic things that we're still working on: how people deal with each other and why.

Q: These are basic social conventions that old societies take for granted, and, nowadays, are trying to drop, or at least deregulate and water down.

A: Yes. We have conventions too, but some of them are so brutish they should be changed. A lot of Jamaican women, especially working-class mothers, have this unbelievably harsh way of treating their daughters. They curse and speak to them in the most dreadful, degrading kind of way. I will bring twenty Jamaican women into this room right now, and all of them will have the same experience. How do you raise a daughter in conditions of slavery? She's going to be confronted with a lot of brutality. It's as though they're conditioning you beforehand, getting you used to what you should expect. Perhaps the only way mothers could help you to survive was to prepare you for it themselves.

Q: Batter you?

A: Yes, because the world is going to batter you, and if you're too soft, you are not going to make it. In a way it's a kind of terrible love. It's a dreadful way of helping you to cope, which scars you but keeps you alive.

Q: That is true of Jamaica Kincaid's *Annie John*.[21] The girl in the novel calls her mother Satan and other names; but in fact, what she perceives as ill-treatment might simply have been her mother's way of 'blooding' her for life.

A: That's the conclusion I came to, because it's amazing the kind of experiences that all the women I know of, my age, have had. I was working in an office once and a son of one of the women was getting married, and she said that her husband was upset because their son was only 21 or something, and that it was her fault the boy was getting married so young, her husband felt it was because she wouldn't hire any attractive maids. It was taken for granted that boys in middle-class families use their maids for sexual initiation.

Q: Your stories talk about this, and give me the feeling that women have nowhere to turn, although Delzie in 'The Big Shot'[22] does fight back. She goes after the man who has abused her, and when he loses his sophisticated grip and breaks down in Creole, she feels a sense of victory. Still it is weak sort of victory.

A: No. She finds someone who at least treated her with some respect.

Q: Yes, she meets Lynval. It was a relief for me to find at least one good man [Lynval] in your stories. I don't think anyone has written such stories before. I know we now have Olive Senior, Erna Brodber,[23] and other women writers; but the older generation of Andrew Salkey, Sylvia Wynter and John Hearne[24] did not generally write from a woman's point of view, dealing with such things as pregnancy, preparing food, and childcare – specifically women's experiences that represent a victimized condition. So far such things have not been adequately rendered in Jamaican or Caribbean fiction. You put these experiences within the right context of a feudalistic, chauvinistic, authoritarian social structure that functions alongside communal ethics, and the influence of the Bible to make up local Jamaican manners.

A: There are all kinds of unconventional strategies which women use to cope, although they seem helpless in face of the patriarchal superstructure. They win small, weak victories like Delzie making Albert break down; but there are other victories too as in 'I Come Through', where the woman narrator withdraws in order to claim what is rightfully hers.

Q: As with so many of your women characters she 'have no luck with man'.

A: The situation in which she finds herself could have totally overwhelmed her, so she retreats and gathers her strength in order to come back stronger.

Q: Yes, she regains her strength in the country with her grandmother; then she comes back and can face her situation again. That is a recurring pattern in your work. I mentioned earlier that 'The Road of the Dread' talks about dangerous forces that beset the persona who then gets a vision which finally gives some relief or some sense of security. That is really the same pattern. Generally, your women characters become victims without being able to overcome their victimizers; but even in their victimized condition, they exhibit toughness. That comes through in characters who appear to say: 'I can take it. I can take more. Give me all you've got, and I will take it and not break.' Maybe I was wrong at first to say that they love it. It is more a sense of 'I can take it' or 'I can cope with it.' I suppose their strategies of coping were not too clear to me.

A: They are very much internal strategies.

Q: Also, you are using a form that is short. Since you don't have the scope of a novel to develop the strategies of coping, your stories tend to repeat this message of coping. This is not a flaw in the stories themselves; it may only appear as a flaw because the stories are collected in one place, and are read one after the other. If each of these stories was to appear separately in a magazine, the effect would be different.

A: The ordinary life of coping in Jamaica defies belief. It is extraordinary what our people live through – things that would destroy the 'ordinary' person.

Q: You fully capture that human capacity to bear tribulation and not to be beaten down completely.

A: To defend themselves, there are spiritual devices that people some-times use. In 'Follow Your Mind'[25] the pregnant woman has nothing, and her husband is in jail; yet she has the courage to defy this priest who is using her as a bad example when he should show compassion to her.

Q: Yes, she rejects his charity with: 'I don't want it.'

A: I think sometimes just being able to do something like that energizes you in a very powerful way.

Q: I agree. It's a gesture of defiance.

A: Sometimes the defiance gives you a kind of spiritual energy. It makes you strong.

Q: I can see how it could energize her spiritually. But it is not just your subject. Someone could have the same material and not tell as good a story. Technically, 'Follow Your Mind' is well constructed. It is compact.

A: That is the Sufi influence: the stories are concise in form, but have a lot of things in them. I'm relieved that you saw these things in them, because I've never discussed these stories with anybody. I wrote them almost furtively, because I didn't think I was a short-story writer. I'm still not sure I am, but I felt that these women wanted me to talk about these things.

Q: I think your stories have a sense of revelation of the inner and outer lives of both men and women. But you are part of a very recent develop-ment in Jamaican and West Indian writing. Up to the 1950s and 1960s West Indian writing was dominated by men. Do you see women writers coming out now as the result of a particular movement or attitude?

A: I'm sure the general wave of feminism that swept the world had some effect on us. I spent a year at Radcliffe, at the Bunting Institute, which is a sort of bastion of feminist thought, but I would not say that I am a 'feminist'. It just seemed to me that I lived in a situation, in Jamaica, that was demonstrating feminism in action. Many women that I know in Jamaica assert themselves and take responsibility for their lives in powerful ways. They have no time to sit down and theorize about it: they just live it.

Q: What passes for feminist theory here does not seem to have any particular application to Jamaica?

A: Not that much. The feminists I know are the higglers in Jamaica who support their families themselves by selling bundles of scallion in Grand Cayman, and using the money to buy goods that they can sell in Jamaica. The route they travelled became known as the 'scellion run'. It made some of the women quite wealthy.

Q: Technically, your poems do not appear to follow any regular pattern. Each poem dictates its own metre and form, so that we get a mixture of one-word lines or short and long lines. Rhymes are used occasionally, and there are some stanzaic divisions. Otherwise it's unbroken free verse. You don't seem to be working within any fixed technical pattern, but your poems emerge whole and self-contained. They are also quite versatile: some are descriptive, while others are narrative, and yet others are shorter and more impressionistic, evocative. I particularly like your coinage of words some of which are very original. You talk about 'soupberb, ghettogreen, coloured people, and crowdapeople'.

A: 'Crowdapeople' is a Jamaican word. It also takes on a bigger meaning. It's what the entertainers use when they are referring to the audience.

Q: Your coinages add freshness and uniqueness to your poems. They support my general feeling that there's nothing derivative in your work, and that you have a voice of your own. What is the significance of the titles of your books? Why *Tamarind Season*, for instance?

A: 'Tamarind season' means hard times. The tamarind season is when a lot of other food doesn't grow. I have moved away from a traditional or linear view where you start somewhere and arrive at this great place at the end. I think there is life, and sometimes heaven makes vertical interventions. It comes and goes.

Q: You mention Africa often – Ethiopia, Benin and the Nile – and, of course, South Africa. Is this simply because you feel sympathy for the underprivileged of the world, all who are victims? Africa seems more special than that in your writing. Maybe the simple answer is that the Jamaican people are predominantly of African descent. But the African references seem to come so effortlessly.

A: They do. Sometimes I don't even know what they are doing in my poems, but they come constantly. It's just one of the currents that is consistent in my work. It is just there. I like African music; it just speaks to me in a particular way. I get a little homesick when I hear it.

Q: You've never visited Africa?

A: No, I've never been. I know I'm going to go. I had a very interesting experience when Wole Soyinka[26] came to Jamaica. He had heard me read my 'Bedspread'[27] poem in London and was generous enough to say that he had been influenced by it. It said something powerful to him.

Q: It is a powerful poem.

A: I used to feel that I had almost a mission to read that poem everywhere I went. But I don't read it anymore. I just feel that it was given to me for a period to read and now I don't have to do it anymore.

Q: That makes it sound as if your work is limited to a particular time and situation.

A: No. I won't have to read it right now; maybe another time.

Q: One reason why I don't believe that 'Bedspread' is limited only to Mandela's[28] political situation is because it acknowledges the power of dreams:

> They and their friends are working
> to arrest the dreams in our heads
> and the women, accustomed to closing
> the eyes of the dead
> are weaving cloths.[29]

Dreams might help to solve a political problem. They can do other things as well.

A: Dreams are the only country some people have to live in. Can you imagine what it would be like if those in abject poverty or other terrible situations were not able to dream?

Q: It's their only weapon.

A: Dreams can transport them to a place where they don't have to deal with their reality for a period.

Q: That might very well be one of the strategies of coping used by characters in *Baby Mother and the King of Swords*?

A: Perhaps. I've also wondered how my characters could articulate profound thoughts about love. They should be able to articulate such things, or their articulation should be made valid. There is the story of the man who felt that his girlfriend looked so pretty that he boxed her down. That was his way of showing his appreciation. At one level that is funny; it is also terrifying.

Q: It is terrifying and it reminds me of Frenchie in your story 'By Love Possessed'. He is humiliated by a stranger in a bar who calls him a 'batty man', but he doesn't fight the stranger – his real enemy – he goes home and takes it out on poor Dottie, his girlfriend, breaking all her precious things. Frenchie is admired for his mindless and cowardly violence. You say that 'nobody had ever seen anybody in such a glorious temper' (p. 55). Even

Dottie, his victim, 'remembered him for his glorious temper', and 'would like to have told the story of how bad her man was and the day he broke everything in her China Cabinet and boxed her down the steps' (p. 55). That seems masochistic, although, as you explained earlier, it may be a self-defensive posture conditioned by post-slavery mores. This is widespread in the Caribbean and does not only influence male/female relationships. Naipaul mentioned it in *The Middle Passage*[30] where people had paid for a performance by an American singer, Sam Cooke, but the promoter had disappeared and the singer failed to turn up. One woman didn't feel she was robbed: 'She feel she pay two dollars for the intelligence' (p. 82). The entertainer's or promoter's 'intelligence' is similar to Frenchie's 'glorious temper', an example of cowardly, criminal, and destructive behaviour that is admired by people who are too demoralized by the after-effects of slavery to notice. But to get back to your point – the man boxed his girlfriend down because he was inarticulate.

A: Yes. Jamaicans have a way of saying: 'Bwoy, yuh nuh see it!' That is supposed to express worlds. In fact, they are inviting you to see what they see, because they don't know how to tell you what they see. I write because I want them to know that I see it.

Q: I suppose artists and writers in all societies articulate things which ordinary people cannot express. Is it that West Indians are specially inarticulate?

A: We can articulate certain things like cricket, but not emotions such as love and tenderness, or deeper thoughts.

Q: Yes, such thoughts come out in rather unorthodox ways. But what do you think about the development of West Indian or Jamaican writing at its present stage? When I lived in Jamaica in the late 1950s, there were only people like Vic Reid, Andrew Salkey, John Hearne and Roger Mais[31] – all middle-class people – often writing about the poorest classes of Jamaicans.

A: You need a lightness of being to enter into someone else's experience, and bring it out purely. You don't have to have the experience necessarily: you need the ear and the heart. Your heart has to be open in a certain way, and you have to love the people; then secrets will open up to you. I applaud Roger Mais for writing about those people, being who he was; but I can't bear his language. Those people don't speak like that. His situations and descriptions are brilliant; but not his language.

Q: So you must be pleased with Jamaican writing today – its variety, accuracy and vigour, and so many women.

A: There are people coming from different perspectives. There is Olive [Senior] coming from one way, and Erna Brodber and Michelle Cliff[32] from different ways. In my case, I am concerned about the truth of what I'm saying. I pray that nothing will make me succumb, and not write it as it truly is.

Notes

1   The *Sunday Gleaner* is the Sunday issue of the *Daily Gleaner*, the longest running daily newspaper in Jamaica.

2   Lorna Goodison, *Tamarind Season* (Institute of Jamaica, Jamaica, 1980).

3   *Jamaica Journal* is a magazine published quarterly by the Institute of Jamaica. It covers a broad range of subjects including history, art, culture, music and literature. Along with *Caribbean Quarterly* (which is more academic), it is probably the most respected journal of arts and culture in the English-speaking Caribbean.

4   Neville Dawes is a well-known poet, novelist and critic who lives in Jamaica. He was born in 1926, in Nigeria, of Jamaican parents, and has worked in both Nigeria and Jamaica. His novels include *The Last Enchantment* (1960) and *Interim* (1978).

5   In *Tamarind Season*, pp. 22–3.

6   In *Tamarind Season*, pp. 46–8.

7   In *Tamarind Season*, p. 50.

8   In Lorna Goodison, *I Am Becoming My Mother* (New Beacon Books, London, 1986), p. 10.

9   The Jamaican elections in 1980 were notorious for violence in which gangs loyal to the People's National Party and the Jamaican Labour Party engaged in open street-warfare.

10   Walt Whitman, 'A Song of Myself' (verse 48), *The Oxford Book of American Verse* (Oxford University Press, New York, 1962), p. 349.

11   In *Tamarind Season*, p. 32.

12   Jean Rhys (1894–1979) was born in Dominica but went to England at the age of 16. Between the World Wars she produced several works of fiction in which the victimization of women was a central theme. Then in 1966 her novel *Wide Sargasso Sea* appeared and confirmed her reputation as a classic writer.

13   See Index for Earl Lovelace.

14   For Jamaica Kincaid, see Chapter 11.

15   Lorna Goodison, *Heartease* (New Beacon Books, London, 1988).

16   Trappists are a reform community of monks, founded in 1664, within the Cistercian order which originated in France in 1098. The Trappist community was founded in France, by Armand de Rancé (1626–1700), but it exists today in many other countries. Trappists practise austerity of diet, penitential exercises, and absolute silence. They abstain from flesh, fish and eggs, and live mainly on bread, fruit and vegetables.

17   Thomas Merton (1915–1968) was an American author who was ordained as a Catholic priest in 1949. Merton chose the solitary life of a Trappist monk while he produced poems, essays and autobiographical works. His writing is both secular and religious, and is often critical of contemporary culture. The broad scope of Merton's religious interests may be seen in the title of one of his volumes, *Mystics and Zen Masters* (1977).

18   It was in the eighth and ninth centuries AD that Islamic mysticism became known as Sufism. Sufis are Islamic mystics who aspire to absolute spiritual purification, and extinction of the ego. Sufis have produced many writers, such as Ibn Al-Farid (1182–1235), whose verse is regarded as the finest expression of mystical aspiration in Arabic, and Jalal-ud-din Rumi (1207–1273), one of Persia's (Iran's) greatest mystical poets.

19   Lorna Goodison, *Baby Mother and the King of Swords* (Longman Jamaica, Jamaica, 1990).

20   'I Come Through' in *Baby Mother*, pp. 12–17; 'By Love Possessed' in *Baby Mother*, pp. 50–6.

21   For *Annie John*, see Chapter 11, note 1. Cf. Chapter 10 for Dionne Brand's comments on resilient women.

22   In *Baby Mother*, pp. 37–45.

23   Olive Senior and Erna Brodber are both Jamaican. Olive Senior is an editor and author. Among other works, she has produced one collection of poems and two collections of stories, *Summer Lightning* (1986) and *Arrival of the Snake-Woman* (1989).
     For Erna Brodber, see Chapter 2, note 10. Cf. Caryl Phillips's comments on his play *Strange Fruit* in Chapter 14, Part One.

24   For Salkey, see Chapter 4.
     For Hearne, see Chapter 4, note 22.
     Sylvia Wynter is a Jamaican novelist and critic who was formerly married to Jan Carew. Her novel *The Hills of Hebron* appeared in 1962.

25   In *Baby Mother*, pp. 21–8.

26   Wole Soyinka, the celebrated Nigerian author, poet, playwright and critic, won the Nobel prize for literature in 1988. Soyinka is the author of numerous distinguished plays, novels and non-fiction works.

27   In *I am Becoming My Mother*, pp. 42–3.

28   See Chapter 7, note 39.

29   In *I am Becoming My Mother*, p. 43.

30   See Introduction, note 11.

31   For Reid, see Chapter 5, note 31.
     For Salkey, see Chapter 4.
     For John Hearne, see Chapter 4, note 22.
     For Roger Mais, see Chapter 4, note 19.

32   Michelle Cliff is a young Jamaican author of six books including the novels *Abeng* (1984) and *No Telephone to Heaven* (1987). She now lives in the US.

CHAPTER 13

David Dabydeen: Coolie odyssey

David Dabydeen was born in Guyana in 1955 and emigrated to England in 1969. He studied at Cambridge University, before completing his PhD at the University of London. He then served as Research Fellow at Wolfson College, Oxford University. Dabydeen next became a lecturer in the Centre for Caribbean Studies at the University of Warwick, where he established a Centre for Research in Asian Migration of which he was Director. Dabydeen's first publication was the collection of poems Slave Song *(1984), which was followed by* Hogarth's Blacks *(1985), a scholarly work analysing images of blacks in eighteenth-century English art. A second collection of poems,* Coolie Odyssey, *appeared in 1988, and a novel,* The Intended, *in 1990. (*The Intended *was awarded the Guyana Prize for Literature in 1992.) A third collection of poems,* Turner, *appeared in 1994. Dabydeen's poetry explores colonial experience with its mixture of oppression, racism and exploitation. His fiction, strongly Conradian in resonance, conveys a bleak vision of inner corruption irresistibly mixed with self-deception. Dabydeen's* Slave Song *won the Commonwealth Poetry Prize. (This interview was recorded at the University of Warwick on 18 April 1990.)*

Q: I always found it puzzling that you came to England so young.

A: I came during the migration from the West Indies to Britain in the 1960s. I was born in Berbice, Guyana, and grew up surrounded by half-eclipsed memories of India that were gained through watching films or through my observations of Hindu rituals: I was fascinated by the fact that every three months or so a pandit would bless something or other. I remember we had moved to New Amsterdam[1] which was largely Afro-Guyanese, and relations between them and us Indo-Guyanese were largely cordial and normal, apart from the normal biases and innocuous prejudices which operate on a day-to-day level. I went to school in New Amsterdam. But in the 1960s I remember all of us had to move from New Amsterdam back to our Indian environment because of race riots.[2] I remember us packing everything that we had in New Amsterdam, getting on a bus, and going back to the Indian villages in rural Berbice.

Q: How old were you then?

A: I was about 7 or 8. I was very conscious of being surrounded by our belongings, of people whispering and being afraid of what could happen to them. These were Indian people. My once nascent sense of Indianness was intensified by this experience of racial hostility. It didn't matter that I couldn't speak a word of Hindi, although my grandmother and my great-grandmother could. The whole environment comprised cows and wooden houses propped on stilts – agricultural patterns of living. My uncle used to live in a mud-hut and owned cows and sheep. People dressed with malas[3] on their head and big silver bracelets on their arms. They were barefooted. This was my sense of Indianness, and it was both intensified and contra-dicted by watching Indian films. We thought of India as being glorious, full of wealth and opulence, instead of mud-huts.

Q: Where exactly was your village?

A: It was called Brighton and was on the Corentyne[4] coast. We stayed there for about three months until the riots were over, then we went back to New Amsterdam. There was always constant journeying back to Brighton village. Every three months, during the school holidays, we went back to Brighton village – that's where most of my family were. In the Caribbean you always return to your grandmother's house.

Q: How long were you at school in New Amsterdam?

A: Until I was about 10. Then I got a scholarship to Queen's College, Georgetown.[5] I was there for about two years.

Q: Did you have family in Georgetown?

A: No, I boarded with people. This was a very important experience for me. There was a very bright Indian boy who was a very good friend in New Amsterdam. We both got scholarships to Queen's College, and went off to Georgetown and boarded separately; but, bright as he was, he could not afford to live in Georgetown, and had to give up the scholarship. That disappointment demolished him. About four years later he had a chance to emigrate illegally. He went to Canada to start a new life, but someone reported him and he had to go back home. When I saw him five years ago in Guyana, he had turned Christian. After preliminary greetings he said: 'Are you saved?' That question meant that our whole boyhood had dis-appeared because of poverty, migration, and the racism in Guyanese soci-ety. Although his family were strong Muslims, he grasped the last straw left to him which was evangelical Christianity. He even joined the People's National Congress[6] which has ruled Guyana continuously for the last 26 years already.

Q: When and how did you come to England?

A: In 1969. My father had separated from my mother and he came to England to make his fortune, as many other West Indians had done. When he had acquired the means to do so, he sent for us. An elder sister came, then me, and then a younger sister.

Q: You went to school here and on to university?

A: I went to Cambridge University.

Q: Then you went on to do a PhD at London University in eighteenth-century literature and art. You were also a post-doctoral fellow at Oxford, and I believe Yale?

A: Yes, I spent three years at Oxford University and brief time at Yale.

Q: Where does your writing come in? What are the beginnings?

A: There were two people who were very influential in my writing career. One was the headmaster in my primary school in New Amsterdam. He was really important to me in terms of wanting to achieve things. He had been abroad and would tell us stories about how things were done there. So at a very early age he sowed in my mind the idea that I had to go abroad to see how things were done. He pushed me, as he pushed many others towards scholarships, etc. Another person who taught me English at Queen's College, made us set up a newspaper with stencils to type, and gave us stories to write. If we wrote a good story or poem, he would let us read it to the class. So he was an extremely creative teacher who inspired us all to write. He had asked us to write a story about a day in the life of a frog, and I had written one of the best stories. He read it to the class, which gave me an audience for the first time, and the pleasure has stayed with me.

Q: Were those the only literary influences in your life that you can recall?

A: The most important influence of all was my family who saw education as absolutely important and urged me to achieve. I was lucky in that one of my uncles had already gone to Oxford University – straight from the bush. He grew up in Brighton village, went to school there, then to Berbice High School,[7] where he won a scholarship to Queen's College. He did his A-levels and went on to the University of the West Indies where he got a first-class honours degree in history. This was during the late 1950s and early 1960s. He then went on to study for his doctorate at Oxford. So there was already someone in the family who had ventured out, all the way from Brighton village to Oxford. I grew up under that influence. Uncle Raja was a little God-figure to us.

Q: You felt inspired by him?

A: Yes. When I went back in 1976 to Brighton village, I saw some of the books that he had read for A-levels, for example, *The Liberal Imagination* by Lionel Trilling. I was in my second year at Cambridge University before I came across Trilling. Guyanese of my uncle's time were far more advanced than we were. What rather saddens me is that under this PNC Government[8] that we have had for so long, although we had the reputation of being the intellectuals and writers of the Caribbean, we Guyanese are now statistically at the very bottom of the examination leagues in the Caribbean. The greatest indictment against this government is that they have not just impoverished the people economically: they have impoverished their capacity for expression.

Q: Is *Slave Song*[9] your first book? I assume by that time you had already written your PhD thesis.

A: No. *Slave Song* was written while I was at Cambridge. I was about 20 or 21 – still an undergraduate. It was published six years later.

Q: When you say 'written', do you mean in the form in which it finally appeared?

A: I had written four or five of the poems in *Slave Song* while I was an undergraduate at Cambridge. During that time I had the chance to return to Guyana. It had been about ten years since I had been home. Leaving as a boy and going back as an adult was probably the most creative process that I've been through. I spent three months at home as an adult. I had also gone back with Western modes of behaviour, including reading, and I think the tension between these modes and the home environment just created poetry. I immersed myself in that atmosphere for three months, and found that going back to Cambridge also released an enormous amount of creative energy. It reminds me of what C. L. R. James[10] says about West Indians – we have the privilege of being insiders as regards English society, but we are also outsiders. It is the same with our homes and villages: we are insiders and also outsiders, and that tension makes for excitement.

Q: Did the poems in *Slave Song* come in exactly their final form, or were they changed much afterwards?

A: They were written in the form that they are in at the moment, but obviously they were revised and shaped as they were being written.

Q: And what about the notes that followed?

A: I thought of three things in writing an extensive introduction and a series of notes: it was a literary joke – hence I referred twice in *Slave Song* to T. S. Eliot, because Eliot had also joked and provided a kind of spoof gloss to *The Waste Land*. On another level, we had been arguing for a long time that Creole was a distinctive language. It was part of the nationalism in the 1960s. We had our own airline, environment, landscape and fruit, therefore we should have our own language. If we were going to take that seriously we should provide translations to our poems. But the third reason is more serious. I wanted to write in a minimalist fashion, question the relationship between the work of art and the critical industry that arises because of the work of art. In other words, I was being the critic and the artist together in one book. It was in the 1970s when I went to Cambridge that modern critical theory – structuralism and deconstruction – was taking root. Art was being eclipsed altogether. Therefore, I was engaged in that whole Cambridge mood where the artist was being eclipsed and the critic became the re-writer of art. *Slave Song* came out of the intellectual environment of Cambridge; but it was also obviously nourished by the Guyanese imagination. It was a deliberately conscious work of literary criticism. It posed the question, which is so central now with Jacques Derrida, the French philosopher/deconstructionist and others, about the relationship between the artist and the critic, and between creative and critical work.

Q: What do you think would have happened if those notes and translations were not there?

A: I think the notes and translations take the poems into the realms of prose – very fine, elegant English prose. This brings up questions about the relationship between the prosaic nature of the English language and the intense, rhythmic nature of Creole. I see *Slave Song* as a whole book of poems; but it is also a book with literary criticism in it. I don't see how you can separate the two. I'm glad that Wilson Harris,[11] in his review of the book, actually pointed out that it is the juxtaposition of the prose and poetry that creates an added dimension of excitement. It's mixed media. Just as there is poetry and paintings, this is poetry and literary criticism.

Q: English readers would respond more warmly to this mixed-media presentation because it includes explanation and interpretation, and it is therefore easier to follow. But don't you run the risk of the West Indian reader being alienated, perhaps even being irritated by the fact that he can understand the Creole language directly, yet he has to face the intrusion of explanation and interpretation?

A: I don't think so. I see that Brathwaite, in *X Self*,[12] has followed me in providing a series of extensive notes even though he has abbreviated them. I think that *Slave Song* did have an impact. Don't forget that in the eighteenth and nineteenth centuries, this kind of writing was not unusual: you had poetry but also extensive introductions. In Pope's case, for instance, we supplied massive notes to his already extensive footnotes. Pope's own introduction to his poetry tends to be very detailed, and he also footnoted his own poetry. I'm not saying that we have to go back to the eighteenth century. What I am saying is that it has influenced people like Brathwaite – whether they wish to acknowledge it or not – in terms of how they present their own poetry to the West. More importantly, I do not think that our own people, because we happen to be West Indians, understand our own language, or indeed the nuances, or evocations of our language. Just because you can speak a language doesn't mean you can inhabit it creatively and intellectually. I think West Indians will benefit from the notes, if they benefit at all, or they will benefit as much as the English. The notes depart from the poems at a certain stage and take off in their own direction. They are little prose pieces by themselves.

Q: I found the sexuality of the poems very interesting. I was particularly interested in what you call 'the erotic energies of the colonial experience'.

A: I think that the empire has been looked at from the perspective of sociology, history, political economy, etc.; but the empire was also an enormous erotic project. I was interested in bringing to the surface the latent eroticism of the encounter between black and white, because it seemed to me that that would be revealing a relatively unexplored aspect of imperial relations. I know that Vic Reid had written a book on the Mau-Mau called *The Leopard*[13] which looked at this matter. But it was sensational. It wasn't playful enough. What I did with my re-formation of the eroticism of plantation life was in fact to contextualize it in English medieval traditions of romantic expression. So that you get a Creole poem that quotes the ballad tradition of medieval poetry. One has to be playful with the potentiality of eroticism, otherwise one can get into a very ugly and sensational way of writing. I distanced myself from the eroticism by overlaying the poems with references outside the plantation experience.

Q: You leave me somewhat confused about the exact object of this erotic type of writing. As you say, writing about colonialism has traditionally brought out aspects of economic exploitation, and of the enormous physical abuse of slavery. I am a little confused about the playful treatment of the erotic aspect of writing poetry.

A: First of all one has to say that the pure delight of writing in Creole about erotic experiences is a very sensuous pursuit. It helps you to strip away the surfaces of colonial relations, also reveal what takes place at the basest level of human emotions and actions, in the same way that Conrad's *Heart of Darkness* ceases being an exploration of a different geography and landscape, and becomes a Freudian exploration of the energies that people exchange. In other words, Africa ceases to be a geographical entity and becomes the territory of the human subconscious. Now that is revealing something else about our colonial relations.

Q: It was something inward-looking and subconscious in a Conradian sense, a dark secret concealed by a shining exterior?

A: I think that it was also linguistically important. I was a bit disappointed in a lot of Creole poetry, including my own and Brathwaite's, because I felt that the poets were largely using Creole in a social-realist manner, without a sense of its psychic energy and disturbing quality. They didn't take Creole to the very edge of breakdown because they didn't have the themes, and unless you stretch a language to its very limits in the way that Salman Rushdie[14] is stretching the English language at the moment, you cannot see its full potentiality. Now the theme that I had, which was eroticism, allowed me to adventure with language and 'pervert' it, which was opposite to Eddie Brathwaite's desire to purify it.

Q: You speak of vulgarity of the language and of pushing it to a breaking-point. You also mention exploring the extremities of language. I would have thought that that was exactly what Brathwaite has done: to mix Creole with Standard English, and marry that mixture with music. So in fact he was pushing beyond linguistic borders into the realm of another medium – music.

A: Brathwaite's project was absolutely innovative, and he's the best poet we've got. But at the end of the day, his Creole is still what I would call polite. It still works within boundaries, and it isn't until you take the language to the very edge of the boundaries of expression that you really see its potential for literature. I think Brathwaite was absolutely important in validating the use of Creole. He is superb in the way that he marries Creole with Standard English and imposes a jazz rhythm on to that, but even that is still conventional; it is not adventurous in a literary way. It works within a limited context and has a limited achievement. You have to use language as Joyce does, or as Rushdie does, or as Lawrence tore and perverted the language in *The Rainbow* and *Women in Love*. In other words, you have to take the language far ahead of the description of social conditions, or indeed of the intellectual projects which seek to marry Standard English with Creole and jazz. That is still a very intellectual project, and can betray an absence of feeling for Creole. I think that Brathwaite's poetry, para-doxically, has a feeling for the Creole language; but it doesn't possess the language instinctively. His reputation is partly based on the use of Creole, but if you look carefully, he cannot feel that language in the depth that Wilson Harris can. Harris has creolized the English language from a differ-ent perspective. This is why people say they find it difficult to understand Harris: he has creolized the English language, confused all the clauses, let the sentences run on endlessly. He has stretched and pulled the language everywhere; I don't think Brathwaite has done that. This is an enormous charge to make against a major literary figure, also a major Black literary figure whose Creole has always been seen as a province for the expression of Black things. I am of Indian stock. I am not re-colonizing Creole; neither do I want to appropriate it. It is, or used to be, my language, and the language of my family.

Q: There is tension between Indo- and Afro-West Indians in Guyana and Trinidad. Do you think this tension is represented in the language spoken by either group? Are there significant differences between the Creole of Indo-West Indians and the Creole spoken by Afro-West Indians?

A: Brathwaite did make a call a few years back for people to start researching Indian contributions to the creolization of language in the Caribbean, because all the research is really about the survival of African retentions. I would hope that what *Slave Song* does is to show how Indian the Creole is, not just in the use of Indian diction – there are many Indian words like *chamar*, *bela*, *pookne*[15] – but also in the whole setting of cows, and houses on stilts, and savannahs and paddy-fields. That agricultural experience is very Indian, and it is arrogant to marginalize us, to think that we can be on the land, day in and day out, since 1838, and not feel for that land and not belong to that land. When you are in the city you don't belong anywhere because you are metropolitan. You are marginal. It is those city-based populations in the West Indies that are the most marginal people. They are the non-West Indians, for they have imbibed all the metropolitan values. We who cut cane and grow rice and get bitten by snakes, are the West Indians who inhabit the spirit of the land, certainly in Guyana. I can't speak for Jamaica and other places where agriculture was sustained by non-Indian traditions.

Q: Roy Heath[16] has also spoken of the urban experience reducing people to a sameness like other urban experiences. The very title 'Slave Song' encourages me to think about the African experience of slavery in the Caribbean, and there are some poems about slavery and master–slave relationships in the book, but the poems which leap at me as most deeply inspired are the Indian poems. I realize that this has come about because of a specific historical context in which African slavery and the plantation system created an environment into which Indo-Caribbean experience was fitted.

A: To describe the Indian experience you really have to start with the parent experience. In other words, what I was trying to do in *Slave Song* was to see a continuum of slave and indenture experience.

Q: Is it not dangerous to speak of different Caribbean experiences as if one set of people suffered more than another?

A: If I am writing about an Indian on a plantation, I will inevitably also convey echoes of the African on the plantation. But if Afro-Caribbean experience is only an echo in my work, it doesn't mean that I am marginalizing the African. It just means that my theme is Indian. There are echoes of Africa always in writing about the Caribbean plantation, but they're becoming more and more inaudible because the African has moved away so far and so fast from plantation life, certainly in Guyana, that the African presence is probably an intellectual memory now.

Q: When V. S. Naipaul produced *A House for Mr Biswas*,[17] he was attacked for being ethnocentric, and he replied by saying that Indo-Trinidadian experience was all that he knew. There is no doubt that this experience was conditioned by such factors as displacement, exploitation, and alienation, which also influence Afro-Caribbean experience. But he had to write about what he knew. For this reason, it is not hard to understand why the strength of your inspiration is in your Indian-based poems. Perhaps it is for the same reason that I was very impressed by the success of your novel, *The Intended*,[18] in capturing the context of Indian life in the Caribbean. I don't think previous writers have captured quite the same mixture of drunkenness, wife-beating and violence with ambition and economic cunning. Having access to this raw, Indo-Guyanese experience, are you now to be considered a black British writer or a West Indian, or Indo-Guyanese writing in England? Your descriptions of the contradictions between Caribbean and British experience, or of people caught in the contradiction are superb.

A: Writers are privileged when they have a variety of sources to draw from, for example, a variety of landscapes that they have lived in, sometimes partially, or in a variety of languages they have spoken, even though they may overlap, like Creole and English. Writers thrive on this kind of plural, complex, contradictory background. Art is nourished by paradox. So in terms of self-definition I am glad I'm a three or four-footed creature, a kind of latter-day Anansi [19] as many West Indians are, a spider-figure with one foot planted in Africa through my scholarship. My doctoral research considered the representation of Africans in Western Art and Literature. Intellectually, therefore, I have a foot planted in Africa. I certainly have one foot planted in India because I can only recapture India in an intellectual way through books, or by visiting Indian friends; because I am Indo-Guyanese I am already removed from India. And certainly one foot is planted in Europe because, as C. L. R. James says, we are very much created by Europe, not wholly but partially: we grew up with Shakespeare; we see the English countryside as Naipaul does in *The Enigma of Arrival*,[20] through the lens of Constable and Wordsworth. We can't just have a direct relationship with the English countryside. We must see it through literary or visual texts. So we've got one foot in Africa, one in Europe, and one in our own society, Guyana, which has its own foot planted in South America. So it is potentially an endless series of poetic feet, landscapes, modes of feeling and thinking, and experiences that are available to us. We should see it as such a privilege. Instead, we see it as a grievance. Historically, some West Indians have said 'Oh God, why can't we go back to Africa? Why can't we go back to India?' To me that is a negation of the imagination, or the sign of an impoverished imagination, an atavistic impulse. It is refusing to see that we are modern people in the sense of having the potential for living in complex states. But we refuse to be complex. This is why in England we set up silly little political parties, or fall back on narrow nationalisms like the Montserrat Association, the Barbados Association, the Trinidad Association. When we are not terrified of our complexities, we turn them into a source of grievance.

Q: Historically, they have been a source of grievance.

A: I think so, but I also think the middle passage was profoundly and paradoxically creative. It wasn't meant to be creative, but by removing the African and Indian from home it set up all kinds of tensions. Diaspora set up all kinds of tensions and possibilities for growth. The middle passage was creative by liberating the imagination from home. Writers have to live outside before they can write about inside; you need that distance. The middle passage gave us a distance from Africa and India. But also it liberated us physically as well. I lost all sense of caste-affiliation. I would not have lost that if the British had not moved us to the Caribbean. I would have been possibly a peasant labouring under one of the most oppressive systems on earth which is the caste system.

Q: You lost your caste but you also lost your language.

A: We lost our language, and it is an irreparable loss. It's a very felt loss to me. I've always wanted to learn Hindi or Urdu. But you have to use what you have.

Q: I accept that the complexity of Caribbean experience may include certain benefits. But living here in England as an Indian-looking person, without an Indian language, are you not at a disadvantage, when you are subjected to racism, for example? Would it not be an advantage to have a language other than English to express your difference?

A: Yes, but I think I can try to express my difference using the English language. All I am saying is that if I had Hindi with the same fluency that I have English, then I would have felt more strengthened, more whole. But possibly even more confined because in a sense by only having the English language to express my difference means that I have to be fantastically creative with the English language. I have to do things with the English language that it may not have the 'natural' capacity for. English does not really allow me to express my Guyanese experience. I have to force the weight of my experience on it and therefore modify the language. New challenges arise out of being trapped in mono-language and having to express differences in it. That in itself creates wonderful tensions that can be exploited by the writer.

Q: You're speaking of literary advantages.

A: Yes, but I see myself as having the protection of a creative imagination. I draw a distinction between the artist and the immigrant. If I didn't have art, then I would be an immigrant, and I would have nothing to console me in this society which you say is so racist.

Q: Since you don't live here as an isolated artist, but among people like yourself, I may ask what is your responsibility to these people who look like you, but don't have the literary advantages to express themselves creatively in the English language, and have to suffer from English racism?

A: But the artist has to go out there and suffer the same. I have to wait at bus stops and sit on trains. The whites don't know that I am an artist, and they don't necessarily care anyway, so in certain situations I am treated like other immigrants in this society. When I speak of the 'protection of the creative imagination', I mean an awareness of, or confidence in the self, which means you *can* speak out, or write out. But you have to see all these things in context. I come from a society, Guyana, which is as racist and traumatized by race, perhaps more traumatized than British society. Even if we argue, as some historians have, that it was the British who created racism in the Caribbean, I was born into a racist society, one in which race was a very important and privileged factor. Coming here for me has, in fact, been as liberating as it has been oppressive. There has been a deep liberal mood in Britain from Magna Carta days to today. The British initiated and participated in the slave trade. At the same time, the abolition of the slave trade was the first major philanthropic movement in this country. So whilst there is racism, there has always been a liberal mood, and we have to exist in it. So I wouldn't dismiss England as a racist society. That is too simplistic. It is racist; but it also has anti-racist elements, and it is our responsibility as immigrant writers to support, sustain, and contribute to anti-racist elements in the society, by helping to develop the society as a whole, and by contributing our arts, sciences, education, business skills and whatever else; for this is our home.

Q: So the future is here?

A: There is no other discernible future except Britain. This is home now, and we have to make it home. I am not arguing for indiscriminate integration, or for abandonment of the cultural baggage that we brought to this country. What I am arguing for is our contribution to all aspects of society, even while bearing with us a sense of our difference. And I do believe that England is spacious enough to tolerate difference in the society; it is big enough to want difference. In the West Indies – those tiny islands, if you are different you are a lunatic; you are ostracized, and called an artist or a madman. That is why Naipaul's fiction is so full of different people called 'mad'. In this society you have greater allowance to be 'mad'. This society is much more liberal than our own society. When we riot in England, sometimes for very good reasons, it is also a refusal to contribute to society. Riots are as negative as they are inevitable.

Q: That's realistic. Whatever the colonial past, it has happened already. People who have come here must accommodate themselves to conditions here. I agree with you. And whereas I am aware of racism in this society, I think you are right to acknowledge anti-racist and liberal elements working against that.

A: I also agree with E. P. Thompson[21] who said that there have always been common decencies operating between people in England. People might be racist in a philosophical or abstract sense. They might talk about Pakis in the abstract sense, but if they sit down side by side in a bus, or if they encounter a Paki in the street, through personal contact, the racism diminishes, and it is not as intense or as overt as you might think it would be.

Q: These prejudices stem from an intellectual dislike produced by histor-

ical factors which are themselves the product of narrow and ignorant attitudes about cultures. Still, as you say, there is a commitment to normal,
social exchange.

A: That's at one level. At another level, this is a society of books, a textual
and artistic society. It's a contradiction to say that a society of books is a
society of hatred: it has its hatreds, but it also has its books.

Q: You sound like V. S. Naipaul in the early days when he first came to
England and encountered civilized social decencies which he had not experienced at home in Trinidad.

A: I wouldn't say that I never experienced it at home, because I've
experienced great acts of generosity in both societies.

Q: But the generosity at home is more personal.

A: Yes, it is more personal and family-based whereas the generosity here
is more social. We must have the confidence and courage to keep saying
that this is our society, even if a lot of white people say it is not. We must
keep saying it is our society, and believing it, not only in the abstract, but in
the way that the Asians coming from Uganda and Kenya in the 1960s did,
despite disadvantages of an alien language, alien foods and ways of dressing. Eventually, they made enormous waves in the cities, and created
businesses that are now major employers in Britain. We West Indians can
learn from the Asians. It seems a tragedy that Indians have become alienated in the West Indies. What Indians did to the Caribbean was quite
revolutionary. In spite of conditions of indenture they brought a sense of
voluntary labour, the feeling that labour merits rewards. Up to 1838 labour
did not bring rewards in the West Indies, because the people were slaves.
We brought back the work-ethic into the West Indies. Why is it that we
don't have a major publishing house in the West Indies?[22] That shows
you how impoverished we are as a region. There's an ambiguity in West
Indians, particularly Guyanese, attacking England. We don't even have
our own publishing house to give expression to our works, in Guyana,
because we spend lavishly on our army as a way of stemming the political
fury that could come from being so backward and incompetent. It's not
enough to continue to blame whites for messing up our society. They may
have introduced elements of the mess, but we completed that job with
superb finality: that is why everyone in Guyana wants to leave.

Q: By way of defence, I can say that, in the twenty-five years or so since
white rulers formally left the Caribbean, the structures of colonialism have
remained in place in social and economic terms.

A: All over the Caribbean we had the middle-classes inhabiting positions
that the whites had vacated, and behaving just like the whites at their
worst. I think that the scholarship of our own economic analysts shows that
we lost economic markets, not because these markets were dominated by
the West, but because we didn't have the capacity to fulfill the demands.

The Lomé Convention guarantees that the EEC will purchase our sugar.[23] But we cannot produce that sugar. Why? Because of administrative and ultimately political incompetence.

Q: Let us get back to your novel *The Intended*. It has an authentic sense of Guyanese life. But how does the structure work? Is there a pattern or significance in the relationship of the Guyanese sections and the English ones?

A: The narrative structure of the novel has no focal point. It's an unstable narrative. I think that one has to exploit the creativity inherent in creolization, by which I mean that there is a confusion of the past, present and future tenses in the Creole language, and I wanted to exploit the space that the confusion offers. So there is no linear narrative in the novel, even though there is a certain direction to the constant flashbacks and flashforwards. They are related to one's linguistic condition – Creole with its confused tenses. I also wanted to convey the immigrant experience, which is not linear, because immigrants are liable to appear and disappear. This is what migrant life is: you appear in one society, then you disappear; you are always moving on. That's the structure. The novel is set on buses and trains, and there is a lot of waiting at bus-stops, a constant sense of travelling which ends up with a boy waiting for a taxi. There are taxis, buses, planes and trains, which represent the constant affliction as well as the creative potential of migration or diaspora. Therefore a kind of intellectual migration is going on as well. The main character migrates to England, but in England he migrates away from his friends.

Q: You have a very good passage on that, with the hero reflecting on British security and his own insecurity, and the mixture of feelings that that produces.

A: I didn't want to get involved in the parade of grievances. One of the old themes in West Indian literature is the crisis of identity. I have a multiple identity. There is no crisis. There is a kind of delight as well as anguish in jumping from one identity to the next. It's like electrons which have their own energization circles. Sometimes they jump from one to the next and release an enormous amount of energy; then they jump to another circle: little electrons jumping.[24] That is not a crisis. That is delight and poignancy, and hopefully a release of energy. To see it as a crisis would be to invest in historical grievances. To call myself a black, and to hate whites is to get back to Manichean systems of operating in the world. It seems to me that our West Indian writers have invested too heavily in the monolith of 'the folk'. This is not true for Wilson Harris and V. S. Naipaul,[25] who came from different positions, one cynical and the other Blakean, yet both making the West Indian feel that he/she is on the threshold of some capacity.

Q: The names of Naipaul and Harris have recurred throughout this interview. But Harris can be so remote, and his writing so inaccessible. How is it that he is so influential?

A: I think Harris's ideas are very stubborn; and ideas have to be converted into art. D. H. Lawrence said that the business of the novelist is to reconcile his metaphysics with his actual sense of living. I think that Harris does this brilliantly at times when you get the most sensuous passages about Guyana and the Guyanese landscape. Then sometimes, there is a sudden loss of sensuousness replaced by a struggle for formulation of philosophical ideas which ought to belong in an essay rather than a work of art. I think that when Harris succeeds there is nothing like it in West Indian literature. There are sudden ideas which emerge from what he calls a half-eclipse. In the middle of a novel an idea will surface, or a few sentences will be thrown up which will suddenly open up a whole new way of seeing things. These fantastic illuminations always come with Harris. The prose is always being illuminated although it is so dark and dense at times.

Q: We used to talk about the fragmentation of colonialism and now this is being interpreted in a more positive way as multiplicity. It is as if the old fragments can now nourish each other in loose association rather than remain broken or useless as in the previous interpretation. Does Harris's work reflect this positive interpretation of multiplicity? Was that there from his first book, *Palace of the Peacock*?[26]

A: I think Harris has seen, in the deepest, most uncanny way, the potential of this fragmentation or multiplicity. All his novels really are about a kind of quantum imagination, as Michael Gilkes[27] calls it, where there are no physical laws that are rigid. There are no identities which cannot be transferred or modified. This is what he struggles to convey in his novels. Whether he succeeds is another matter. I think he does mostly. All art fails ultimately, or fails at critical times. At least Harris has taken a different position from Naipaul. Naipaul's position strikes me at times as being similar to that of Négritude,[28] in searching for a stable community or a stable set of ideas. The search for stability is always in Naipaul. To me that can show an unwillingness to adventure into realms of anarchy and confusion which is the modern condition, which is why Naipaul always seems so magnificent, so nineteenth-century in the impeccable, chiselled nature of his prose. His writing seems so colonial as opposed to post-colonial. Post-colonial writing is one of confusion. It has thrown up its own literary form of 'magical realism'.[29] Naipaul does not see in the confusion the possibility of a new regrouping of citizenship, of a new language emerging or indeed of old languages co-existing. Why does Babel have to fall down? I still agree with Enoch Powell,[30] whose position in politics seems similar to Naipaul's in literature. I also think of Brathwaite's Babel in his poetry, although he drew boundaries. All this revelling and confusion can, at one level, mean an enormous loss of the self or self-confidence. In other words, you cannot be cultural unless you have a sense of boundaries. Brathwaite drew African boundaries in the Caribbean, and Naipaul shows the terror of an absence of boundaries. Harris revels in the absence of boundaries, and that can be very dangerous. It can mean that you are a dilettante, that you are loose and have no roots or attachment or commitment. But I do hope that I can be intensely Guyanese, or intensely Berbician, or English, or European. In other words, one has the possibilities of inhabiting different masks intensely.

Q: What you express is a protean vision of something that is remade constantly even while being broken. You envisage a process of constant dissolution and regeneration.

A: The amoeba never breaks its boundaries, it always has a skin, a shell. You always have the nucleus of your soul.

Q: From the very beginning Harris has always talked about singularity: a unity within diversity. There is always a nucleus.

A: Sometimes the nucleus shifts within the body of the amoeba, but the nucleus is always there, and there is always a skin or boundary.

Q: So that the person is still whole. The self is still whole.

A: Lamming[31] sees the skin as a castle. He would see colonials constructing their skin out of stone. But stone is not fluid. You can either just obey a stone or you can destroy it and make it crumble. I prefer to think that the boundary of your skin is not made out of stone, and that it is not something that you have to blow trumpets at and smash down like the walls of Jericho. It's amoeboid.

Notes

1 Cf. Chapter 5, note 12.
2 Race riots erupted in Guyana during 1962–64, mainly because of opposition to the government led by Dr Cheddi Jagan. Racial clashes between Indians and Africans, the two major races, resulted in Indians moving from areas where they considered themselves vulnerable, e.g. New Amsterdam, which was predominantly African.
3 A 'mala' was a garland made from freshly-cut flowers. When worn on secular occasions its function was mainly decorative or ceremonial, but it carried spiritual significance when worn at religious rituals.
4 This is also the setting of Mittelholzer's *Corentyne Thunder* and partly of Carew's *The Wild Coast*.
5 Cf. Chapter 9, note 45.
6 See Chapter 1, note 13.
7 Cf. Chapter 5, note 1.
8 See note 6 above.
9 David Dabydeen, *Slave Song* (Dangaroo Press, Denmark, 1984).
10 For C. L. R. James, see Chapter 2, note 15.
11 For Harris, see Introduction, note 7.
12 Edward Brathwaite, *X-Self* (Oxford University Press, Oxford, 1987).

13   See Chapter 5, note 31.

14   Cf. Chapter 4, note 17.

15   These are Hindi words. A *chamar* is a leather-worker and therefore, in Hindu terms, someone beyond the pale, a social outcast; a *bela* is a wooden rolling pin; and a *pookne* is an empty metal cylinder used for blowing air and stoking up open wood-fires.

16   See Roy Heath's comments in Chapter 7.

17   See Chapter 1, note 12.

18   David Dabydeen, *The Intended* (Secker & Warburg, London, 1991).

19   See Chapter 4, note 31.

20   See Introduction, note 10.

21   E. P. Thompson was a British Marxist historian and author, well-known for his numerous publications, including *The Making of the English Working Class* (1963). He was also an active campaigner for international peace.

22   Cf. Roy Heath's comments in Chapter 7 at note 9.

23   The Lomé Convention was signed in 1975 between the European Community (EEC States) and an ACP Group of African, Caribbean and Pacific countries. Among other things, the Convention guaranteed purchase by the EEC of ACP sugar at EEC prices.

24   Cf. Chapter 13 at note 19.

25   For Harris and Naipaul, see Index.

26   For *Palace of the Peacock*, see Introduction, note 7.

27   In Michael Gilkes, *Wilson Harris and the Caribbean Novel* (Longman, London, 1975).

28   Cf. Chapter 8, note 23.

29   Cf. Chapter 4, notes 16 and 17.

30   Enoch Powell is a former British politician and member of the Conservative Party. He achieved notoriety in the 1970s by warning against the presence of increasing numbers of blacks and Asians in Britain. In one speech, he warned of 'rivers of blood' as a consequence of the racial conflict that would follow from unchecked immigration. Powell proposed a scheme encouraging non-white immigrants to return to their homelands through funds provided by the British Government. The scheme was not implemented.

31   For Lamming, see Index.

CHAPTER 14

Caryl Phillips:
The legacy of Othello, Part (1)

Caryl Phillips was born in St Kitts in 1958 the same year that his parents emigrated and took him to England. Phillips grew up in Leeds, and later attended Oxford University. His writing career began with plays such as Strange Fruit *(1980) and* Where There is Darkness *(1982). He also wrote scripts for film, television and radio. His first novel,* The Final Passage, *appeared in 1985, and was followed by other works of fiction, including* Higher Ground *(1989);* Cambridge *(1991);* Crossing the River *(1993); and a volume of essays,* The European Tribe *(1987). Phillips's writing renders Caribbean immigrant experience in England with great insight and versatility, evoking themes of exile, alienation and restlessness. He has the rare ability to see this experience from within and without, and to interpret the complex relations between the immigrants and their children who have grown up in England. Phillips lives in London, but maintains a house in St Kitts as well. He now teaches at Amherst College in the US. (The interview in Part (1) was recorded on 15 October 1986, and that in Part (2) on 1 March 1991; both interviews were recorded in Toronto.)*

Q: Some West Indian writers like Wilson Harris, V. S. Naipaul, and Roy Heath[1] have been living in Britain since 1950. You represent a younger generation that includes such writers as Mustapha Matura, Linton Kwesi Johnson, David Dabydeen and David Simon.[2] Is the writing of Harris, Naipaul, and others of their generation important to you?

A: The writers who were initially important to me were African-American writers, largely because Ralph Ellison's[3] work was available in Penguin Modern Classics, and James Baldwin[4] was an international figure. The fact that Lamming, Selvon and Harris[5] actually existed was more important to me than what they were writing. The only works of their generation towards which I had any real empathy were those that related to England, like *The Emigrants*,[6] and *The Lonely Londoners*.[7] Works that were rooted in the Caribbean meant nothing to me. I felt much more in tune with the urban jungle that Ralph Ellison or Richard Wright[8] would describe, because I lived in an urban jungle myself.

Q: My first impression of your work was that it didn't fit my experience in the West Indies, but it did coincide with the world of African-Americans, that is to say, the experience of black people who had been westernized in a metropolitan, Euro/American context. Your writing deals with black people who have been Westernized in a similar context.

A: Actually a novel that I now recognize as great, but which didn't mean anything to me at first, was *In the Castle of My Skin*.[9] Richard Wright's *Black Boy*[10] was phenomenally important to me because I could understand the pain and despair of actually growing up in the South, and having to deal with white society. Lamming's book about a Caribbean childhood was remote from me, while Richard Wright's book was closer, since it was about being young and feeling utterly out of tune with the society around me. In *In the Castle of My Skin* Lamming was describing the process of growing up in the bosom of that society, with the rich smells, outdoor nature, and so on which was very remote from my experience.

Q: Lamming and Selvon wrote about West Indian immigrants arriving in Britain with false expectations and attitudes. These immigrants encountered discrimination. Their warm, sunny temperament and flexible Caribbean attitudes came into conflict with more rigid, metropolitan, cultural habits. The result of the conflict was negative, but at least there was hope that things might change later on. Your books give me a sense of what has happened later on, after your characters have lived in Britain for twenty years. They still think about going back home to the West Indies. There is still the same rage, bitterness and dissatisfaction with Britain. Have twenty years made no difference?

A: In terms of the British attitude towards black people and towards West Indians in particular, I would say it has changed since Lamming's day when there was curiosity, then hostility. In my day, I think the hostility is almost distilled. There is no longer any curiosity about black or West Indian faces. I think part of the anger or hurt which may permeate my work comes from the fact that when I look at the life of my parents and of people of my parents' generation, I feel they have been given a terrible deal in Britain. I also feel that it would be very difficult for me to see a future for myself in England if I was a married man with children. Looking ahead now, I feel slightly angry and upset at the fact that I won't be comfortable bringing up another generation of West Indians who, because of intractable British attitudes, will have to go through the same problems I went through. These are the same problems that were depicted in *The Lonely Londoners* thirty years ago.

Q: In *Where there is Darkness*,[11] Albert is preparing to return home. In *Strange Fruit*[12] Alvin goes home, and in *The Final Passage*[13] Leila is set to go back to the West Indies.

A: My novel *State of Independence*[14] concerns a man who has spent twenty years in England, and also decides to go back to the Caribbean. The novel actually begins with him on a plane circling over an island. It's about the first three days after his arrival, and his reflections on how he has spent twenty years in England. He has not kept in touch with anybody. He feels some bitterness about England, and a kind of romantic love toward the Caribbean. In him I have pulled together all the strands in my plays, and tried to examine the question of what happens to the man who tries to go back. I have never really felt that it is possible to go back. The bleakness in some of my work perhaps comes from the fact that to reconcile yourself to not going back is to accept a situation that is, unfortunately, permanently unhappy. That's the experience of my generation in Britain. The writing of my contemporaries is about the struggle to be accepted, which, considering the work already done by those writers who came over in the 1950s and 1960s, and the pioneering work of my parents and other parents like them, makes it all seem futile. The question leaps out: 'When will it end?'

Q: No responsible person could suggest emigration from Britain as a solution – 'repatriation' – as Enoch Powell[15] calls it. But, in an artistic way, you could dramatize a situation which encourages people to consider the implications of 'repatriation'.

A: West Indians or most West Indians in Britain remember the Caribbean and have the idea at the back of their minds that perhaps one day they can go back. The problem occurs when you don't have any memory of the Caribbean, and you have been told that's where you are from. That's why Alvin in *Strange Fruit* goes back to the Caribbean, returns to England, and actually discovers that the Caribbean is not for him. It's a real problem to have no memory of the Caribbean; and it's a problem to have a memory of the Caribbean. If you seek to discover the Caribbean as somebody growing up in North America or Britain, then nine times out of ten you will be disappointed.

Q: I seem to detect parallels between your work and Paule Marshall's. Did reading *Brown Girl, Brown Stones*[16] have any effect on you?

A: I don't think it had an effect on me, because I wasn't aware of Paule Marshall in the context of West Indians in the States. I am now aware of her perhaps because *Brown Girl* has been issued again, but also because of people like Jamaica Kincaid,[17] who are beginning to look at the West Indian experience from an American point of view.

Q: You seem particularly hard on women in your books, for instance, the mother and the girl Shelly in *Strange Fruit*. I feel a little uncomfortable about the intensity of victimization which the women seem to suffer in general – both black and white. In the case of Shelly, she seems so utterly hopeless. Nobody wants her: her parents don't want her. I agree the boy's mother offers her something and gives her the key to her house. But Shelly's situation is one of real desperation.

A: I am glad you mentioned the mother giving her the key. The mother could never convince her two sons of how much she loved them. Somehow, by giving Shelly the key, I wanted to show her capacity for love. The second thing is that I wanted to examine the whole question of a mixed relationship. The third thing I attempted to depict was the situation of being desperate. I wanted to throw into relief the idea that all black people are directionless, and all white people have a sense of purpose and direction; because you know as well as I do, that there are white people who are more screwed up than black people. Those three factors contributed towards my presentation of the mother and Shelly.

Q: Don't West Indian women take an excess of blows, both emotional and physical, in their relationships with men?[18]

A: I don't know enough about West Indian domesticity in the islands. In the case of West Indians in Britain, it seems to me that the women have taken more blows than the men. The Caribbean is a matriarchal society; white Europe is patriarchal. I think this vicious shift from one form of behaviour between men and women to another in Europe produced an irresponsibility in some West Indians which no generation could afford to endure. After all, when you are going through problems of adjusting to a society which in many ways and forms is rejecting you, it doesn't really help if your father, for whatever reasons, decides to leave the family.

Q: This happens quite often, doesn't it?

A: It happened in my family. But that's not why I am concerned with examining it. I am concerned because there are very few of my West Indian contemporaries in England who actually grew up in a stable family background.

Q: When I first looked at your work, I felt you knew the metropolitan situation of the black minority and white majority very well. The relationships, language, dialogue and tensions were exactly right. Then I noticed that in writing about people in the West Indies, there was the same authenticity. Your control of two contrasting milieus impressed me. I suppose the fact that you have gone back regularly to visit the Caribbean might help to explain it.

A: In writing *State of Independence*, a novel with a contemporary Caribbean setting, I felt that some of it must be related to the politics of Independence. I think my publishers and perhaps readers were surprised, because they assumed I would continue the story from *The Final Passage* not necessarily using the same characters, but using a setting and characters that would bring my sensibility further and further into England. In fact, the reverse has happened. I do feel, for a number of reasons, that I desperately want to address the Caribbean situation, as much as I do the British one, and for me, quite frankly, it is a matter of research. It is a matter of exposing myself to it.

Q: I would think that there is a difference between experience that is learnt or researched and experience that is lived, that you grow up in.

I wonder that I don't detect a difference in authenticity between your rendering of these two types of experience.

A: The two types of experience are not considered by my contemporaries in Britain, not in David Simon's work, or Linton Kwesi Johnson's or the work of any of the younger playwrights. Nobody addresses the Caribbean at all. It's difficult to explain to people that I was born in the Caribbean, whereas three of my younger brothers weren't. I have always clung to the fact that even though I hadn't visited the Caribbean as a mature person, I did originate there. Maybe if I had been born in Britain, and not had to go through my childhood with the knowledge that I was born in the Caribbean, I may now be addressing the British situation with more vigour. But for me it has always been a safety-valve against the 'rivers of blood' type of speeches, against social pressure. It has always kept me sane, the fact that I was born in the Caribbean. I will always pay my dues towards that.

Q: If you were born in England and wrote the type of literature which largely addresses the problems of minorities and so on, how limiting would you find that? What exactly would be the limitation? Authors who write like that are performing a social function of setting injustice right, or expressing protest against injustice.

A: I suspect it would be totally limiting. I think it would be impossible or, at the very best, extremely difficult for me to address the situation in Britain only. To limit myself to Britain only for my subject matter would make me a protest writer, merely an extension of the university sociology faculty, which would prevent me from being seen as a writer *per se*. Linton [Kwesi Johnson] is a very good example of this. He feels as though he hasn't even begun writing, despite his established reputation. He doesn't feel he knows his craft. That's perhaps another reason why I am not prepared to limit myself to the British situation, because eventually there will come a time when the idea of rage – which is what Baldwin was talking about when he criticized Richard Wright – the idea of rage would become my theme.

Q: That itself would be limiting.

A: That, in the end, would probably stifle whatever talent I have.

Q: Since you mentioned this question of rage, I want to bring in Naipaul[19] who has also studiously avoided rage as his main theme. This has made him greatly hated, or at least controversial. But I don't see in you that hostility towards Naipaul that I detect in many West Indians and West Indian writers?

A: No, because I think Naipaul's talent is unquestionable. But he made a decision or perhaps he didn't make a decision – perhaps he didn't have a choice of how he wanted to be. But he's been consistent in it. He's never actually strayed into the territory of becoming a spokesperson. He's never jumped on a convenient platform. He has remained detached, and you have to respect the man for his consistency. I don't particularly like Naipaul's view of Africa. I certainly don't like his view of the Caribbean; but I respect his talent and his consistency. He doesn't bring out any bile in me because I don't feel he's interested in the areas I am interested in. Writers are very territorial animals, and I think I could understand why a Lamming or a Selvon might feel very bitter about a man of their own generation achieving the stature that Naipaul has. Economically, he must be comfortable for the rest of his life. When people hold a festival, for example, and they need someone who has written from the West Indies, they are more likely to ask Naipaul than they are to ask Lamming. After a while, it would piss me off if I was Lamming. But Naipaul is not a competitor in my area.

Q: From the beginning of *Where there is Darkness*, there is a flashblack, with constant interchanges between contemporary and past action throughout the play. Where does that technique come from? Are you following a particular trend in contemporary drama?

A: The play was inspired structurally by *Death of a Salesman*, in which Arthur Miller tried to examine the life of a man who was dangling by a string, and the string is about to break. That's the dramatic situation, and the only way you can contextualize the man's life is by seeing what happened before. It was a very convenient dramatic structure, theatrically, from a West Indian point of view, because it is striking to first see the gloomy, cold English lighting, then after the sets and stage revolve, to suddenly see the bright, Caribbean sunshine. Dramatically, the technique is much more powerful when you are given two cultures and two different types of sunlight. Of course the very term 'flashback' comes from the cinema. Arthur Miller's career was deeply involved in the cinema as well.

Q: It's all right to say that you were born in St Kitts, grew up in England, and that now you are recovering the Kittician experience so that you can consider both your British residence and St Kitts origin in your work. But the fact remains that you live in Britain; you publish in Britain. People will call you a British writer. You will be compared with the people writing in Britain today. How do you see your position *vis-à-vis* native British writers?

A: As I said, writing is competitive. My development as a writer runs parallel with the development of younger British writers. I look at what they publish and think I'd better make sure my next book is up to scratch. So I do feel an affinity with contemporary publishing in Britain. However, I think it is an advantage to be liberated from some of the nonsense and parochialism produced not only by living in Britain, but by British incestuous publishing itself. I feel I have a territory or subject matter which is more international than that of my British contemporaries.

Q: How does your British/Caribbean perspective give you an advantage over them?

A: Most of them think that I am a bit crazy, because I don't just write about Britain. This affinity for black subjects and writing is only one thing that distinguishes me from my British contemporaries. The other thing is a group of novels which affected me when I was growing up. These were novels by David Storey, Alan Sillitoe and John Braine[20] who dealt with the problems of growing up in the working class. Those novels affected me because they portray class and culture dislocation that I could relate to very easily. When I look at the work of my British contemporaries – people like Ian McEwan and Graham Swift,[21] who are still in their thirties and who are fine writers – their subject matter doesn't engage me in the same way as the subject matter of novelists who came a generation before them. So it's not simply because they are British; it is also their subject matter that distinguishes me from them.

Q: Your position is unique in that you can write with equal conviction from within British as well as Caribbean society. When Naipaul tried to write from a British perspective in *Mr Stone and The Knights Companion*,[22] I don't think he was nearly as successful as in his West Indian novels.

A: Yes, but my uniqueness places a special responsibility on me. Both Caribbean and British societies have many things wrong with them that need to be examined and exposed. I can see historical connections between the two societies, and I can see contemporary reverberations between them. I also feel very comfortable, culturally, in both societies. I can build bridges, and help to cross-fertilize the two. Given the history of slavery, colonialism and modern-day neo-colonialism, there's a whole range of explosive, political and social subjects that I think I am probably in a good position to explore.

Notes

1 For Harris, Naipaul and Heath, see Index.
2 Mustapha Matura is from Trinidad and lives in England. Some of his best-known plays include: *As Time Goes By* (Calder and Boyars, London, 1972); *Independence* (Methuen, London, 1982); *Playboy of the West Indies* (Broadway Publishing, New York, 1988).
    Linton Kwesi Johnson is from Jamaica and has established a reputation as a leading black British poet based largely on recordings of his poetry accompanied by music.
    See Chapter 13 for David Dabydeen.
    David Simon was born of West Indian parents in Paddington, London. He is the author of the novel *Railton Blues*.
3 Ralph Ellison is the author of *Going to the Territory* (Random House, New York, 1986); *Invisible Man* (New American Library, 1952); *Shadow and Act* (Random House, New York, 1964).
4 For James Baldwin, see Chapter 11, note 27.
5 For Lamming, Selvon and Harris, see Index.
6 George Lamming, *The Emigrants* (Michael Joseph, London, 1954).

7   See Chapter 6, note 11.
8   Richard Wright is the author of *Native Son* (Harper, New York, 1940); *The Outsider* (Harper, New York, 1953); *Black Boy* (Harper, New York, 1945). Cf. Chapter 8, note 21.
9   See Bibliography under Lamming.
10 See Chapter 6, note 11.
11 Caryl Phillips, *Where There is Darkness* (Amber Lane Press, London, 1982).
12 Caryl Phillips, *Strange Fruit* (Amber Lane Press, London, 1981).
13 Caryl Phillips, *The Final Passage* (Penguin, Harmondsworth, 1990).
14 Caryl Phillips, *A State of Independence* (Faber and Faber, London, 1986).
15 Cf. Chapter 13, note 30.
16 See Introduction, note 4.
17 See Index and Chapter 11.
18 Cf. similar comments by Lorna Goodison in Chapter 12.
19 For V. S. Naipaul, see Index.
20 David Storey was born in 1933. He is a novelist and playwright who also worked as a professional footballer. He came to notice with his first novel, *This Sporting Life* (1960). Alan Sillitoe was born in 1928 and achieved popularity in Britain with novels such as *Saturday Night and Sunday Morning* (1958), and *The Loneliness of the Long Distance Runner* (1959).

    John Braine (1922–1986) was one of the provincial British novelists who were regarded as 'angry young men' in the 1950s because of their radical views. Braine achieved fame with his novel *Room at the Top* (1957). In his later novels, Braine was hostile to the radical views he had expressed earlier.
21 Ian McEwan is an English fiction and screenplay-writer known for his macabre and grotesque characterization and imagery. His works include *Or Shall We Die?* (1983) and *The Innocent* (1990).

    Graham Swift is an English novelist. His psychologically intricate novels include *The Sweet Shop Owner* (1980); and *Waterland* (1984).
22 V. S. Naipaul, *Mr Stone and the Knights Companion* (André Deutsch, London, 1963).

CHAPTER 15

Caryl Phillips: The legacy of Othello, Part (2)

Q: Since I spoke to you last you've written *The European Tribe*, *Higher Ground* and *Cambridge*.[1] I have already said that I see your work as interpreting the fate of black people in the modern world, that is to say, in an international context. In *The European Tribe*, among other things, you define the specific problem of blacks who feel British, yet are told that they don't belong to Britain. You illustrate their problem through the image of a transplanted tree that failed to take root in foreign soil. In *The European Tribe* you also offer perceptive commentaries on British colonial experience in places like Gibraltar, the Falkland Islands, and Northern Ireland – some of the last appendages of empire. I particularly like your chapter on Othello, 'A black European Success', because it seems to deal with one of your central concerns – the options for a black person from the colonies, nowadays from the third world – who has been made or shaped in the developed world. In the Persian Gulf War[2] that is currently being waged, General Colin Powell, who is the military head of US forces, was born in the Bronx of Jamaican immigrant parents. He is leading mainly white forces which have dominated the world for five hundred years, and in the process, slaughtered many people, including aboriginal Americans and African-Americans like Powell himself. In the battle of Omdurman,[3] fought one hundred years ago, Kitchener slaughtered thousands of Sudanese using Anglo-Egyptian forces, in the same way that the Americans are using other Arab forces against the Iraqis today.

A: I think the diaspora experience has always produced ironies some of which are humorous, and some not. I think the figure of the black person of African origin who is used as a weapon against non-Europeans did begin, in a literary context, with the figure of Othello. At Oxford University I read Shakespeare's *Othello* with a very different feel than most of my contemporaries. I remember my tutor telling me that he didn't have anything to say about my essay on *Othello* because it was so personal. He hadn't thought about Othello as a man who was being used by society. My tutor approached the text through the easier prism of Desdemona or Iago; but I approached it through the magical window of a man who, whether he liked to or not, continually made references to his origins through the imagery in his speeches. What frightens me is the huge irony of the legacy of Othello.

Q: Do you see us completely trapped by a Eurocentric power-block that is secure in its ability to dominate powerless groups of the third world?
A: I don't think it is secure. Half the problem is its desire to co-opt or involve black people in a struggle against other black people. It's symptomatic of a lack of security. If Venetian society had been more secure, they wouldn't have asked a black man to run their army for them.
Q: Is there a parallel here with Colin Powell and the US army?
A: We should be careful not to confuse the European black diaspora experience with the American black diaspora experience. The American situation is much better-documented and has a more enduring history.
Q: I agree about the differences between the European black experience and the American black experience. As you suggest, there are historical reasons for it. Also, there is a larger number of blacks in the US – at least 12 per cent of the population. There's nothing like that proportion of blacks anywhere in Europe; and there may be other reasons as well. But in interpreting that European black experience you found it useful to read about American blacks.
A: I see the links and the way in which the European black experience and the black experience in North America and the Caribbean feed off each other: they're vitally interrelated. But to begin that debate or the retelling of that story from a European perspective will make them feel uncomfortable because there isn't an ongoing history of debate on such subjects, and there isn't a visibility of black people in Europe, in positions of authority, to make the debate possible. The European identity is still insecure. You have to bear in mind that these countries, for the most part of their history, have been at war with each other. France has been fighting Germany; everybody's been fighting the Soviet Union; Poland has been invaded several times. Now, you have the almost unbelievable spectacle of them banding together, not just politically and economically, but to a certain extent culturally, inasmuch as soon you won't even need to show your passport to actually go across these borders. It seems to be symptomatic of the fact that they're trying to find a more secure identity by clinging on to each other. The notion of a United States of Europe would have been unthinkable twenty years ago when they still had this concept of self which was reinforced by colonial outposts like New Caledonia, in the case of the French, or the Falkland Islands in the case of the British. But once you start to lose those colonial possessions which give you a sense of identity, you have no choice but to bury the hatchet and cling to each other. France and Germany have fought each other three times in the last century.
Q: And France and England, for centuries.
A: Now they're digging a tunnel between the two countries. This seems to suggest a European crisis of identity which is, of course, compounded by

the fact that they have these blacks – Indians and Africans – in their presence now.

Q: President Bush now talks about a New World Order.[4] In some ways this could be very sinister so far as the fate of third-world peoples is concerned. However fragile European unity is, it is still dominant.

A: Europe's relevance in the world is only going to survive if it hangs together. Now the way in which this works in terms of lining up against the third world probably supports your thesis. What I'm saying is that Europe's role in that lining-up against the third world only has significance if Europe is united. Power is deeply rooted in the United States of America, and Europe has been outstripped economically by countries like Japan and even Korea.

Q: *Higher Ground* utilizes the Jewish experience of victimization that you mention in *The European Tribe*. I realize that when you grew up in England, one of the more spectacular examples of racism was the Jewish holocaust, and that since you already knew about the black holocaust, it was natural for you to link the two. I suppose this explains your choice of subject in the third section of *Higher Ground*, where you portray Jewish victimization in similar terms to black victimization. But the State of Israel is an eloquent example of how victims can turn into victimizers.

A: You see the same thing unfortunately in South Africa today. You'd have thought that, given the historical evidence of what's happened to blacks in South Africa, people would have learned; yet brother is fighting brother. Sadly, people don't learn a lot from history.

Q: *Higher Ground* and the first section of *Cambridge* reveal a distinct interest in historical subjects. As an interpreter of the fate of contemporary blacks and other powerless peoples, is there a reason for going back to historical subjects?

A: As someone trying to write creatively about a diaspora history, it seems to me that there is so much misunderstanding of the role of people of the African diaspora, particularly Caribbean people in the world, that I feel a sense of responsibility almost as much to history as to literature. Writing about the contemporary scene is something which I'll continue to do; but I find that I do that more easily in dramatic works. When I think about prose, I find myself always looking somehow to redress historical events, or re-address historical facts, as well as trying to create characters who can communicate with the audience. This comes from an awareness of the debased, undervalued and misunderstood historical position from which we have all emerged. People don't understand. I want to look back at historical events and, at the same time, entertain people and make them think. I want to make them realize that the history of what happened on the west coast of Africa in the eighteenth century is at least as interesting and vibrant as the history of what was happening on the east coast of the United States or in England at the same time, although only the white history has been written up to any extent.

Q: Can we expect this trend to continue, with your interest in contemporary subjects being expressed in dramatic works, and your interest in historical subjects taking the form of fiction or non-fiction?

A: The easiest thing to level against the Caribbean is that it's a place of no history, because when you're getting on a plane to go down there, you still have some tourist asking you what language to speak or what money to use. They would never do that getting on a plane to Spain, because they would either know, or would have had the generosity to find out. But they'll never do that for the Caribbean. They assume that there is no history there, and that whatever they find they will be able to impose their history, or US dollars, or language upon it. Columbus found the Caribbean before he found America.[5] So when we talk about a New World, the Caribbean is older in the consciousness of the modern world than the United States of America. But you wouldn't believe so if you looked at the literature or at the histories that have been written. I feel very strongly that the key to redressing this is by actually trying to display the fact that there is a complex history to the Caribbean which paradoxically involves tourists, whether they like it or not.

Q: Many years ago Chinua Achebe made the same point in claiming that one purpose of his writing must be to advance the idea that African 'societies were not mindless but had poetry and, above all, they had dignity'.[6]

A: Africa has produced committed writers of world stature who have taken up the mantle of redressing their countries' history through literature, and trying to forge coherent and sound literary traditions in that way. I think partly because of its diaspora nature, *vis-à-vis* writers, and partly because of the small size of the place, the Caribbean really hasn't taken that on yet. The first serious attempt to make people aware of a classical history of black people in the Caribbean is Walcott's *Omeros*.[7] This poem is an extraordinary attempt to try and make people aware that Homer's *Odyssey* applies as much to West Indians as it does to Greeks.

Q: As you know, there have been other attempts to re-create West Indian history in fiction, for example, several novels by DeLisser,[8] Ada Quayle's *The Mistress*,[9] Orlando Patterson's *Die The Long Day*,[10] and Jean Rhys's *Wide Sargasso Sea*.[11] There are strong parallels between *Wide Sargasso Sea* and *Cambridge*, not only the young white female protagonists, but interchanging narrators as well. Was *Wide Sargasso Sea* an influence?

A: No. I don't know why at this stage of my career I'm finding it easier to write in the first person. Perhaps this has something to do with the whole nature of the Caribbean experience, in so far as I do feel strongly that to adopt an authorial position of third-person narrator is to somehow reduce the complexity of the Caribbean. I like the idea of different voices, because that's what I hear when I go to the Caribbean. That's what I feel about the Caribbean. It's made up of different individuals, and I don't feel that I can easily apply an authorial position of the third-person narrator to a society which is made up of so many different voices and experiences.[12] There's something about writing in the first person, whether one interchanges narrators or not, which seems to give a more urgent and lyrical voice to Caribbean experience.

Q: The narrative in *Cambridge* is lyrical and does have a sense of urgency. It is history successfully transformed into fiction. I think it was John Hearne who called Patterson's *Die the Long Day* regurgitated sociology. I don't think that anyone will say that either *Higher Ground* or *Cambridge* is unconvincing as fiction: both are lyrical, dramatic, wholly convincing narratives.

A: I am disturbed not so much by what people are writing about, but by how they're writing about it. What I find slightly problematic with my forebears in the West Indian literary prose tradition is that formally they are so conservative. Any writer gets to a certain stage where they realize that they have developed skills to tell a story, and they have to find ways to achieve more insight and precision. It becomes a matter of wanting to tell your stories in ever-increasingly poignant, disturbing and challenging ways. When I look at the historical form of the West Indian novel, I often feel that it is stuck in a documentary mode of storytelling. I don't see this in the Spanish writing of the Caribbean. Even though the stories of the Spanish Caribbean writers sometimes don't interest me very much, I see invention in the works of Alejo Carpentier, Carlos Fuentes, Octavio Paz and obviously Márquez[13] who describe themselves as Caribbean, because they are indeed Caribbean writers. Their experience is very similar to ours. I went to Venezuela last year. Caracas is a Caribbean capital with a similar ethnic mix, the same vibrancy and mood. These writers are applying themselves to basically the same historical material; but they are using some of the inventiveness and varied mix of the Caribbean in their literary form. When I was preparing for *Cambridge* I couldn't see any English-speaking writer who had ever tried to dwell both at the level of language and the consciousness of a nineteenth-century English woman. My editor in New York told me that he didn't think that many black Americans would have attempted to tell the story from that point of view either. Of the last three West Indian writers I talked to, Derek Walcott aside, all are learning Spanish.

Q: Who are the other two?

A: Fred d'Aguiar and Joan Riley.[14] And why? For the same reasons: because they're trying to look at the writing of others who consider Caribbean experience, but draw on techniques deriving from more than just the

English tradition. It's a way of telling a story which feeds as much from Borges in Argentina,[15] as it would from Cela in Spain.[16] It's just to try to expand the parameters of how we express ourselves in what are some of the most culturally and racially heterogeneous parts of the world. To apply a rather restricted, almost Jane Austen-type English to a novel dealing with a part of the world which is far more complex than that seems to be self-defeating.

Q: It points to the recognition of a common historical and cultural reality, a New World civilization which evolved out of European colonization, the mixture of races, exploitation, and all that. C. L. R. James[17] had a vision of the Caribbean that cut across linguistic and cultural boundaries. It stretched from the English-speaking Bahamas in the north right down to French-speaking Guyane in the south. He felt it was all one place. Lamming has also said as much in his lecture 'Concepts of the Caribbean'. [See Chapter 1.]

A: It is one place. But there's more than one language: that's the thing. As English-speaking Caribbean people, we've inherited a certain insularity which the English themselves have always had. Linguistically, the English are incredibly conservative; they're equally unadventurous in the form of their literature. The most adventurous British writers have been Irish – Joyce, Yeats, Beckett. I think, given our history, we have to learn from writers like Joyce and Beckett, who decided they were not going to buy the traditions which were handed over to them by the English who had colonized their country. They took to the wing and flew in a different direction, and I think it's about time that we in the Caribbean realized that we also don't have to buy the English literary tradition, because it is not applicable to our circumstances as a people who are a mix of aboriginal American, Carib Indian, African and European. It would be a long, hard struggle, but I have some hope because I see many of my contemporaries at least becoming aware of this. For this reason Caribbean writing is actually a lot healthier now than it was ten years ago.

Notes

1   Caryl Phillips, *The European Tribe* (Faber and Faber, London 1987); *Higher Ground* (Viking Penguin, London, 1989); *Cambridge* (Bloomsbury, London, 1991).
     Although *A State of Independence* (1986) is mentioned in Chapter 14, it had not actually appeared at the time of that interview.
2   The war was fought through February 1991 against Iraq, by a coalition of forces led by the US, with the purpose of dislodging Iraq from its illegal occupation of Kuwait.
3   The *Encyclopedia Britannica* (1968) refers to Kitchener's 'tremendous slaughter of Arabs at the battle of Omdurman': and comments, 'Despite the ruthlessness of his methods, Kitchener's victories thrilled the empire during the period of Queen Victoria' (p. 393).

4 The New World Order emerged after the collapse of communism in the USSR, and the disappearance of a bipolar world order dominated by a capitalist USA on one hand and a communist USSR on the other.

5 Cf. comments by Lamming (In Chapter 1), and Walcott (in Chapter 3) on the age of the West Indies.

6 Chinua Achebe, 'The Role of the Writer in a New Nation', in G. D. Killam (ed.), *African Writers on their Writing* (Heinemann, London), p. 8.

7 Derek Walcott, *Omeros* (Farrar, Straus and Giroux, New York, 1990).

8 H. G. De Lisser (1878–1944) wrote several novels re-creating the history of Jamaica, while injecting a good deal of suspense, romance and adventure that were less historical. De Lisser was also editor of the *Daily Gleaner* for many years.

9 Ada Quayle, *The Mistress* (MacGibbon & Kee, London, 1957).

10 Orlando Patterson, *Die the Long Day* (William Morrow and Co., New York, 1972).

11 Jean Rhys, *Wide Sargasso Sea* (André Deutsch, London, 1966). Jean Rhys incorporates rich and complex images into an insightful portrait of post-slavery Caribbean society. Cf. Chapter 12, note 12.

12 Cf. Chapter 13 at note 19.

13 For Carpentier see Chapter 4, note 16.

Carlos Fuentes was born in 1928 and is a leading Mexican novelist; Octavio Paz was born in 1914. He is one of the best-known Latin American poets; For Márquez see Chapter 4, note 16.

14 Fred d'Aguiar was born in London in 1960, but grew up in Guyana, before returning to London in 1972. He is the author of two collections of poems, *Mama Dot* (1985) and *Airy Hall* (1989). *Mama Dot* won the Guyana Prize for Poetry in 1987.

Joan Riley was born in Jamaica but lives in England. She is the author of the novel *The Unbelonging* (1985).

15 Jorge Luis Borges (1899–1986), the Argentinian poet, author and editor, is perhaps the most important literary figure in his country. His work is distinctly anti-realist.

16 Camilo José Celá was born in 1916 and has dominated Spanish literature since the Second World War. He is a novelist, scholar and editor.

17 For C. L. R. James, see Chapter 2, note 15.

Select bibliography

Braithwaite, E. R. *To Sir With Love* (Bodley Head, London, 1959).

Brand, Dionne, *'Fore Day Morning* (Khoisan Artists, Toronto, 1978).

_____ , *Earth Magic* (Kids Can Press, Toronto, 1980).

_____ , *Primitive Offensive* (Williams-Wallace, Toronto, 1982).

_____ , *Winter Epigrams & Epigrams to Ernest Cardenal in Defence of Claudia* (Williams-Wallace, Toronto, 1984).

_____ , *Chronicles of the Hostile Sun* (Williams-Wallace, Toronto, 1984).

_____ , *Rivers Have Sources, Trees Have Roots – Speaking of Racism* (Cross Cultural Community Centre, Toronto, 1986).

_____ , *Sans Souci* (Williams-Wallace, Toronto, 1988).

Brathwaite, Edward Kamau, *Rights of Passage* (Oxford University Press, London, 1967).

_____ , *Masks* (Oxford University Press, London, 1968).

_____ , *Islands* (Oxford University Press, London, 1969).

_____ , *The Arrivants: A New World Trilogy* (Oxford University Press, London, 1973). (Includes *Rights of Passage, Masks, Islands.*)

_____ , *X-Self* (Oxford University Press, London, 1987).

Carew, Jan, *Black Midas* (Secker and Warburg, London, 1958).

_____ , *The Wild Coast* (Secker and Warburg, 1958).

_____ , *The Last Barbarian* (Secker and Warburg, London, 1961).

_____ , *Moscow Is Not My Mecca* (Secker and Warburg, London, 1964; Stein and Day, New York, 1965, as *Green Winter*).

_____ , *Grenada: The Hour Will Strike Again* (The International Organisation of Journalists, Prague, 1985).

Clarke, Austin, *The Survivors of the Crossing* (Heinemann, London, 1964).

_____ , *Amongst Thistles and Thorns* (Heinemann, London, 1965).

_____ , *The Meeting Point* (Heinemann, London, 1967).

_____ , *When He Was Free and Young and He Used to Wear Silks* (Anansi, Toronto, 1971).

_____ , *Storm of Fortune* (Little, Brown, Boston, 1973).

_____ , *The Bigger Light* (Little, Brown, Boston, 1975).

_____ , *The Prime Minister* (General Publishing Company, Ontario, 1977).

_____ , *Growing Up Stupid Under the Union Jack* (Casa de las Americas, Havana, 1980).

Dabydeen, Cyril, *Poems in Recession* (Georgetown, Guyana, 1972).

_____ , *Goatsong* (Mosaic Press, Oakville, Canada, 1977).

_____ , *This Planet Earth* (Borealis Press, Ottawa, 1979).

_____ , *Still Close to the Island* (Commoner's Publishing, Ottawa, 1980).

_____ , *Elephants Make Good Stepladders* (Third Eye, London, Canada, 1982).

_____ , *Islands Lovelier than a Vision* (Peepal Tree Press, Leeds, 1986).

_____ , (ed.), *A Shapely Fire: Changing the Literary Landscape* (Mosaic Press, Oakville, Canada, 1987).

_____ , *To Monkey Jungle* (Third Eye, London, Canada, 1988).

_____ , *The Wizard Swami* (Writers Workshop, Calcutta, 1985; Peepal Tree Press, Leeds, 1989).

_____ , *Dark Swirl* (Peepal Tree Press, Leeds, 1989).

_____ , (ed.), *Another Way to Dance: Asian Canadian Poetry* (Williams-Wallace, Stratford, Canada, 1990).

Dabydeen, David, *Slave Song* (Dangaroo Press, Denmark, 1984).

_____ , *Hogarth's Blacks: Images of blacks in Eighteenth Century English Art* (Dangaroo Press, Denmark, 1985).

_____ , *Coolie Odyssey* (Hansib and Dangaroo Press, London, 1988).

_____ , *The Intended* (Secker and Warburg, London, 1991).

Dathorne, O. R., *Dumplings in the Soup* (Cassell, London, 1963).

_____ , *The Scholar Man* (Cassell, London, 1964).

Goodison, Lorna, *Tamarind Season* (Institute of Jamaica, Jamaica, 1980).

_____ , *I am Becoming My Mother* (New Beacon Books, London, 1986).

_____ , *Heartease* (New Beacon Books, London, 1988).

_____ , *Baby Mother and The King of Swords* (Longman Jamaica, Jamaica, 1990).

Harris, Wilson, *Palace of the Peacock* (Faber and Faber, London, 1960).

_____ , *Black Marsden* (Faber and Faber, London, 1973).

Hearne, John, *Voices under the Window* (Faber and Faber, London, 1955, 1985).

Heath, Roy A. K., *A Man Come Home* (Longman Caribbean, London, 1974).

_____ , *The Murderer* (Allison and Busby, London, 1981).

_____ , *From the Heat of the Day* (Allison and Busby, London, 1981).

_____ , *Genetha* (Allison and Busby, London, 1981).

_____ , *The Shadow Bride* (William Collins, London, 1988).

James, C. L. R. *The Black Jacobins* (Random House, New York, 1963).

_____ , *Minty Alley* (Secker and Warburg, London, 1936; New Beacon Books, London, 1971).

Kincaid, Jamaica, *At the Bottom of the River* (Farrar, Straus and Giroux, New York, 1983).

_____ , *Annie John* (Farrar, Straus and Giroux, New York, 1985).

_____ , *A Small Place* (Farrar, Straus and Giroux, New York, 1988).

_____ , *Lucy* (Farrar, Straus and Giroux, New York, 1990).

Lamming, George, *In the Castle of My Skin* (Michael Joseph, London, 1953).

_____ , *The Emigrants* (Michael Joseph, London, 1954).

_____ , *Of Age and Innocence* (Michael Joseph, London, 1958).

_____ , *The Pleasures of Exile* (Michael Joseph, London, 1960).

_____ , *Season of Adventure* (Michael Joseph, London, 1960).

_____ , *Water with Berries* (Longman Caribbean, London, 1971).

_____ , *Natives of My Person* (Longman Caribbean, London, 1972).

Mais, Roger, *The Hills Were Joyful Together* (Jonathan Cape, London, 1953).

_____ , *Brother Man* (Jonathan Cape, London, 1955).

Mittelholzer, Edgar, *Corentyne Thunder* (Eyre and Spottiswoode, London, 1941).

_____ , *A Morning at the Office* (Hogarth Press, London, 1950).

_____ , *Shadows Move Among Them* (Lippincott, Philadelphia, 1951).

_____ , *The Life and Death of Sylvia* (Secker and Warburg, London, 1952).

_____ , *Of Trees and the Sea* (Secker and Warburg, London, 1956).

_____ , *A Swarthy Boy* (Putnam, London, 1963).

Naipaul, V. S., *The Mystic Masseur* (André Deutsch, London, 1957).

_____ , *Miguel Street* (André Deutsch, London, 1959).

_____ , *A House for Mr Biswas* (André Deutsch, London, 1961).

_____ , *The Middle Passage* (André Deutsch, London, 1962).

_____ , *An Area of Darkness* (André Deutsch, London, 1964).

_____ , *The Mimic Men* (André Deutsch, London, 1967).

_____ , *The Enigma of Arrival* (Viking Penguin, London, 1987).

_____ , *India: A Million Mutinies Now* (Heinemann, London, 1990).

Phillips, Caryl, *Strange Fruit* (Amber Lane Press, London, 1981).

_____ , *Where There is Darkness* (Amber Lane Press, London, 1982).

_____ , *A State of Independence* (Faber and Faber, London, 1986).

_____ , *The European Tribe* (Faber and Faber, London, 1987).

_____ , *Higher Ground* (Viking Penguin, London, 1989).

_____ , *The Final Passage* (Penguin, New York, 1990).

_____ , *Cambridge* (Bloomsbury, London, 1991).

_____ , *Crossing the River* (1993).

Quayle, Ada, *The Mistress* (MacGibbon & Kee, London, 1957).

Reid, Vic, *New Day* (Knopf, New York, 1949).

_____ , *The Leopard* (Heinemann, London, 1958).

Rhys, Jean, *Wild Sargasso Sea* (André Deutsch, London, 1966).

Salkey, Andrew, *Escape to an Autumn Pavement* (Hutchinson, London, 1960).

_____ , (ed.), *West Indian Stories* (Faber and Faber, London, 1960).

_____ , *Hurricane* (Oxford University Press, London, 1964).

_____ , *Earthquake* (Oxford University Press, London, 1965).

_____ , (ed.), *Stories from the Caribbean* (Paul Elek Books, London, 1965).

_____ , *The Late Emancipation of Jerry Stover* (Hutchinson, London, 1968).

_____ , *A Quality of Violence* (Hutchinson, London, 1969).

_____ , *Jamaica* (Hutchinson, London, 1973).

Selvon, Samuel, *A Brighter Sun* (Allan Wingate, London, 1952; Longman, London, 1971).

_____ , *The Lonely Londoners* (Allan Wingate, London, 1956; Longman, London, 1972).

_____ , *Ways of Sunlight* (MacGibbon & Kee, London, 1957; Longman, London, 1973).

_____ , *The Plains of Caroni* (MacGibbon & Kee, London, 1970).

_____ , *Moses Ascending* (Davis Poynter, London, 1975).

Walcott, Derek, *Epitaph for the Young* (Advocate, Bridgetown, Barbados, 1949).

_____ , *In a Green Night: Poems 1948–1960* (Jonathan Cape, London, 1962).

_____ , *Dream on Monkey Mountain and Other Plays* (Farrar, Straus and Giroux, New York, 1970).

_____ , *Another Life* (Farrar, Straus and Giroux, New York, 1973).

_____ , *The Joker of Seville and O Babylon!* (Farrar, Straus and Giroux, New York, 1978).

_____ , *The Star-Apple Kingdom* (Farrar, Straus and Giroux, New York, 1979).

_____ , *Midsummer* (Farrar, Straus and Giroux, New York, 1984).

_____ , *Omeros* (Farrar, Straus and Giroux, New York, 1990).

Wynter, Sylvia, *The Hills of Hebron* (Jonathan Cape, London, 1962).

Index